Post Mortem

Post Mortem

Why Canada's Mail Won't Move

David Stewart-Patterson

Macmillan of Canada
A Division of Canada Publishing Corporation
Toronto, Ontario, Canada

Canadian Cataloguing in Publication Data

Stewart-Patterson, David, date.
  Post mortem: why Canada's mail won't move

Bibliography: p.
Includes index.
ISBN 0-7715-9504-2

1. Postal service — Canada — History.   2. Postal service — Canada — Management — History.   3. Canada Post Corporation.   I. Title.

HE6655.S84   1987   354.710087'3   C87-094216-6

All inquiries regarding the motion picture or other dramatic rights for this book should be addressed to the author's representative, The Colbert Agency Inc., 303 Davenport Road, Toronto, Canada, M5R 1K5. Representations as to the disposition of these rights are strictly prohibited without express written consent and will be vigorously pursued to the full extent of the law.

Design by Craig Allen
Edited by Kathleen Richards

Contents

To Cleve and Alison,
who delivered me into this world,

and to Ivanka,
without whom I would be lost.

Acknowledgements

It would be difficult to thank all those who helped in the creation of
this book. Those who wished to keep a low profile would not like to
see their names here, and it would be unfair to list only those whose
names appear in the text. Let me therefore thank all of them, and
add a special note of gratitude to two people who were crucial to my
documentary research: Geoff Bickerton, the research director for
the Canadian Union of Postal Workers, and Jean Weerasinghe, the
librarian at Canada Post Corp.

I must also thank my employer, *The Globe and Mail*, along with
its managing editor, Geoffrey Stevens, and its business editor, Tim
Pritchard, for allowing me the time necessary to complete this
work. My friend and colleague Michael Harris is due a fine bottle of
wine for encouraging me to take the plunge.

My agent, David Colbert, has been a constant source of positive
criticism from the day he dissected my vague ideas and told me to
put together a proposal. His assistance throughout the process of
negotiation, writing, and editing has been invaluable.

At Macmillan, I would like to thank Anne Holloway, whose prompt
and positive response to my proposal got the project moving, and
my editor, Kathleen Richards, who stayed with me cheerfully through
the inevitable crises of a first book.

And finally, of course, I have to thank Ivanka, who didn't let a
book deadline get in the way of our decision to marry, and whose
love and support never faltered during the long winter weeks when I
seemed to have no time for anything except my computer.

Preface

While I was a student at the Carleton University School of Journalism, I remember going one night to see the movie *Dirty Harry*. It was one of those cheap showings in a classroom, and the amateur projectionist found that he didn't have the right lens. If we wanted to see the movie, we had to watch it squeezed, so that people appeared tall and stick-thin, and cars turned into squat little boxes.

Michael Warren reminds me of that stretched Clint Eastwood. Tall and thin, he has that unmistakable Eastwood brow and those gunfighter's eyes. But when he opens his mouth, the whole image changes. It is as if Dirty Harry wore a three-piece suit as he walked up to the punk and inquired smoothly, "How may I make your day?"

When I first met Warren over lunch in the dining-room of the Four Seasons Hotel in Ottawa, an expense-account eatery known for its elegant 300-calorie creations of *nouvelle cuisine,* the president of Canada Post Corp. was still in the early stages of his four-year journey through the strangely distorted landscape that is Canada's post office.

At first I wondered why a man with a mission to chop an impossible deficit would spend company money on fancy lunches, but I soon realized that this was part of his vision of how to survive in a place where he could have few friends. His job was to turn around the financial numbers; his priority was to turn around people's ways of looking at the organization that produced the numbers.

I had returned to Ottawa from Toronto in 1982 as a business reporter on Parliament Hill for *The Globe and Mail*. One of my tasks was to take a closer look at some of Canada's Crown corporations.

Warren caught my attention that first day during a conversation about the state of the post office before it became a Crown corporation. In the early 1970s, he said, "the best managers in the post office were running the unions." It seemed a strange thing for a president to say. Like the man himself, it was a simple enough remark on the surface, but it hinted that there was a much more complex mystery to be unravelled.

The post office was at first interesting to me, and then intriguing, simply as a management problem. It was, and is, a business unlike any other. And the more I delved into its affairs, aided by Warren's penchant for throwing out gobs of information that could be used to figure out results he had not intended to divulge, the more my fascination grew. By the time Warren resigned in 1985, I had come to realize that even in the 3,000-word magazine piece I had written on his departure, I was only scratching the surface.

The result of my interest was this book. It is not about Michael Warren, nor is it about Canada Post Corp. They are both prominent players, but this is really the story of Canada's love-hate relationship with its post office, seen through the eyes of its Cabinet ministers, its senior bureaucrats, its corporate executives, and its union leaders. It is a story not so much of numbers as of people, their hopes and fears, triumphs and frustrations, and their impressions of what happened and why.

Many others before me — commissions and committees, study groups and task forces — have examined the post office and its problems. This is a study of its people, the ones who fed it, nursed it, cursed it, and, together, helped it crumble.

I don't expect many of them to be entirely happy with the result. Passions have flared too high for anyone caught up in the post office to remain neutral. I have tried to understand the feelings and motivations of each person involved, but I have also exposed them to the criticism of others. The result is not a diatribe against any one individual or group. Many people have made decisions and pursued different policies with the best of intentions. In that constant clash of interests and intentions, however, lie the reasons for the collapse, first of the post office as a federal government department, and then of its incarnation as a Crown corporation. There too lie the clues that, if heeded, could yet lead to its revival.

The Crowning Touch

■

The hills and trails of the Gray Rocks resort, an hour's drive north of Montreal, are popular year round. The small group of postal managers gathered there in the spring of 1981, however, paid scant attention to the scenery.

For three days they took turns. They tossed out problems, scrawled on scattered ranks of flip charts, and played with each other's suggestions. There were no harsh denunciations or scathing comments: it was what Jim Corkery called a "greenlighting" session. "You're trying to tumble out all the ideas you've got and then you start to say what are the pluses and minuses of that idea versus that idea. If you've got somebody with a good idea, you don't want it shot down before it's been explored."

No one there doubted the importance of their gathering. Corkery was the deputy postmaster general, the top civil servant at the post office. The rest of the men in the room formed his senior management group. In less than six months, their department would be wrenched from the bureaucracy and turned into a Crown corporation. The ideas and decisions that emerged from this meeting would set the agenda for the corporation's first five years.

The top-level planning session had been in the works for some time. So many changes would be involved. The post office would have to learn to manage its money, run its real estate, and haggle with its employees. All those jobs had been handled by other departments. Now it would have to hire new people and do them for itself.

There would be more freedom, but more responsibilities, too — many, many more. A new board of directors would fill the gap between postal managers and politicians. The idea was to make the mail run more smoothly by keeping the two groups apart. But the new company and its board would have to show the Canadian people that it deserved that freedom by making a dent in its huge financial losses and doing something to improve the country's mail service.

The meeting had another purpose, one that added an unexpected air of tension. That came from the presence of a gangling but elegant man who said little but watched and listened a lot at the meeting. At six feet six inches, Michael Warren has difficulty being unobtrusive at any time, but at Gray Rocks his presence loomed over every manager present.

"It was a little strained initially because I was a stranger to them," says Warren. "There were sort of two bosses there. Corkery was the deputy minister . . . and here was this new guy from Toronto coming in, sitting in on the meetings."

Warren had been picked as the new president of Canada Post Corp., and, as he watched each man talk and scribble and listen, he was beginning to make up his mind which of those postal executives would keep their jobs and which would have to go. "It gave me an insight into some of the key people. They were all very loyal, they were all very conscientious. Many of them had been hurt, really badly hurt. And some of them simply didn't have that sort of commercial orientation. . . . I wouldn't think that more than two people in the room could read a balance sheet."

Many, including Corkery, would not survive. Of the top ten postal bureaucrats, only two would sit among the ranks of the vice-presidents of the new corporation.

"He just sat there at that one, because that was my meeting," says Corkery. "We walked through the five-year plan as we saw it. He did very little, if any, influencing of that first block. That was an education meeting for him, to sort of get a feel for the organization and where we would go, where we could go, and what the pieces were of the puzzle. What we were trying to do was identify the areas of concentration that had to take place . . . to try and lay out within each of the segments of the organization what we thought had to take place.''

As civil servants, they still felt their prime duty was to deliver a service on behalf of the government, and their self-image had taken a battering from the labour conflicts of the past decade. "It scarred them. This was the first set of meetings where I found that the past so dominated the people involved, the past had been so painful, so without a win, so unrewarding, so the people at this meeting who were concerned with labour relations, they were giving approaches to the future which were very much subdued by the experiences of the past,'' says Warren. "Their creativity had been warped and contained by the structure of the institution.''

Corkery himself already knew his days were numbered. "I was expecting to take it on for the first period. Stupid expectation, because the politics of the situation were just stacked against it. I think they made a political decision. The first I knew that it was going to happen was I saw an ad in the paper, looking for a president through an outside recruiting agency.''

He phoned Michael Pitfield, the country's top bureaucrat as Clerk of the Privy Council and the man in charge of handling appointments to senior federal jobs. "What the hell's going on?'' Corkery asked. "He said, well, the Cabinet had decided to see what was in the market. Was I considered? You could be a candidate if you wished. So I got the message at that stage that they had decided politically that they were going to put new blood in.''

Hugh Mullington, a senior bureaucrat at Treasury Board who had been responsible for post office affairs for many years, said the government felt that "if you're going to go to a Crown corporation, you've got to be seen to be making a major change, and therefore you have to change management. I can't deny the optics, but I think in hindsight it was a dreadful decision. I felt badly for Corkery, because I think Corkery could have done a great deal. And I think if anybody was equipped to effect a turnaround, it was Corkery.''

Corkery stayed on as Warren's number two to help with the transition from department to corporation, but not for long. Warren says he wanted the benefit of Corkery's knowledge for a while, but "I think we found eventually that it was tough to have two cooks in the kitchen, because he had been head of the organization. So he and I both agreed after four or five months that it was probably best that he find something that he could go and head, and call the shots."

A rather bitter Corkery headed off to become master of the Royal Canadian Mint. "I probably would have stayed as chief operating officer, which is what I was for the first six months, but Warren decided that it would be a dumb move to have me around, because I knew too much. Although I wasn't an objectionist by any means, Michael likes to be the big cheese and the king and nobody else. To have somebody else that knew more than he did was inappropriate for him. So he said I had to leave. Actually, it was a good decision. I could not have worked for him."

Going outside the post office for a new batch of senior executives had been done once before, in the late 1960s. Corkery, an engineer and manager with twenty-five years of experience at Canadian General Electric, had been part of that group. In all, the government had used private-sector talent to fill more than fifty top jobs at the post office in the late 1960s and early 1970s.

The private-sector recruiting had been part of an ambitious set of plans to yank the post office into the twentieth century. Instead, Canadians got a peanut-butter sandwich without the bread. It still tasted about right, but it proved to be a sticky mess. The flavour of the private sector that had been brought into the system found no backing, and the new postal managers were forced to rely on the old ways.

In 1968 a Crown corporation had been a good idea; a decade later it had become vital for the survival of the post office. After years of dithering, the Crown corporation was born of one man's irritation. "It was Trudeau that did it," says Corkery. "Trudeau just sprung it one day. He said, 'I've had enough of the debate in Cabinet on labour relations in the post office. I've had it. Let's Crown it.' And that was it, so then we started."

Prime Minister Pierre Trudeau gave no warning. He dropped

his decision into the middle of a televised speech on the need for cutting the size of government, having told his postal minister, Gilles Lamontagne, only a day earlier. "The situation in the post office is intolerable and has been for some time," he said. "Canadians are losing patience. They are increasingly fed up. So am I."

The announcement caught bureaucrats by surprise as well. "There was absolutely no planning that went into it up to that point," says Mullington. "It had not been identified as being the best alternative."

As Trudeau made his announcement, a three-man task force run by Alan Darling of the Privy Council Office, Bill Kelly of the Department of Labour, and John Uberig from the post office was putting the finishing touches on a study that set out various ways that a Crown corporation could be established. Even when their report was finished, it only laid out options without making any recommendations.

It was the right decision, but it was too late, and for the wrong reasons. That in turn meant that it was set up the wrong way as well. After using the failures of state corporations in other countries as excuses for not setting up a Canadian postal corporation, the federal Cabinet ignored the lessons it could have learned from those mistakes.

Corkery and his fellow managers had waited for years for that precious signal from the top, and they did not really care about the circumstances. Even so, the lack of preparation meant that three years and two changes of government would pass before the Crown corporation was actually born.

Yet as they went about fashioning their new rose, the politicians were sowing the seeds that would sprout into a suffocating growth all around it. The concept survived and the Crown was created. But along the way, the government made some crucial decisions that would have a devastating effect on the corporation's ability to do its job.

The first of these was a political move to make sure that the idea of a Crown corporation kept the full support of the postal unions. They had been pushing for a Crown corporation since 1975 because they felt it would improve their chances at the bargaining table. When Trudeau handed the job of setting up Canada Post Corp. to André Ouellet in 1980, Ouellet made sure that the unions got all the input they wanted.

"The legislation itself was negotiated word for word between the unions and André Ouellet. It was not given to Justice to draft the legislation. The final details of the legislation were drafted in the fifth-floor boardroom of the Canadian Labour Congress right next door here, with André Ouellet sitting there and his lawyer and our lawyers, and we laid it out in detail, each and every single word, semicolon, colon, right from front to back, the legislation was drafted with the minister and the unions," says Ron Lang, the CLC research director who co-ordinated the union's efforts and later sat on Canada Post Corp.'s board of directors. Lang took part in every discussion leading to its creation, along with Ouellet, CLC vice-president Shirley Carr, and representatives of the postal unions.

"I literally sat with the unions and drafted the legislation with them," agrees Ouellet. "We had many, many meetings involving Shirley Carr and the representatives of those unions because I wanted them to feel that it was a piece that they would be satisfied with."

"There was a great deal of trust built up between the minister and the unions," says Lang. "When Ouellet said what he was going to do, gave his word that he would do something or follow a certain procedure, gave a commitment on some aspect of the legislation, he never once fell down on that commitment. So the unions have a lot of time for André Ouellet, and when he said something, they knew that that's the way it was going to be."

"All the wording has been well thought out so that there would be no confusion or misinterpretation," Ouellet told the House of Commons when he brought the bill forward for a second reading in October 1980. "I am not suggesting the bill is perfect, but it represents as never before the collective efforts of the administration and the postal unions."

The collective effort had certainly been made. But the wording was more than imperfect. It contained fatal flaws, ones that had been clearly exposed by Great Britain's experience in turning its post office into a Crown corporation ten years earlier. And Ouellet himself quickly compounded those mistakes as he chose the new managers to run the post office.

The initial flaws lay in the way the corporation and its actions would be controlled by the government. Its spending would be subject to review, and its rates — the very basis of its income — would still need the green light from the Cabinet. And the wording of the bill left a vague but wide-ranging power in the minister's hands to tell postal managers to do whatever he wanted as long as it was in the national interest. The failure of the government to set up the corporation, tell it what to do, and then get its hands off, would undo those plans in very short order.

Even so, the government might have been able to make its misshapen creature fly if it had chosen the right people to be directors and executives and given them the right instructions. Instead, the process of selecting new men and women to run the post office got tied down by patronage and affirmative action. Then the government compounded its folly by confusing those it had picked about what it wanted from them.

Warren, who was picked for the top job through a professional head-hunting firm, was no fool. He had been a deputy minister in three departments of the Ontario provincial government. He knew about political realities. He had also been the chief general manager for the Toronto Transit Commission. He knew about the conflicting pressures on managers of an essential public service, where higher prices and labour strife are equally likely to cause loud complaints from the public.

By the time he signed on, he had in his hands a one-page mandate for Canada Post Corp. It contained three basic instructions: the same ones laid out in the bill creating the Crown corporation, but with a different emphasis because they stood alone. Warren was told to get the Crown corporation on a self-sufficient basis, to preserve labour peace, and to improve service to the public. Since those goals often conflict, the choice of which ones would get the most attention first was left up to him — or so he thought.

The emphasis quickly became clear when finance minister Allan MacEachen pushed for a quick end to the postal deficit. ''I have to admit, I was the guy that effectively said, you've got to put a carrot out in front of this corporation,'' says Corkery. ''Five years, it's got to break even, knowing damn well that it might not. But it doesn't make any difference. What you're driving for is forcing the system to say, you've got to break even. You've got to have a motivator there to get out from all this other crap.''

To get the Crown corporation on the right track, the government had already decided on a big boost in postal rates. The increase from 17 cents to 30 cents was supposed to go through before the Crown corporation was set up. Instead, it took effect January 1, 1982, just months after Canada Post Corp. was born. Canada Post had to live with the criticism, but Warren at least was able to use the jump in revenue as evidence of the work he had done to bring down the deficit.

Ouellet, meanwhile, had told the unions nothing about any deadline for self-sufficiency. He may have talked over every sentence in the bill, but the bill said nothing about when the corporation was to end its losses. Due regard to finances was only one of five points the corporation was directed to take into account while providing traditional levels of service.

The minister also made no mention of a financial deadline in 1980 as he led off the second-reading debate. He did emphasize that the beginning of the clause containing the reference to good financial results — ''While maintaining basic customary postal services'' — was a guarantee to Canadians that they would not see a reduction in services.

When the unions discovered the unexpected deadline in the corporate mandate, they were outraged. ''The words 'basic customary postal service', we thought we understood what was meant by that,'' says Lang. ''Once you've changed it over, and you have someone coming in from the outside who was not part of the original bargaining, didn't understand what went into the formation of the Crown corporation, and had his own ideas from the private sector of how to run a corporation, well, that's when the parting of the ways started. That's when the thing started to come unravelled. Our idea of what we had agreed upon and what Warren's idea was, it wasn't the same damned idea.

''Why did the politicians have to overlay every consideration with this goddamned bottom line of the deficit? Once you have done that, most other problems become secondary. That was the one constant factor in every discussion that came before the board and every discussion with the minister subsequent to that. . . . The goddamned deficit was becoming the operational mode and principle upon which Canada Post was based.''

Other promises also fell by the wayside. Although Ouellet told the House that postal rates would be sent to the Canadian Transport Commission for approval ''to protect the interest of the people and to establish the necessary arm's length between the corporation and the government'', they remained political decisions for the Cabinet, and provided an unending source of frustration to the new managers.

The conflicting intentions and actions of the Crown corporation's birth would only get worse as the Conservatives succeeded the Liberals in the 1984 election. Ouellet at least knew what he wanted to do and what trade-offs he was willing to make. The new ministers had to start from scratch as they made the change from criticizing to ruling.

In the promised rose garden of the Crown corporation, Ouellet and Warren were able to keep their prize plant looking presentable by snipping and pruning and fertilizing. As the new Tory gardeners dug into their books to decide what to do, the barely suppressed weeds sprang up with a vengeance. Canada Post was soon locked in a death grip.

1
Mail
Supremacy

■

It is almost two o'clock in the morning as the Lufthansa jets come thudding down onto the runways of Frankfurt airport. Like a latter-day recreation of the Berlin airlift, they appear out of the night in a steady stream. From all corners of the compass they come: from Hamburg and Hanover, from Cologne and Stuttgart, from Munich and Berlin.

Once on the ground, they shun the welcoming light of the terminal buildings. Instead, they gather in a circle out on the tarmac. They open their bellies to the eager hands of a scurrying crowd of workers, and the circle takes on the air of a poker game in which every player deals at once. Here the cards are shiny aluminum containers, being rolled out of each plane and shoved back into others. An hour later it is over.

The doors slam shut, and once again the scream of jets stabs into the night. One after another the planes zoom into the air and head back whence they came. Nothing remains but a fading roar in the sky, floating across the next-door American air base and the long-suffering suburbs of Germany's banking centre.

This nightly routine at Germany's busiest airport is made possible by a unique deal between the German post office department and the national airline. Each night the trucks drive from each of Germany's major postal plants to the nearest airport, where a Lufthansa jet is waiting. Into each plane go the containers of mail for other parts of Germany, marked with the

name of the postal plant nearest the destination of the mail it
contains. When the planes arrive at Frankfurt, the ritual exchange
of containers fills each plane with letters and parcels destined for
the area it left. The mail for each city and town in the country is at
the nearest plant by the small hours of the morning.

Such service is not cheap. The German post and telecommunications ministry gets no money from the taxpayer except in
an emergency. The phone system makes a great deal of money
for the government, but it also needs more and more cash for the
latest in electronic technology. The post office loses money —
and lots of it. The losses are covered by the profits from the
phone system, but they eat into the money that the government
would prefer to spend on the electronic side. So far, the postal
minister has set a limit on postal losses of DM2 billion a year. In
1985, the post office squeezed under the wire with a loss of
DM1.8 billion, about $1 billion.

What impact do postal efforts have on the German public?
"Our mail service is terrible," gripes one resident of Bonn, the
capital city of some 300,000 people. "It can take me eight days
to get a letter across town."

The German experience illustrates two things about postal
customers. No matter how efficient a postal service is, there will
always be enough mistakes for people to remember. And no
matter how good the service, it will never be good enough to
match people's expectations.

The public still expects the dedication chiselled into the stone
of the New York post office: "Neither snow nor rain nor heat nor
gloom of night stays these couriers from their appointed rounds."
In Canada, as in the United States, the history of the post office
resounds with the adventure of the frontier and the primal
conviction that "the mail must go through."

Former postmaster general André Ouellet told a 1973 gathering
of postmasters that the post office was "the finest personal
communications network so far devised. Personal — that's the
key word. A lot of people don't like the government. It's too
impersonal. It's too big. It makes them feel small and helpless.

"But everyone knows his post office. It's a building you can't
mistake. The only building in town with a flagpole, a sign and a

mailbox in front . . . about the only federal building that most people feel at home in. And everyone in little towns and villages knows his postmaster. People know you by your first name. They deal with you person-to-person. They think of you, rightly or wrongly, as their personal link with the government, a little peephole into that great big Ottawa beehive. . . . The post office is familiar. It cuts the government down to size. It's a reference point in that huge federal landscape.''

Because it is so personal, the post office has become the easiest way for individuals to judge their government. A Canadian may not care about international crises or be able to fathom complex federal grants to the oil patch or tax aids to industry, but his daily mail tells him whether or not those folks in Ottawa have their act together.

''Members of the public are able to monitor the performance of the post office to a degree that is impossible with the activities of any other department,'' the consulting firm Kates, Peat, Marwick and Co. noted in a 1969 study of the post office. ''Every citizen can recognize a delayed letter, a misdirected letter and inefficient delivery service.''

''It's a great way to take a whack at the current government,'' says Jim Corkery, the former deputy postmaster general. ''You can't manage the post office, so how the hell can you run a government? And you can always find something that's gone wrong.''

Customers in other countries feel the same way. ''The postal business is ubiquitous,'' wrote British author Michael Corby in *The Postal Business*, his book about the first ten years of Britain's experience with a postal Crown corporation. ''Directly or indirectly, it affects the lives of everyone in the United Kingdom. There can be few people who do not, one way or another, use its mail and counter services. The postman is one of the best-known figures in any community and the royal mail vehicles with their red livery are as familiar as the London omnibus. The organization is cursed when things go wrong, and taken for granted when it performs successfully.''

Griping about the mail has a long and honourable history in Canada. One of the first complaints on record was in 1822 when the governor general himself, Lord Dalhousie, objected to the way the mail packets from Britain bypassed New York and delivered mail for Canada via Bermuda and Halifax.

Mail for Canada used to go to New York, then up the Hudson River and over the border into Canada by way of Lake Champlain. When British and American troops started marching back and forth across the border shooting at each other during the War of 1812, the Royal Mails had to find another route. The alternative, however, took the mail by sea to Halifax and then overland to Quebec City, an arduous trek that usually took at least a month. Lord Dalhousie complained that his dispatches from England sent in November 1821 did not reach him until the following February. Orders sent in February did not reach him until May.

He and other users of the mail packets, the fast ships used for official mail, were also less than impressed with the prices they paid for this transatlantic service. According to a postal history written in the 1930s, customers paid the equivalent of 92 cents to send a single sheet of paper weighing less than an ounce from London to Quebec City via the land route from Halifax. It cost 96 cents to reach Montreal, $1.04 to get as far as Kingston, and $1.12 to York, all in the days when a dollar was a considerable sum indeed.

Speed, ease of use, reliability, and price: from century to century, from country to country, the mournful lament remains the same. In the eyes of postal customers, the reputation of modern postal systems is undone by a combination of two things: the legendary proportions of their past and the unalterable realities that rule their present.

In Canada, the post office not only provides a ready source of complaints, but also allows Canadians to send their complaints to MPs for free. The combination of mistakes that are easily seen and complaints that are cheaply made has put the post office on the top of the gripe list for many politicians.

The number of complaints to politicians is one measure of postal efficiency. The service they receive as MPs is another, and that has been tainted over the past two decades by the extraordinarily bad showing of Ottawa's own post office, Alta Vista. In 1985, for instance, Ottawa West Tory MP David Daubney complained that mail from his constituents, living less than two miles from Parliament Hill, took an average of nine days to reach him.

Former postmaster general Jean-Jacques Blais remembers the day when one of his Liberal colleagues, Scarborough MP Martin O'Connell, came storming into his office. He was just back from his riding, where he had held a public meeting at which his constituents were free to show up and talk to him. "Christ, there was nobody there. I had five of my executive there. I sent the notices out, but nobody got any notices. I sent them out three weeks ago. I want you personally to do an investigation."

Blais, dumbfounded that O'Connell could have sent out thousands of letters and not had one reach its destination in three weeks, promised to do just that. He went over to the Alta Vista postal terminal and soon found the problem scrunched up underneath one of the sorting machines. Because all the notices were sent out from one office, they had been bundled into a single sack which would not need sorting until it reached Scarborough. "Somebody had shoved the damn sack right underneath the machine. They just saw that it was an MP."

The Alta Vista plant has been no respecter of party lines. Mississauga North MP Bob Horner, a Tory from the other side of Toronto, says he once sent out a batch of 77,000 letters to his constituents at the end of 1984 to wrap up the year. The letters took sixty-two days to reach them. "You put in a New Year's message and people get them in the end of February. . . . I'm fed up with the post office, because aside from other things that come and go in my riding, the post office is a constant irritation."

There have been many theories as to why the Alta Vista plant swallows up mail — especially MPs' mail — with such glee. Senior managers, both under the old department and under the new Crown corporation, have never been able to pin down the cause. And while federal politicians may get a distorted impression of postal service as a result, the problems in Ottawa's plant cannot account for the nation-wide discontent so clear in MPs' mailbags.

Even when postal employees are inspired to do the extraordinary, some customers figure it must be a front for something fishy. In September 1986 the managers of the Cathedral Station Post Office at 215 West 104th St. in New York hit on a novel way to clear up their growing backlog of bills, entreaties, postcards, and periodicals — they sent postmen out for an extra round on Sunday.

"I've been sitting on this stoop on Sundays for over fifty years," 86-year-old Jack Ryan on West 109th St. told the *New York Times*, "and this is the first time I've ever seen it happen. I thought to myself, 'Either I'm crazy or that mailman is.' "

"We don't have a doorman, so the mailman always rings our apartment to get in the building," said Gregory Simmons. "When he rang today, my mother didn't believe him. She thought he was a really dumb burglar pretending to be a mailman, and she wouldn't let him in."

The Canadian post office adds its own touches above and beyond the call of duty. Even Santa Claus has his own postal code (H0H 0H0), and although the post office doesn't promise next-day delivery, many postal workers chip in their free time to make sure those letters to the North Pole get answered. In 1982, for instance, 3,900 postal employees with the help of other volunteers penned 457,000 replies on behalf of St. Nick to children at home and abroad.

And Canada is not without its modern-day postal heroes, even if little is heard of them. In a 1974 speech, Ouellet singled out Fred Quinn, a postal clerk in Halifax who had not taken a day's leave since 1952; Brian Bedard, an Ottawa letter-carrier who noticed smoke coming from a window, checked and discovered a burning mattress, and called the fire department in time to prevent a major loss; and Tom Elsdon, who ran the mail between Calgary and Bragg Creek, Alberta. "When the blizzards blow, his mail truck is often the sole vehicle on the road. At spring runoff, he uses two trucks for one stretch. He leaves one truck on the far side, parks the other on the near side, and wades through the quagmire with the mail. I think we can assume that he's conscientious."

Corkery says the post office is sometimes able to do the almost impossible in tracing people who have moved without leaving a forwarding address, or recovering items lost somewhere in the mail system. "There's still lots of them that really care."

"I think that the devotion of managers and employees at the post office is fantastic," says former Canada Post executive André Lizotte. "They're so badly criticized that they stick together. I've seen this right across the nation."

In the endless fight for better service, Canadians have never been happy except when the government gives them more. In the days before Confederation, the postal service was run from London, and the British Postmaster General gave strict orders that no new postal routes were to be allowed unless his Canadian officials were absolutely sure that the revenues to be gained from those new routes would cover all the extra costs.

Throughout the first half of the nineteenth century a political battle raged between London and colonial politicians. Not until 1847 did Lord Elgin arrive as the new governor general with authorization to hand over control of the postal system as soon as the provincial legislatures had agreed on a uniform system. By 1851 the deed was done.

Complaints about service quickly died down. Those early days were heady ones of full-scale expansion, fulfilling the long-suppressed desires of the Canadian people — a letter in every pot, a post office in every town.

The united province of Upper and Lower Canada had a total of 601 post offices when it gained control in 1851. A year later the total was already up to 844, and by Confederation in 1867 it had reached 2,333. In Nova Scotia, the number doubled in the first four years and quadrupled in fifteen years to reach 630 at Confederation. New Brunswick's network jumped from 100 to 433 over the same period.

The other factor in the rapid expansion was the spread of the railways. From a mere 66 miles of track in 1851, they grew to cover more than 1,400 miles by 1857. The completion of the Grand Trunk and Great Western railways between Quebec and Windsor cut the time it took to send the mail between those two cities from ten and a half days to only forty-nine hours.

It was a time of innovation as well as expansion. Registered mail was started in Nova Scotia in 1852. Money orders were first tried in 1855. Parcel post started in 1859. In the same year, the post office first put letter-boxes on the streets of Toronto.

On October 1, 1874, customers in Montreal began receiving free delivery of their mail by letter-carrier. In the following year, this privilege was extended to residents of Toronto, Quebec, Hamilton, Ottawa, Saint John, and Halifax. Until then, letter-carriers had always collected a fee from those who received letters at their door on top of the price paid by the sender.

Something for nothing has always been a sure winner with voters, and when the United States began experimenting with free delivery to rural residents as well, it did not take long for the idea to spread. After becoming a major election issue in 1908, free mail delivery was ordered for rural routes as well.

The first route, with thirty-seven mailboxes, was opened on October 10, 1908, between Hamilton and Ancaster, Ontario. "A red mail collecting wagon of the style familiar to the residents of the large cities left the Hamilton post office at 2 o'clock with letters and papers for the people living along the route," the Woodstock *Sentinel-Review* recorded. "This was driven by Capt. W. R. Ecclestone, of the Hamilton post office, who will be remembered for his excellent postal work with the Canadian troops in South Africa. No letters were gathered until the 25th box — that of Mr. Walter Vansickle — was reached at the junction of the Dundas and Ancaster roads."

By April 1, 1912, when a separate branch of the post office was created to look after rural routes, there were 900 of them, with 25,000 boxes in use. By November 1913 that number had doubled, and by the dawn of the 1980s, contractors in cars and trucks were delivering letters to more than 1,000,000 addresses on more than 5,000 rural routes.

Through the early days, technology and political pressures combined to cut the cost of mailing letters drastically. As the post office grew larger and more bureaucratic, customers would find it more difficult to wangle new and better services, and prices would head back up.

Much has changed since then. Just as the couriers in their canoes were taken over by the railways, the famous brigades of railway mail clerks, sorting away at fifty miles an hour, have been wiped out by the airplane. Many of the postal clerks, flipping letters into slots with practised skill, have been replaced by machines that can scan tens of thousands of letters an hour.

Yet now, to the puzzlement and anger of postal customers, the advances in technology do not have the same effect as before. Instead of resulting in faster mail delivery, the use of machines seems to make the system slower. Instead of the lower prices made possible by earlier technological advances, the modernization of the post office leads to a never-ending stream of postal-rate increases. Customers have a hard time understanding why the post office finds the mail so tough to deliver. It looks so easy.

The post office has taken to blaming many of the delays on its customers. They use envelopes that are too small or too large. They get the address wrong. They forget the postal code, or make a mistake in writing it down. They don't put enough stamps on it. They stick in odd-shaped objects which give the sorting machines hiccoughs.

The post office, however, can cast blame where it will. Its customers will make their own judgments, based on what they see. And they lay the blame at the feet of those red mailboxes and the people who take care of them. If a person can pick up the phone, punch a dozen numbers, and within seconds talk to someone almost anywhere in the world, it seems inexplicable that a simple letter cannot make it across town overnight.

Moving the mail is a process that has grown increasingly complex over the years. When there was only a relative handful of people in the country sending a fairly small volume of mail to a limited number of destinations, it was pretty simple to keep track of all the pieces and get them to the right places. This century, however, has seen an explosion in the number of people, the number of letters they send, and the number of destinations to which they must go.

A letter passes through many hands, mechanical and human, in what is supposed to be its brief journey. The voyage usually starts in one of those red boxes on the corner, or perhaps in a slot in the local pharmacy, from which a postal truck will take it to the nearest sorting station.

Not all mail can be handled the same way. Large packets and boxes will not fit through the machines, and have to be sorted by hand. Some envelopes are too small for the machines. The job of sorting out ''normal'' letters from the large, small, and strange is done by humans and by a machine called a Culler-Facer-Canceller, or CFC for short.

As its name implies, this machine does other jobs as well as culling — getting rid of the unusual envelopes. It then turns the envelopes so that they all face the same direction and are right side up. This is important, because a later machine looks for the postal code as the last item in the address — the part closest to the bottom of the letter and furthest to the right. Finally, the CFC looks for the fluorescent stripe that appears on every legal Canadian stamp. If a letter is properly stamped, it then cancels the stamp with a postmark, which both makes the stamp impossible to reuse and shows the date that processing began.

The next machine is the one that looks for the postal code. It is called an Optical Character Reader, or OCR. Now that all the letters are right side up, it looks at a one-inch slice of the envelope across the bottom of the address seeking the six-character pattern of three letters and three numbers that make up the Canadian postal code.

The OCRs are far from perfect. They can only cope with so many of the ways to print, type, or write each letter or number. Canada's first machines can read only about one-quarter of the letters fed into them. None the less, it is faster to run all the letters through the machine than to try and figure out which ones it can read and which ones should go straight through to be read by human sorters.

If the OCR can read the postal code on a letter, it sprays it with a pattern of thin and thick bars in a fluorescent orange or yellow ink. This pattern reduces the written code to a series of zeroes and ones which can be understood by the scanners and computers of sorting machines.

Letters that fail to gain the stamp of approval from the OCR are fed into manual-coding desks. At these desks, arranged in banks of twelve, letters pop down one at a time in front of a postal worker who reads the postal code and types it into the machine. Then the letter is whisked off, is sprayed with the orange bar code, and rejoins the successful OCR graduates.

Once coded, the letters go into the first of the sorting processes. The first three characters in the postal code determine whether the letter stays in the same city or goes somewhere else. Letters for other plants are called forward mail, while those that stay in the same plant are known as local mail.

Forward mail is processed first, because this is the mail that must catch flights or make it onto trucks in order to reach the destination plant in time for local sorting. As soon as the forward sort is finished, the computer switches the sorting machines over onto local patterns that will split the mail into smaller and smaller batches which can be sent to individual post offices.

Then it gets tossed back into bags and is taken by truck to neighbourhood postal stations. There the letter-carriers who walk the nation's streets do the final sorting to organize the mail on their routes. Finally, it is out into the rain or sleet or hail or sunshine. With a thunk or a clatter, the mail goes through once more. Another Canadian has his chance to curse the way the post office has blown it once again.

The system has many ways to fail. Letters have been known to get stuck in the crannies of mailboxes, and in one U.S. case were eaten by a rat that was also trapped and had nothing else to satisfy its hunger. When the bags are dumped out in the postal plants, letters can get caught in the folds, sometimes never to be found again unless a prison inmate comes across them when resewing a worn-out bag.

Both machines and men make mistakes in reading and typing the postal code. This sends the letter off to unknown reaches of the postal system. In fact, although postal officials are loath to say so loudly, a letter with a wrong postal code will take longer to process than one sent without a postal code. The latter will flow through the manual sorting process, which may take longer but still works, while a mistake in the code will not be caught until it arrives at the wrong destination and then gets filed back into the manual sorting process to have the code corrected.

Under the old manual system, a letter would be handled by about twenty different sorters. "Every time you did it, you had a check, because if you found an error, it got picked up at that stage," says Corkery. "With post coding, you don't have that. You get one reading, and then you don't have anything until it gets to the letter-carrier. Once that [set of] darn little yellow bars is on the bottom, if it isn't right, it's gone to Timbuktu, and until Timbuktu finds it and gets it back into the system, it's written off.''

When Corkery worked in the manufacturing business, it was all right to make mistakes on five per cent of the items. ''You couldn't tolerate a five-per-cent error rate in sortation. You would be dead. You're talking half of one per cent per sorter. Even that is a horrendous number, and the bloody thing is spread across the deck, so that every customer's got one error and so you've got 200,000 to 300,000 a night that are screaming blue murder.''

Even when the operators or the OCRs read the postal code correctly and the machine sprays on the right sequence of bars and spaces, the sprayed code may not be readable. That happens most often when the envelope contains something bulky, even a thick letter of too many pages, which is significantly smaller than the envelope. A bump or slope on the front surface of the envelope means that the code bars may get sprayed on at a slant which becomes unreadable by the letter-sorting machines. Such letters are rejected and have to go back and be done again — sometimes much later.

For one letter, the system would work easily. For twenty-five million a day, it gets trickier. What makes a good performance toughest of all is that, while twenty-five million a day may be average, Canadians are far from consistent.

Someone who wants to fly from Ottawa to Vancouver books a seat. If there are no seats left, too bad. A Bruce Springsteen fan lines up for concert tickets. If he is not fast enough, he either stays outside or pays a huge sum to a scalper. Canadians have never been asked to book passage for their letters, and only recently have they begun to pay scalpers' prices to private courier services.

In fact, many business customers of the post office insist on waiting until the end of the day to mail their letters. The evening pick-up collects about eighty per cent of the daily volume. Postal plants have from then until 10:30 to sort all the letters headed for out-of-town destinations. Letters that have not made it through the mill by then will miss the last flights out of town at about 11:30.

"So you've got about five hours to sort, and that's all you've got, a little tiny window," says Jim Corkery. If letters are going to be delivered the day after being sent, postal plants have to work through the night. As soon as the mail going out of town is taken care of, the local mail has to be sorted. Before that is finished, the letters from other towns and cities begin to arrive. It all has to be finished by about six in the morning for the letter-carriers to do the final sorting into their shoulder-bags.

"The other big difference, and this is the one that we just never found a solution for, no country has found a solution for, you cannot forecast what sort of volumes you're going to get. Traditionally, you get a swing over a two-week period of forty per cent [from highest- to lowest-volume days]. That's unreal when you try to say, I've got to staff for that. . . . You can't control your product."

In the manufacturing business, everybody puts in a regular shift. If machines break down or orders suddenly surge, you ship out the extras stored in the warehouse out back. If all your customers go on holiday, you can let the warehouse fill a bit before you worry about laying off workers.

A postal manager really has four choices: pay too much every day to have a large staff on hand; bring in casuals when needed and fight with the unions; pay union members lots of overtime; or use enough workers to handle an average load and let the rest of the mail slop over into the next day, hoping that the next day will have lighter volumes on its own.

With co-operation from customers, there are ways to ease the variations from day to day. About four-fifths of the mail goes to or from businesses, and much of it comes in big batches of bills and junk mail. Big mailers like the phone, hydro, gas, and credit-card companies really couldn't care less if their bills take one day or four to reach their customers.

The post office can therefore use this kind of mail to level its load from one day to the next. As long as the bulk mail is pack-aged on its own, the post office can tuck it into a "warehouse" on a busy day and get it done the next. Of course, those big customers want something for their co-operation. The post office, for instance, can offer to come and pick up their mail in the morning, right off their computer printout. Now that it is a Crown corporation, it can also offer discounts on the price of mailing those bills — an option it did not have while still a government department.

One of the ironies of modern postal service, however, is that while the bulk of the mail is handled faster and more accurately, the letters about which customers really care are most likely to be abused. Personal mail, such as hand-addressed birthday cards, thank-you notes, or get-well-soon cards, tends to be oddly sized, illegible by machine, mistaken by coding-desk operators, and to have wrong or missing postal codes. The modern sorting system has little or no tolerance for such flaws.

Most of the mail does move quickly. What ruins the post office's public image is the sheer volume of letters. The Crown corporation set an objective of delivering 90 per cent of letters on time: the day after mailing within cities, two days between most major centres, and three days from coast to coast. That standard was applied to more than seven billion pieces of mail a year.

Even if the post office reached its target of 90 per cent on-time delivery, 10 per cent would have arrived late. For the fiscal year ended March 31, 1985, that would have been 730,000,000 late letters — two million for every day of the year. Putting it another way, every man, woman, and child in Canada would have received an average of twenty-nine late pieces of mail a year.

Canada Post did not meet that target. During 1985, it dipped below 80 per cent on-time performance. Personal mail makes up only a fraction of the total mail — about one-fifth, of which half are Christmas cards. But because the machines have trouble digesting it, personal mail inevitably makes up a much bigger chunk of the late mail.

The sheer number of late letters means that some will either be very late, or be sent to people who keep a close watch on the travel time of their mail. A really late letter can stick in the mind for years, and taint a customer's perception of postal service long after any changes for the better may have taken place.

The troublesome number of late letters is one thing. The problem gets worse when customers no longer believe the numbers. And the post office's record gives them good reason to be suspicious.

In 1981, the year the Crown corporation was born, Auditor General Kenneth Dye severely criticized the accuracy of the National Evaluation of Postal Service (NEPS), the system used by the post office to measure the speed of postal service.

All NEPS tests were handled internally. There were no outside, independent checks. The tests used specially prepared test letters that were correctly addressed and bore the postal code. The test letters were mixed in with the regular mail at postal plants, and delivered to postal boxes in post offices both within the same city and in other cities.

Yet NEPS measured only certain kinds of mail. In particular, it only looked at perfectly "machinable" mail. Most third-class (advertising mail) and about half the first-class letters — any that had to be manually processed — were not counted. Those personal letters not only were the most prone to delays, but also tended to slip between the cracks of the postal measurement system.

Using his own procedures for a three-month test of the mail in early 1981, the Auditor General came up with much the same results as the post office for mail sent between cities: about 50 per cent of the letters arrived on time.

When it came to local mail, however, the Auditor General found that actual delivery times were much slower than those claimed by the post office. In Ottawa, the Auditor General said only 85 per cent of local mail arrived the next day, while NEPS claimed a success rate of 90-93 per cent. In Toronto, the Auditor General's results varied between 77 and 80 per cent, while NEPS said 86 to 90 per cent of local letters were on time. And in Vancouver, the third city tested, the government auditors found that only 68 to 72 per cent of mail within the city was arriving at its destination the next day, compared with the 81 to 82 per cent claimed by the post office.

There were other problems with the post office testing process as well. The most significant was that while NEPS did measure what percentage of the mail arrived on time, it paid no attention to how late the rest of the letters arrived.

For postal managers, the test procedures created a dangerous sense of satisfaction. No other means of measuring the speed and reliability of the mail were being used, so the NEPS figures became the balm that soothed the harried brows of those facing the never-ending barrage of public complaints. ''Nobody is perfect,'' they could say, ''but our figures show that we are doing a good job.''

The most serious damage was done outside, both to the post office's image and reputation in the eyes of the public, and to the public's willingness to trust the post office when it did try to improve. When the Auditor General himself, that staunch defender of the public purse, came right out and said that the post office was lying with its figures, postal credibility was dealt a mortal blow. It would have devastating consequences for the new managers of the Crown corporation when they not only continued to use NEPS internally but made it their public measure of improved performance.

The resulting practices were laid bare after a Toronto postal clerk, Aditya Varma, went public with a variety of charges against the post office. He was fired, but was reinstated on the orders of the Prime Minister's Office early in 1985. The government ordered an investigation by the consulting firm of Laventhol and Horwath. Its report found most of his charges groundless, but confirmed flaws in the testing system.

Among the documents found by the consultants was a December 5, 1979, memo from the regional general manager for Ontario to the directors of all his plants. ''It has come to my attention that some officers, in their zeal, are identifying test letters at some point in the operation and searching for any that may be missing. Not only does this practice compromise the results, but it uses time which can be better spent getting our customers' mail out.''

In February 1982 the Quality Assurance Branch of the new corporation did some extra tests of its own in the wake of the Auditor General's report. They showed that NEPS overestimated post office performance by more than 15 per cent for local mail and by 10 per cent for mail sent between cities.

In February 1984 the Internal Audit division did a confidential report on the operations in Halifax and recommended major changes in the testing procedures.

In June 1984 the manager of service-performance research in the Pacific Division wrote to the manager of the Vancouver sorting plant: "I regret to have to advise you that I have a further report from one of my officers who outlined in detail how the tampering with test mail is conducted in your plant."

Laventhol and Horwath found that the purpose of the figures changed dramatically as soon as the post office began publishing them. "NEPS letters were easily identifiable and some plants established procedures to ensure that these letters received priority treatment. . . . When NEPS results were presented to the public as an indication of the performance provided by Canada Post, pressure was felt by the supervisors in the plants who were made accountable for achieving high NEPS test results. . . . By holding plant personnel accountable for the achievement of satisfactory performance figures, management may have unwittingly encouraged practices designed to inflate NEPS test results."

As a result of all the public furor, Canada Post did adopt better testing procedures, eventually handing the entire job of testing to an outside agency, but the damage had been done.

There is more than one way to make postal performance look better than it really is. In his book *The Postal Business*, Michael Corby found that the British post office had managed to improve its on-time performance by easing its standards. During its first decade as a Crown corporation, the British post office started clearing street mailboxes earlier in the day, reduced some of its evening collections, and abolished all collections on Sunday. If it had kept the same standards, said Corby, the Royal Mails would have delivered only 84.3 per cent on time in 1975/76, rather than the 92.6 per cent the corporation reported. Similarly, while more than 90 per cent of second-class mail was being delivered within two days after mailing when the Crown corporation was set up in 1969, a decade later the post office reported that 95 per cent was "on time" — within three days of posting.

In Canada, when the government announced a new five-year plan for Canada Post in 1986, it promised to boost on-time performance to 99 per cent by July 1987. The catch was that the deadlines had been pushed back by a full day. On time now means two days for local delivery, three days between most major cities, and four days across the country.

In 1980, the post office department reported to André Ouellet as he became postmaster general for the second time that 92 per cent of local mail was being delivered the next day and 99 per cent within two days. Seventy-nine per cent of mail to other destinations was arriving on time and 96 per cent within an extra day. In other words, before the Crown corporation even started, the post office said it was delivering 99 per cent of local mail and 96 per cent of out-of-town mail within the standards Canada Post Corp. adopted in 1986 — if you believe the test results.

Still, that 99 per cent sounds pretty good. But even a mere one per cent of seven billion letters is seventy million pieces of mail that will fail to meet the new, more generous deadline. If there is anything that infuriates a customer more than failing to meet a difficult deadline, it is failure to meet an easy one.

2
Addressing
Change

■

"By the way," Claude Parent asked his old boss, John Mackay, "have you seen the ad in the paper?"

Mackay, then president of ITT Canada, had not seen Parent in what seemed like ages when he bumped into him by chance at the Toronto airport in early 1969. Parent had quit his job as corporate secretary when the company moved its head office to Guelph, Ontario. He wanted his children to have their schooling in French, so he joined the federal government in Ottawa at the Public Service Commission.

Now the PSC wanted someone to fill a brand-new job at the post office. The ad Mackay had not yet seen sought a regional general manager for Ontario. This person would be told to fix the post office in the province his way, with unprecedented freedom from meddling by Ottawa.

To take on the job, the government, and Postmaster General Eric Kierans in particular, wanted to find a private-sector executive who could wake up the tradition-bound department and bring it into the twentieth century as a business. "I said, 'So?' " recalls Mackay. "He said, 'Well, that's just up your alley, 'cause you'd love that.' It was one of those shots out of the dark."

Mackay was not overly excited, but he was a little worried about his future with ITT. He was scheduled for a move to a new post fairly soon, and the company wanted him to go to the United States. Neither Raleigh, North Carolina, nor either of the company's two sites in Tennessee really appealed to him as nice places to live, but ITT was the sort of company where even well-respected executives could not afford to say "No" very often.

Because of that, Mackay did not reject Parent's suggestion out of hand. He asked his former subordinate to let him know more about the job, and then forgot about it. Mackay soon got more than a letter. That summer, he was called by David Morley, the chief head-hunter for the Public Service Commission. Morley wanted him to visit Ottawa and come in to talk about the job. "I wasn't that excited about it, so I said, 'Why don't you send me some literature on it?' "

Mackay could be excused for playing the reluctant bride. Ever since the Second World War, the post office had been considered anything but a great place to go by public servants with ambition. Until Kierans came along, there was little interest in even trying to recruit managers from the private sector. When the government did try, its recruiters were rarely met with great delight. In Mackay's case, though, Morley was persistent, and since Mackay happened to be going to Ottawa on a business trip the week he was called, he agreed to stop by Morley's office.

Morley had already called in the heavy artillery. While in Ottawa, Mackay got a phone call from Kierans. The two men launched into a long chat. Mackay had bumped into Kierans before, during a speech in Toronto by the minister where the ITT president had asked a tough question that got Kierans worked up. He went over to the minister after the speech, and after the two had talked for a while, Kierans popped a pointed suggestion. If people like Mackay thought things could be done better, he said, they should be willing to join the civil service and help set things straight. "He sort of shut me up," says Mackay. "I thought: Work for the government? That's crazy."

The suggestion came back to him when Kierans renewed his assault in Ottawa. "He was the greatest personnel head-hunter that you could come across. He talked with great exuberance about government, what people should do for the government," Mackay says of Kierans.

Money was a problem. The government could not afford to pay Mackay as much as ITT did. But Mackay was just turning forty and not too worried about the size of his retirement bank account. What made up his mind, aside from Kierans' persistence, was a combination of excitement and worry. He was increasingly hesitant about going to the United States, and increasingly intrigued by the idea of doing something that had never been done before.

He quickly got more than he expected. Less than a year after taking on the job in October 1969 to run the experimental Ontario region, the top job at the post office fell vacant with the departure of Paul Faguy. Mackay was invited to move to Ottawa and take the top slot.

"I was one man and a girl in the Ontario region in Toronto and I said, God, I don't really know that much about the post office," he recalls. But he had been in on much of the consulting work being done at the time, and he felt he could handle the job. On September 1, 1970, he started work in Ottawa. He would keep the job for the next six years, through some of the most turbulent episodes in Canada's postal history.

"The most important objective that Kierans gave yours truly was: 'Mechanize the post office and put a postal code in. And if you do that, Mackay, that's all I'm hiring you for. That's the main thing.' "

To achieve that goal, the department put more ads in the papers. "We were looking for bargaining people, operational people, for the regions, and industrial engineering and the whole gamut," says Mackay. Over the next couple of years, some 55 to 60 private-sector executives were dropped into the top post office jobs. Another 100 or so, including a handful from his old company, were hired at lower levels. The influx was quickly dubbed — among other labels — "the ITT Mafia", a label that became particularly pointed when the post office later chose ITT machines as part of its plans for mechanization.

The new managers came for all kinds of reasons from all kinds of backgrounds. Jim Corkery, who first filled Mackay's slot in Ontario and later succeeded him in the top job, came to the post office after twenty-five years at Canadian General Electric. He was a professional engineer who moved into management. He knew about running large plants with assembly-line workers and a tough union.

He came to the post office because he had felt it was time to leave what he calls "a dying business": manufacturing television picture tubes and radio tubes. "My job was to fire about two thousand people, close down three plants. And I didn't like it, because I'm three generations out of GE. My father worked for them and I knew a lot of these engineers when I was in knee pants following them around through the factories. I decided when I looked at GE that there was more of the same that should take place. Somebody had to be the hatchetman and that's a terrible job. I got a feeling that this company would be using us somewhere else. . . .

"I was mad at the company, too, because I didn't think the company did a very fair job in treating their employees, I think they just threw them to the wolves. Just when I was in this sort of mind-set, an ad appears in the paper for a regional general manager for Ontario for the post office. The description of what they were looking for was my background completely because I came out of a heavy mechanization/automation kind of industry. I said, Hey, that's me. I don't know anything about the post office, but it's about time I changed.

"So I threw my hat into the ring, and there were two hundred of us that applied for the job." He was picked to go before the selection board. After talking to Mackay and Bill Wilson, an earlier deputy minister, they offered him his choice of three regions needing new top bosses. Corkery decided to stay in Toronto and take the Ontario region.

Other private-sector talent had volunteered. Gordon Sinclair had been working in the gas business in Washington, D.C., when the racial unrest of the sixties reached its peak. With four girls in the family, the forced-busing issue made him think of going home, and he fired off a letter to Edgar Benson, then head of the Treasury Board, saying he was available. "Next thing I knew I had several entreaties from the federal government."

He settled on a job as a director in the Department of Fisheries, with the mission of making the changes recommended by the

Royal Commission on Government Organization, the Glassco commission, in 1962. He came to the attention of the post office in 1968 when he was pressured by his boss into being interviewed by a board for a job in the Department of Indian and Northern Affairs.

It was a job he did not want. Perhaps as a result, the interview went badly as he got into a verbal fight with the deputy minister. However, Sinclair now suspects he was sent there for the benefit of one of the other members of the board, the assistant deputy minister for finance at the post office, who was on the verge of retiring.

A week later he got a phone call from Paul Faguy, the deputy postmaster general, who asked him to come in for a chat about working for the post office. "I had the beginnings of the flu and I was starting to take chills and it was about minus twenty-five Celsius . . . anyways, I went." Just after Christmas, in the middle of the holiday season, the Public Service Commission called and offered him the retiring assistant deputy's job.

His job in Fisheries was far from finished, but the jump to assistant deputy minister was a big promotion. It was a case of being in the right place at the right time. Kierans had already started his recruitment campaign, and the Public Service Commission was anxious to show him that the public service already had the kind of person he wanted.

Sinclair admits he didn't really know how big a job he had agreed to take on until he got there. "Nobody really appreciates the size and the scope of the post office until they begin to look into the beast. Then it gets to be monumental."

Others poured in from all over the country — John Uberig, vice-president and treasurer of Southam Publications; Garth Campbell from the marketing side of Canadian National Railways; Jack Prescott, president of American Air Filter; Larry Sperling, executive vice-president of Consumer's Distributing.

Kierans was relentless in his pursuit of talent, using moral suasion to get what he couldn't buy. Sinclair remembers going on trips to Montreal and Toronto with Kierans and Faguy during which the minister made dinner speeches to business leaders, scolding them into doing their part. "This is the post office problem. These are the kinds of executives we need. You here have an obligation to help the government, the country, yourselves,'' by lending good people to the post office or pointing out those that were available, Kierans would say. "It was an appeal for talent.''

As a group, the people he recruited would have a tremendous impact on the workings of the post office over the following decade. It would not be the kind of impact Kierans had envisioned. The conflict and chaos of the next decade would leave their collective reputation badly tarnished. None the less, by the late 1960s their private-sector experience was badly needed.

The management that prompted Kierans to drastic action was itself the result of decades of slow build-up, in rather the same way that sand and silt and dead bodies drift to the bottom of a lake and, in time, solidify into sandstone. Montreal was a particular trouble-spot, says Mackay. It was "one of the most inbred postal operations across the country. The people had been there for generations. Nobody ever moved in or out.'' Others before Kierans had tried to shake up the organization to get a better handle on postal operations, but no matter how much they stirred up the mud, it all seemed to settle back into more of the same.

Despite decades of efforts to get postal managers in the field to take decisions on their own, the post office remained obsessed with the notion of centralized control. Neither crisis nor opportunity could get fast answers out of Ottawa. "People say that if you wanted a rubber stamp costing $3.50, you had to get a requisition out of Ottawa, and from what documents I saw, I think there was a certain amount of truth to that,'' said Mackay.

The public service was not alone in such practices. ITT, says Mackay, "was very bureaucratic and precise. Everything was laid down in black and white. For instance, ITT had a public image to maintain. They even said what typewriter, what type you had to use in your typewriters, and the type of paper. It was as rigid as that. The big difference, though: it was easy to get a decision. In government, it's not easy, because too many people are involved.''

Even minor matters had to be referred by postmasters to district directors and then to headquarters in Ottawa for approval before any action could be taken, said a consultants' report in

1969. "This includes purchases exceeding $10.00 on First Aid supplies and $50.00 on the repair of furniture and furnishings except in emergency cases."

Just setting up a new letter-carrier route—in accordance with the regulations — required thirteen steps, which involved the local postmaster, the district director, the superintendent of operations, the supervisor of postal requirements, the director of postal service, the assistant director for operations, as well as the delivery requirements division, the installations and staffing standards division, the organization and establishment division, the buildings and accommodation division, either the city services division or the highway and rural services division and the personnel classification branch, and reference to either municipal officials or MPs.

The true state of postal management was not revealed until Kierans took charge after Trudeau's election in 1968. He felt that the post office was in real trouble. In the course of his work on a Crown corporation, he unleashed a bevy of consulting firms to do a series of studies on what was wrong and how to fix it.

Their reports, summarized in an inch-thick document by Kates, Peat, Marwick and Co. called *A Blueprint for Change*, touched on every aspect of postal problems. Their conclusions about the state of management made the case for new blood shockingly clear.

The existing managers were badly educated and they were old. Of about 500 officers of the department at or above the Program Administration 3 level or its equivalent, almost 70 per cent had no more than a high school education. Only 16 per cent had one or more university degrees. In the vital program-administration group, the section that ran postal operations, only 4 per cent had degrees.

Many of the senior managers seemed to have risen to their posts just by being there long enough. Over half of the top 500 officers were over the age of 50, and a third of them were between 40 and 49. The age distribution was even worse in the group responsible for actually moving the mail: 68 per cent of the officers there were over 50 and 92 per cent of them were more than 45 years old.

Kierans says former deputy minister Bill Wilson was an example of what was wrong with the post office. He was a nice guy, Kierans says, but generally satisfied with the way the post office was run. He had worked his way up the ranks from letter-carrier to the top of the bureaucracy. "Nowhere in the period of twenty-five or thirty years had anybody spent a nickel on Bill Wilson" for training in finance, or accounting, or transportation, or human or industrial relations. That prompted Kierans to look at how much the post office as a whole spent on management training in a year. "It was $35,000. You had 40,000 employees, which meant you could have bought them each a hot dog. It was all spent on going to conferences. No wonder you have the problems you have."

Most managers were career civil servants, largely promoted from within the post office. Many still carried the stamp of their military past, although some managers say the extent of military style is overrated. However, it was clear that orders still came from the top, and those giving orders expected them to be obeyed. Personal favouritism played a role in promotions; so did a desire to bribe potential trouble-makers out of the ranks of the hoi polloi.

The result was a system of managers who lacked formal training and were respectful of authority from higher-ups. Indeed, the consultants outlined a fundamental problem of management attitudes: an unwillingness to question traditional ways of dealing with problems, a lack of initiative, an excessive reliance on the rules and regulations rather than on common sense, and an over-all feeling that they were administrators rather than managers.

Theoretically, an ambitious postal manager had the freedom and authority to use his own initiative. In reality, the structures binding the post office also shackled its managers. Bucking tradition, said the consultants, could be "taxing in the extreme and would exhaust the endurance of even the most persevering of executives."

Major changes were clearly needed, and needed soon.

Canada was not the only country with postal problems by the time the sixties rolled around. In the United States and Great

Britain, others had also decided that the end of that turbulent decade was a good time for change.

South of the border, in the midst of civil-rights movements, anti-war protests, hippie communes, and other facets of a culture in transition, a politician did something strange. Lawrence O'Brien, a long-time foot-slogger for the Democratic Party, had been rewarded with the job of postmaster general in President Lyndon Johnson's cabinet. In the spring of 1967, O'Brien told an astounded U.S. public that he felt his job should be abolished.

O'Brien said that the only way to free the U.S. post office from a "restrictive jungle of legislation and custom" was to turn the federal department into a non-profit corporation. The company would be run by a board of directors appointed by the President with the approval of Congress, would have the power to issue bonds to pay for expansion of its plants and machinery, would set its own rates to cover expenses, and would pay its employees by private-sector standards.

By then, the United States postal service employed 700,000 people, more than any U.S. company except AT&T and General Motors. It collected more money in revenue each year than such industrial giants as U.S. Steel and DuPont. Yet on its budget of $6.3 billion (U.S.), it lost more than $1 billion in 1967.

In a line that could have been written for Canadians, the *Arizona Republic* described the U.S. post office as "deeply ensnared in political patronage, a dozen feuding postal unions, antiquated machines and methods, and bureaucratic red tape originating from political pressures." The paper heartily endorsed O'Brien's suggestions.

The Postmaster General had to go to Congress for step-by-step approval of almost anything he wanted to do: building or modernizing post offices, buying new equipment, raising postal rates, or changing employee salary levels. He was beholden to other departments of government for many of his needs. The General Services Administration, for instance, controlled all postal buildings in much the same way that the Department of Public Works in Canada owned all of the Canadian post office's quarters. That meant that the U.S. post office had to ask the GSA any time it wanted to cut a new window in a wall, repair a floor, or improve the lighting in a postal plant.

And, of course, many post office jobs were political appointments, subject to both Congressional whims and high turnover. "About all the Postmaster General can do is preside over the resulting chaos," noted the *Los Angeles Times*.

Congress was not eager to lose such an abundant font of political appointments and patronage contracts. President Johnson did, however, appoint a ten-person commission headed by former AT&T chairman Frederick Kappel to conduct "the most searching and exhaustive review ever" of postal operations.

The resulting 1968 report, called *Towards Postal Excellence*, provided fascinating reading for the Canadian consultants commissioned by Kierans to do the same thing for the Canadian post office in 1969. The folks at Kates, Peat, Marwick were particularly struck by one passage from a Congressional hearing, where the chairman of the House Postal Appropriations Subcommittee asked O'Brien:

"General . . . would this be a fair summary: that at the present time, as the manager of the Post Office Department, you have no control over your workload, you have no control over the rates of revenue, you have no control over the pay rates of the employees you employ, you have very little control over the conditions of service of these employees, you have virtually no control, by the nature of it, of your physical facilities that you are compelled to use — all of which adds up to a staggering amount of 'no control' in terms of the duties you have to perform. . . ."

O'Brien replied: "Mr. Chairman, I would have to generally agree with your premise . . . that is a staggering list of 'no control'. I don't know [whether] it has ever been put that succinctly to me. If it had been at an appropriate time, perhaps I wouldn't be sitting here."

The report of the President's commission was too pointed to ignore. There were too many problems that could be solved. The result was a U.S. form of Crown corporation in 1970.

Much as the Canadian consultants would recommend, the Postal Reorganization Act handed the running of the post office to a board of governors. Its members were appointed by the politicians, but had the authority to tell the post office what to do. The new U.S. Postal Service gained the power to negotiate with its own employees. It took control of its buildings. The right to raise stamp prices was taken away from the politicians and given to an independent Postal Rate Commission.

In Britain, meanwhile, Her Majesty's mandarins had come to similarly glum conclusions about the state of their post office. In 1969, Britain did set up a Crown corporation, and gave it a mandate and legislation similar to that adopted in Canada twelve years later. They allowed it to negotiate with its unions. They kept rate-setting in the hands of the politicians. They told the new corporation to be efficient and improve service.

By the mid-1970s, the post office was in chaos. Service had deteriorated, fiscal losses were sky-rocketing, and another major review committee had to step in to figure out what had gone wrong. The British experience would prove that a Crown corporation in and of itself was not enough to solve the problems of a business like the post office. Yet it would also show Canadian politicians — years before they decided to follow suit — how to avoid some serious problems in the way a Crown corporation was set up.

Those lessons, which could have saved years of grief and untold amounts of money, would be ignored.

Back in Ottawa, the Canadian consulting firms knew Kierans wanted a vision of sweeping change and that is what they produced in *A Blueprint for Change.*

In 1969, their study said, the department was at a crossroads in its history. "Down one road, unless fundamental changes are effected, lie steadily deteriorating services to the public and a mounting annual deficit which by 1980 could exceed $500-million." As it was, the deficit was helped along by inflation, and passed the half-billion-dollar mark by the mid-1970s. By the end of the decade, the losses had actually dipped a bit, but there was little doubt in the public mind that service had only gone downhill.

The consultants, however, were convinced that a better way was possible. Despite all the earlier studies, there had been no real look at why the post office existed. As a government department, the post office can provide superb service, ignore the costs, and still be judged a star performer — if superb service is the government's goal. As a business, it can succeed only if it stays afloat financially. Like any company in the service industry, the post office must pay attention to its customers and what they want. But like any company anywhere, it must also keep its costs in line with its revenue.

A commercially oriented post office, the report said, is one that is "responsive to the needs of its customers, alert to the realities of the competitive environment and provides efficient service at the lowest possible cost. . . . It must be recognized that the opposite to a commercially-oriented post office is a post office that provides an unsatisfactory service that is unduly costly."

A Blueprint for Change said a Crown corporation was the only way to go. To make such a corporation work, many other changes would be needed.

Chief among them was a huge investment in new machinery to automate the sorting of letters. Automation had been one of the perennial victims of the federal budget process. Postal plants were out of date and overcrowded. On the basis of the machine sorting being done in other countries, including the United States, Great Britain, Australia, and Germany, automation in Canada could cut the cost of handling a letter by up to twenty per cent.

A new management structure was also vital. The government would have to restrict its role to that of any other shareholder. It would appoint a board of directors, which would then run the company within general guidelines set by the government.

Directors would have to have proven managerial competence that applied to the post office's major markets. The board must have the authority to hire, fire, transfer, and promote postal employees, the consultants said. It would take over negotiations with the postal unions and look after benefits such as a pension plan.

"We have concluded that constraints are placed on the administration of the post office which prevent fulfilment of their tasks. This is particularly the case in the areas of personnel, facilities and finance." A Crown corporation should have the option of getting other departments to do such work on a contract basis or of hiring people to handle those jobs itself.

The corporation should be set up to be self-supporting, the consultants recommended. The company could keep any profits it made to cover losses in other years. If it made enough money, it could pay dividends.The corporation would also be allowed to borrow money from the government, either for operating costs or for long-term investments.

Above all, the postal corporation must be able to set the rates it needed, they argued. No more would Parliament be left with the job of raising the price of a stamp. Politics had consistently left postal rates lagging behind the costs of moving the mail. For a Crown corporation to succeed, that job would have to be handed to an independent body.

The consultants admitted that even if the corporation took all their advice on improving productivity and cutting costs, stamp prices would still have to go up, and they did not want politicians to be able to derail the plan. "Analysis of the expenditure and revenue forecasts leads unalterably to the conclusion that the economic fate of the Post Office rests squarely with the flexibility and freedom to adjust rates to cover expenditures."

To make all this work, the consultants said, new managers with new ideas were an absolute must. Training programs for the managers already there were needed too, but the ambitious sort of program they wanted to see would be impossible without tough, competent, and experienced help from the private sector. The recruitment efforts were supposed to bring people into the operations branch with experience in fields alien to the bureaucracy: industrial engineering, traffic and transportation, production control and distribution, business administration, and sales and marketing.

The consultants recognized that it would be tough to get good people to move to the post office. "Prerequisites to attracting top calibre executives with proven experience are competitive salaries, freedom of action within agreed policies, budgeting controls and clearly defined objectives and goals, and possibly most important of all, the full support of a board of directors."

What the consultants had presented as a carefully-thought-out package became a political shopping-list. The government decided to spend lots of money on new machines and buildings. It hired its legion of private-sector managers. It played with new organizational structures.

The new team of postal executives was, in the end, cut adrift in the bureaucratic sea. Their boat had enough gas to run for a while, but then they found themselves trying to use the same old tools as their predecessors. The new managers were trying to paddle their craft through a hurricane. Just like O'Brien in the United States, the new managers had a job to do, but still had no control.

3
Of
Machines
and Men

■

Gerry Fultz was the epitome of the old-style postal manager. He had never finished high school, but he had a natural talent for engineering. After decades in the post office, says his boss, Gordon Sinclair, he had an encyclopedic knowledge of the post office and the way it worked. He was also rough, tough, and abrasive. "He looks like Archie Bunker, he talks like Archie Bunker, and he thinks like Archie Bunker."

One day, Fultz phoned his boss from Vancouver. "Sinclair," he snapped. "Today's my birthday."

"I know that, Gerald. Happy birthday," a bemused Sinclair replied.

"Thank you very much. I just wanted to call you up and tell you something. Today I'm fifty-five years of age and now I've got my thirty-five years in. I just want you to know that I can afford to be as sassy as I please."

"Gerry," shot back Sinclair, "how will I know?"

Bob Rapley was Fultz's opposite, an intellectual man who had worked in management consulting and administration for the air force, the Public Service Commission, and the Treasury Board before joining the post office. "They were like oil and water, except they became fast friends," says Sinclair. Together, the two would lay the groundwork for the mechanization of the post office.

At one time Canada was on the leading edge of work on postal machines. In the late 1950s, the Canadian post office built a machine in its own workshops which was controlled by one of the first computers ever designed for postal purposes. It did not use a postal code, but extracted what it needed from the address. The procedure proved too clumsy and costly and the project was abandoned.

That was the end of work on machine sorting in Canada until it became a centrepiece in Kierans' sweeping vision of change. One of the consultants' studies, done by Samson, Belair, Riddell and Stead of Montreal, looked at the possibilities for coding. A postal code is a vital part of an automated post office because it becomes the part of the address that can be read and understood by the sorting machines.

The new machines, in turn, meant that new plants had to be built. Some could be adapted, but others would have to be scrapped in favour of new sites.

The government wasted no time in moving on mechanization. The Samson, Belair study was tabled in the House of Commons in February 1970, and the post office set up a coding and mechanization branch to run the project in July. By then, the government had already announced that the first postal codes would be released on April 1, 1971. That gave the fledgling team under Fultz and Rapley nine months to learn how to make a code work, design one, and then implement it.

In the spring, postal officials went off to West Germany and Great Britain to see their brand-new machines at work. They made more trips that summer as they settled on the format for a Canadian code. In July, they decided to use the now-familiar six-figure code with three letters and three numbers. The format, known as ANA NAN, where A is a letter and N is a number, was far more flexible than the all-number zip code used in the United States. Even though six letters — D, F, I, O, Q, and U — are not used to avoid confusion, especially with handwritten codes, the format has almost as many combinations as there are Canadian addresses.

By March 1971 the post office had finished turning a map of Ottawa streets into a complete list of codes for the city. Then came Manitoba, Saskatchewan, and Alberta. Parts of Ontario followed, and then eastern Quebec, Metro Toronto, western

Quebec, the rest of Ontario, Montreal, British Columbia, and finally the Atlantic provinces.

Meanwhile, the post office was well along with the job of choosing and installing the machines to do the sorting. Canada decided to forgo the latest thing in postal technology. The Optical Character Reader, a machine that could read printed words or characters and translate them into machine code directly, was still in its infancy. The post office did not want to take chances. The ANA NAN code was designed to be read by OCRs when that technology was ready, but to start, Canada would stick with "coding suites".

A suite is made up of twelve coding desks, where human beings read the postal code and type it into the machine and the machine sprays on the fluorescent bar code. Even with these machines, Canada was determined to stick with a known quantity. "They wanted stuff off-the-shelf, and there were very few companies around that actually made stuff from the shelf," says Mackay. The technology was so new that most machines were custom-designed.

Belgium had begun with a single machine that read only the typeface of its own department's printer on the cheques it sent out. France and West Germany had done some work, and England had bought its first machines, but, like other countries, it was running into terrible problems with its unions. "They mothballed the stuff for months, because the unions wouldn't work on it." Japan had already coded, and Nippon Electric Co., along with a couple of U.S. companies, were ITT's main competition for Canada's business.

The first set of machines was slated for Ottawa, right under the noses of Canada's curious and demanding politicians. Tenders were called in November 1971 and opened in January 1972. The contract went to John Mackay's old company, ITT Canada Ltd., which was acting as the sales agent for an ITT subsidiary in Belgium.

The decision landed Mackay, only recently elevated to the top job in Ottawa, in hot water with Opposition politicians. He faced two grillings at the hands of parliamentary committees looking for evidence that he had fixed the bidding.

"Clinically pure, I was not around when the quotes were given, and ITT was the lowest quote," he says. "It was also probably the most developed off-the-shelf. So they won the contract."

However, he was well aware of the perceptions a successful ITT bid might cause, and he kept Jean-Pierre Côté, the new postmaster general, up to date on the problem. The minister was well prepared for the queries when they came, and kept Mackay from being too badly mauled.

The contract called for delivery of the first machine in January 1972. On January 3, an Air Canada DC8 landed at Montreal International Airport in Dorval with nineteen tons of equipment. It was taken to the Ottawa postal station the next morning — the first working day of the year. The post office wasted no time in setting up the machine, and by August it was handling "live mail" (rather than test batches).

When tenders were called in October 1971 for the machines needed in the other fourteen large postal plants scheduled for automation, ITT came out on top once again. There had been only two bids, and although ITT's equipment was actually more expensive, it needed fewer people to run it, and would be made in Canada.

The first coding desk from the new Canadian plant arrived in Ottawa on June 9, 1973, and by July 25, Postmaster General André Ouellet had flipped the switches on the first two Canadian coding suites and the letter-sorting machines that went with them. By the next winter, special tests on four suites and sorting machines under peak loads had convinced the post office that the machines worked properly.

By then, the training machines were already in place in Winnipeg and the ITT production line was hard at work on the machines for Regina and Saskatoon. There were a few delays — Calgary was late starting up because the new plant was not built in time — but the process of mechanization ground its way inexorably onwards.

Meanwhile, as expected, OCRs were coming on the market, and by May 1972 Canada had decided to buy some. The government called for bids on all optical readers that would be needed for Toronto, Montreal, Vancouver, Winnipeg, and Ottawa.

The post office said the OCRs had to read 80 per cent of all typed and printed fonts (kinds of typefaces) found in the Canadian mail stream. Of that 80 per cent, 60 per cent had to be read, translated into bar code, and correctly pre-sorted. In other words, a satisfactory machine would take almost half of typed and printed letters completely out of human hands.

In March 1973 the contract went to Marsland Engineering Ltd., a division of Leigh Industries. The machines were designed by Nippon Electric Co. of Japan, which would build the first machine and then sell the technology to Leigh. The thirty-three machines would cost $12.5 million.

Canada had taken a middle position in the debate over how much the OCRs should be expected to read. The United States allowed the postal code to be placed anywhere on the envelope; Japan insisted that the postal code appear in a box on the envelope whose position could not vary by more than 1 millimetre. One was easier for the customer, the other simpler for the machine and therefore much cheaper.

Canada decided that the code would be the last item in the address, and therefore required the machines to look only at a one-inch band across the envelope starting three-quarters of an inch from the bottom. It also decided not to bother with handwritten envelopes. "Handwritten addresses are becoming increasingly scarce in our mail system, and the cost of a machine with a handwriting reading capability would be beyond our means," Fultz reported in a 1974 review of progress on the mechanization program.

For all its good intentions, the government never gave the new OCRs the intensive tests it had planned. The post office bought 1.5 million envelopes, and sent letters to 60,000 people asking them to help by typing addresses on 50 envelopes with their standard typewriters. They hoped that half would agree, but the response was abysmal.

In the end, the post office ran its tests with 50 sets of fake mail instead of 60,000. Even though each batch had 8,000 pieces, it meant that the machines were never tested on more than a tiny fraction of the kinds of type used across the country.

Getting machines that did the job was only part of the problem.

As *A Blueprint for Change* had warned: "The introduction of automated facilities presents a major managerial challenge, particularly in terms of relations with employees whose understanding and support of the broad goals and advantages of automation in terms of the employment opportunities are vital." In simpler words, the tough part for managers would be convincing workers that they had more to gain from the machines than they had to lose.

Kierans' consultants felt that postal workers could be persuaded that the new skills would be more useful in other jobs outside the post office than the traditional knowledge of the postal sorting system. "Carefully pursued, the introduction of automation would increase employee identification with the purposes of the service and the overall psychological impact on the employees could prove to be a very real, tangible advantage."

Large-scale automation should "provide minimum disruption to postal service and maximum benefit in the long term to employees." The post office's goal should be to use machines to do the best possible job of delivering the mail while "upgrading the work content, morale and job satisfaction of postal employees."

That was the plan. It didn't work.

In the 1970 contract talks, the post office agreed to "seek ways and means of minimizing adverse effects" of technological change and to "meaningfully consult" with the union about such effects. The first meeting did not take place until December 1971, by which time the government had already ordered the first coding and sorting machines for Ottawa.

Mackay, Fultz, and several other senior officials met with union leaders to run through their plans to bring in coding and sorting machines. They made no secret of the scale of the project, and the Canadian Union of Postal Workers admits that it was told right from the start that mechanization would be put in place in fifteen cities across the country.

"We mapped out where we were going and spelled it out to them," says Sinclair. "They didn't like it. They didn't trust it. They didn't trust us. But they knew where we were coming from."

Aside from the question of trust, the postal workers say they did not really understand what was going to happen. "The information provided was very sketchy and Union officers still did not appreciate the full implications of the mechanization and modernization plans,'' CUPW later reported to its members.

"First of all, there was no requirement to negotiate. There was a requirement to consult," says Mackay. "There were guarantees that no one would be laid off because of that. That was all window-dressing from the union's point of view. They would keep on nattering about that. The trouble was, there was no way we could get them to sit down with us and try and work things out because that was not their philosophy. They used to say, the Jean-Claudes of this world: 'You manage and we're the critics.' You can't operate that way."

Mackay says mechanization only made sense if it was done right across the country. "You don't gain from a mechanized system until you do it nationally because you have the bar code and then you have to read the bar code. If [a letter] then goes somewhere you can't read it, you've not gained anything."

Union leader Joe Davidson credited John Mackay with a "diabolically clever" strategy for sliding mechanization past the noses of postal workers. Part of the plan, he said, was a matter of downplaying the extent of the changes. While politicians made speeches about a program that would cost $96 million, a 1978 report to then postmaster general Gilles Lamontagne put the bill at $200 million for machinery and $700 million to build new postal plants in some cities and fix up those in others. By then, the program had been expanded from 15 cities to 39 plants in 26 cities.

"It became clear to the union that the automation program was far more substantial than they had been led to believe and was constantly expanding," CUPW complained to the conciliation board in the 1977/78 contract talks.

Bringing the machines into one postal plant at a time also concealed the impact on postal workers, Davidson charged. After the Ottawa plant, those in Western Canada were the first to change over, and precedents were set there before the impact of the changes sank in at national headquarters and in the larger and more militant locals in Montreal and Toronto.

"There was no attempt to be smart or clever," says Mackay. As the machines were installed in one plant, the training crews could get to work teaching people how to run and fix the new machines, while the installation crews would move ahead to the next plant in line. Aside from the lower costs of a single crew which moved into one plant at a time, the sequence meant that installers and trainers alike could learn from their experience with each plant and prevent the same mistakes as they moved on to the larger plants. "You've given me a lot more credit than I deserve," Mackay once told Davidson. "We were always one step behind you. We were never one step ahead of you."

Meanwhile, postal ministers also tried to soothe the fears of postal workers as the automation program moved into full swing. Kierans wrote the unions a letter—attached to the 1970 contract —that promised: "The planned modernization program will not result in layoffs of present full-time employees during the life of the present agreement provided that employees will accept relocation, reassignment and retraining." Jean-Pierre Côté confirmed that message after he took over.

It was hardly a blanket assurance. It made no promises about how many jobs might be chopped a couple of contracts down the road once the full network of mechanized sorting plants was in place. Employees might have to move to new plants, whenever and wherever they were built. And to keep their jobs, they would have to be willing to do new jobs, the jobs needed by the machines, and to be trained to do them.

And the consultants who thought mechanization would be good for workers had not reckoned on the behaviour of the Treasury Board. Under the Public Service Staff Relations Act, Treasury Board is the official employer of every government worker. While the Public Service Commission may act as a recruiting agent, Treasury Board handles all contract talks and decides what jobs deserve what pay scales. Its decisions affect pay rates across the federal civil service.

This meant two things. First, Treasury Board was always looking over its shoulder at the rest of the civil service to see what impact any concessions it made to postal workers would have on other federal workers. Second, it stuck to rigid rules of classification. Pay rates were set solely according to the skill and experience needed to do the job.

As the first machines at Ottawa's Alta Vista post office went on line in 1972 during that year's contract talks, workers found out how Treasury Board felt about the new coding jobs. They were outraged.

The job of coding clerk had been classified as PO-1, the lowest possible level in the post office. An experienced postal clerk doing manual sorts was classified at PO-4. The coding jobs would pay only $2.94 an hour, 20 per cent less than the $3.69 an hour that a postal clerk could make.

The post office did say that workers would not have their wages cut if they took one of the new jobs, but they would not get another raise until PO-1 rates caught up with what they were already making. Not surprisingly, few postal clerks were interested in taking the lower-paid and more boring jobs.

In September 1972 the union complained to the Public Service Staff Relations Board that Treasury Board was breaking the rules by changing the terms of work during contract talks. The board ruled that the post office and Treasury Board had violated Section 51 of the PSSRA by not consulting the union in an effort to agree on a salary rate for the new jobs, but said the employer had every right to classify coding clerks at the PO-1 level.

As the consequences of the advent of the new machines sank in, the union began to fight back. It went to the public with a campaign asking customers to boycott the postal code until the government agreed to a deal on technological change. If the plea for sympathy didn't work, there were also veiled threats that frustrated postal workers might deliberately send coded letters into oblivion, while old-style addresses would get better treatment.

The boycott, says Mackay, was a flop. Each month the percentage of customers using the postal code rose. All told, the union was making little progress in its fight against the machines until the management in Montreal got a little too aggressive in April 1974.

Large numbers of postal workers started wearing T-shirts to work with the slogan "Le code, je l'ai dans le cul" (loosely, "Fuck the postal code"), and that proved too much for plant managers to stomach. When workers refused to stop wearing them, many were suspended indefinitely as a prelude to firing, and that proved enough of a provocation for the militant leadership of the Montreal local. The Montreal workers occupied the main Peel Street terminal and said it would stay closed until the suspensions were cancelled.

The message from the government in Ottawa, said Davidson, was to offer no quarter and no compromise. For the militants in the union, it was an all-or-nothing struggle, because the strike was illegal. If they did not reach a deal, all the strikers could be fired and the Montreal local broken for good.

The Montreal workers did not trust their national leaders, and sent former local vice-president and then national chief steward Jean-Claude Parrot to Ottawa to join the talks with Postmaster General André Ouellet. He felt that CUPW president Jim McCall gave away too much too quickly. The Montreal workers decided that only Parrot would speak for them. A humiliated McCall resigned as president of the union and Davidson took over.

On the morning of Friday, April 19, Parrot went to Davidson's apartment. They agreed that they could not afford to have the Montreal local gutted, and the only way to save it was to get postal workers across the country to join the illegal strike. Davidson called Toronto president Lou Murphy and got him to have his members on the street by noon. By evening, the general strike call had gone out. The next day, the letter-carriers reluctantly agreed to join in as well.

That move pushed the government into appointing a special mediator, Eric Taylor, to help settle the dispute. On the evening of April 25, he went to the government with a proposal that included no reprisals against workers for taking part in the illegal strike, a lifting of all the suspensions that had sparked it, and the appointment of a special committee, headed by him, to settle the dispute over how much to pay the coding clerks.

The union was ready with two press releases, one announcing an agreement, the other saying that the strike was still on. At 11 p.m., there was still no reply from the government, so the union held its press conference and issued the release saying there was no deal, and that became the big-breaking story for the nightly news.

At midnight, Taylor came back with the news that the government had agreed. Then, victory in hand, Parrot slid over one last demand. The disciplinary measures against the union and its members had led to a court action which could only be dropped by the Attorney General. "We requested his signature, in order that this thing be valid."

The offended bureaucrats did not want to get the minister out of bed for something they did not believe was necessary. "Our lawyers were there, and realized we were serious," says Parrot. "I'm not sure he was in bed anyway. I think the Cabinet was not in bed that night. They wanted to settle. They were all around." Eventually, a Treasury Board official was authorized to sign on behalf of the Attorney General. "Finally we got it," and at four o'clock in the morning, the union issued its other press release.

Taylor's Special Settlement Committee found an artful way to dodge Treasury Board's authority over job classification. It didn't mention the word. Instead, it just said coding clerks should be paid a certain wage, one that put them somewhere between PO-2 and PO-3. Legally, the coders were still PO-1, but informally they were PO-2⅝. The situation could not last.

By the beginning of 1975, the union and the government had reached a deal. Instead of arguing over the skill involved in reading letters and punching buttons, they agreed to change the job descriptions. All coders had to have all the knowledge of a postal clerk in order to qualify. That satisfied Treasury Board, and coders were classified PO-4. It was no better-paying than the old postal clerk's job, but after thirty months of squabbling, it was no worse.

Postal officials had known from the start that mechanization was a piece of dynamite in terms of labour relations. Treasury Board's intransigence over the classification issue lit the fuse, and the resulting 1974 explosion in Montreal would echo for years to come as the militants gained control of CUPW.

The summer of '74 also brought with it a new minister, Bryce Mackasey, whose self-image as a friend of labour became an open invitation to the unions to forget about talking to the bureaucrats. The next battles over technological change would be fought at the political level, where postal managers would have even less influence.

Mackay says that mechanization had to go ahead in one fell

swoop, but admits that the big new plants may have been a mistake. "I would split them up more. . . . I think the bigger they are, the more problems you have from a labour-relations point of view. They become very cold. One thousand employees is too many."

But management's biggest mistake was its handling of the classification problem. "We argued about that in house," he said. "I'm afraid our friends in Treasury Board who were involved in that classification determination I think overwhelmed us. I don't think we fought hard enough to ensure that it would be at least the same level."

Even though postal managers thought the classification of coders was unreasonable, says his successor Jim Corkery, "the beast was so entrenched. . . . That thing never should have happened and didn't have to happen except for Treasury Board. In effect, you had a strategy which got you into a hornets' nest and eventually you had to face it and say: 'It's a dumb decision. We'll have to get out of it.' We used Taylor to circumvent Treasury Board."

Joe Davidson agreed that the postal managers, if left to themselves, would probably have been more willing to make a deal. "John Mackay and his senior officials may have wished to avoid slugging it out toe to toe with the CUPW over automation, but the whole legal framework gave them no choice but confrontation," he wrote.

Gordon Sinclair, who by then had moved from his job as assistant deputy minister in charge of postal finances to head of operations, was even more blunt about the rigid approach to classification. "The classification scheme didn't really give a sweet damn about the problems of the post office. If that's the job, that's the way it classifies. If that's the way it classifies, that's what the pay scale is. End of discussion. . . . We would have been quite happy to have the coders classified at a fairly high level of sorter. The additional dollars compared to the size of the mechanization program were infinitesimal. But being in the public service, you were a slave to the classification system."

4
Divided
They Fell

■

John Uberig was frustrated. In 1975, it had been three years since he had left a private-sector career where he qualified as a chartered accountant and went on to become vice-president and treasurer of Southam Publications. As assistant deputy postmaster general for finance and administration at the post office, he was desperate to find some way of letting the post office get on with its job.

The problem was the same one that had encircled Lawrence O'Brien in the United States: the post office and its managers had no control of their own operations. The power to get things done had been divided by half a dozen acts of Parliament and handed to as many different departments and agencies around Ottawa. Uberig wanted some kind of special status for the post office that would give back control where it was needed.

As the mechanization program began to come apart with the wrangling over classification, Uberig sent an eight-page memo to Mackay laying out the problems he saw with the existing structure.

Top of the list was the Public Service Staff Relations Act, which he said simply did not work for the post office. "This Act probably is suited to a majority of government employees being white collar workers or typical clerical support staff. But it does not suit the needs of a major portion of postal employees who are involved in a blue collared industrial type setting."

The Financial Administration Act dealt with the related problem that Treasury Board rather than the post office was designated as the employer of all postal workers. "This relationship then gives control of wages, fringe benefits, etc., to a body which is not necessarily conversant with the problems of operating the Canada Post Office."

Uberig said contract talks also ran into trouble because Treasury Board was not willing to talk about new ideas like cutting down on the abuse of sick leave by offering to "buy back" a portion of the unused leave on retirement.

The post office also lacked control over hiring both workers and managers because of the Public Service Employment Act. "Post Office manpower needs must be spelled out to the PSC, who then act as the recruitment agency in a fashion that often seems to be a bureaucratic system of maintaining the bureaucracy."

He became even more caustic in his references to the Department of Supply and Services, set up under the Supply and Services Act to be the purchasing and contract agent, warehouse, and payment authority for government. "It imposes and proposes to impose more and more control on Post Office purchasing and supply operations. Again this is an area where any breakdown in the systems can result in adverse public and labour relations," Uberig griped.

"The Post Office must be able to respond to needs on a quick and flexible basis. DSS by comparison has the reputation of a pregnant elephant — slow, stodgy, continually growing, and difficult to convince that it must change its ways."

The post office was also having major problems in its dealings with the Department of Public Works, which controlled all post office buildings and plants and the money needed to build and maintain them. "Although a degree of co-operation between our departments has been worked out over recent years, there are many conflicts still remaining. . . . Cleaning and repair services, which if not properly attended to can result in public criticism of the post office, are controlled by DPW. Our facilities planning can be upset by the unilateral reassignment of priorities by DPW or Treasury Board, leaving Post Office management to bear the ramifications."

And like other federal departments at the time, the post office was having to cope with the Official Languages Act, and was particularly upset with the way Treasury Board chose to administer it. "For many years we have provided bilingual service in areas where it was a demonstrated need and did so by hiring bilingual people. Now we must offer the job opportunity to unilinguals who are willing to take up to 12 months' language training and, if they are the successful candidates, make alternative arrangements to do the job during this training period. In many cases it is nearly impossible to find alternatives and work that should be done simply slides farther and farther behind. Also, the current exercise of identifying language requirements has resulted in some bilingual employees adopting a unilingual position to the detriment of the service."

All this came on top of the restrictions contained in the Post Office Act itself, especially the one that gave Parliament the sole right to set postal rates. This was supposed to ensure that "overzealous officials will not raise rates out of proportion to needs and service. However, it also stymies deserved and needed rate adjustments by subjecting any proposals to the political arena."

Attempts to give more freedom to postal managers had also been thwarted because of the need to get political approval, and for several years the government had decided that changes to the post office were not important enough to warrant scarce time in the House of Commons. "Therefore, although times and needs have changed, Post Office legislation has not kept pace and deficits pyramid."

Uberig was not the only senior manager complaining about the situation. Gordon Sinclair, his colleague in charge of postal operations, says he was continually exasperated by Treasury Board's attitude. The fight he never won was to revive the old practice of letting postal workers go home as soon as the day's mail had been sorted. This had once been common practice in the days before collective bargaining came to the post office, and had proved to be a good incentive to the sorters to work fast.

"You could say to them, 'There's the mail that just came in off the train,' " adds Jim Corkery. " 'When you've got it all worked, you can go home.' And they worked like beavers. Standard, accepted drill in the post office." People would work twice as hard on the tough days with the understanding that if tomorrow was a soft day, they could go home and play golf. Enforcing a contract removed that flexibility.

Then the Auditor General slammed the post office for paying people for time not worked. The increasing use of trucks and airplanes as well as trains made shipments more frequent. It became harder to tell when the work was done. As contracts came to govern the plant floors, such informal ways of motivating workers ground to a halt.

A 1975 study found that some plants had tried an incentive sort for special occasions, usually sports events like the first Canada-Russia hockey series. Because so many employees did not want to miss them, managers would either bring televisions into the plants or let workers go home early if all the mail had been processed in time.

On a system-wide basis, however, the CUPW's attitude to work measurement, the difficulty of sticking to the same standards at various plants, and the potential abuse would have made incentive sorting tough to revive. No system of rewarding efficiency with time off could satisfy both the union and Treasury Board. The post office, says Sinclair, became "a victim of the average theory, where it is better to be consistently wrong than inconsistently right."

Mackay says the post office ran afoul of Treasury Board on other matters, such as trying to pay letter-carriers a bonus for lugging around bags full of advertising flyers — a measure later adopted by the Crown corporation. "No way would they go along with that because that would create a precedent within the rest of government. . . . Time and time again we'd run into that sort of thing and we couldn't convince the board."

Corkery, in charge of the Ontario region at the time, remembers his run-ins with Public Works over managing postal buildings, especially on weekends. "You run out of oil. There's no heat. Your people are out on the street. DPW is the supplier and he tells you to shove it: 'I'm not going to come in to work until Monday and I'll be in then to see what it's about.' More than one time we would get into this kind of argument, because basically he worked a five-day week and he wasn't going to get off his ass to keep the thing going on a three-shift operation." Corkery finally told his managers: "You're authorized to order it, and pay for it, and we'll fight about it afterwards. You never get caught in another one of those situations."

Keeping buildings in good shape caused other problems. "You'd get into unbelievable conflicts. You'd have a hole in the floor and people tripping on it. It's unsafe. 'Well, it's on schedule but we don't have any money. It'll be four months before it's fixed,' [Public Works would say]."

Because the pay cheques were sent out by Supply and Services, postal managers could not fix any mistakes. Getting pay errors corrected could take months, and upset workers wasted no time in adding to the grievance lists when they did.

Postal managers could not blame all of their problems on other departments and agencies. As the mechanization plans unfolded, another of the recommendations of *A Blueprint for Change* was creating a monster within the postal walls.

Kierans' consultants came to the same conclusions as others before them when they looked at the structure of postal management. There was too much authority at the centre and not enough initiative out in the field. In principle, Kates, Peat, Marwick felt that decisions should be made as low down the tree as possible, and that lower-level managers should then also be held accountable for their decisions to match their greater independence and authority.

To break up the Ottawa monolith, the report suggested creating four regional organizations: Quebec, Atlantic, Ontario, and the West. The various postal districts and individual post offices would be organized under those four groups. Headquarters would shrink and stick largely to staff jobs such as defining what the post office should be doing and planning new services. Within their regions, managers would have all the responsibility for moving the mail.

The government decided the new structure made sense. Along with the structure, it also adopted a philosophy that was to cause untold problems down the road. The consultants had said that since regional managers would be closer to their customers than would the Ottawa mandarins, they should be allowed to follow different policies if they so desired. "The manner in which the postal system operates need not be uniform throughout the country,'' the consultants said, and so it was to be.

''As a result of geographical decentralization, without appropriate management systems, we found that we had four post offices instead of one. And this was three too many,'' said Larry Sperling, who joined the post office in 1975 after twenty years with United Aircraft, IBM Canada, and Consumer's Distributing, and took charge of the post office's marketing arm. The empire of Ottawa became a collection of kingdoms, regional regencies with all the cohesion of feuding medieval barons. Variations in the standards of service were one thing, but autonomy degenerated into a kind of musical chairs with the mail.

Aside from a lack of co-operation between regions, there was also pressure to compete. Normally, a little competition is a healthy thing. When combined with the poor quality of information going to the bosses in Ottawa, however, the pressure tempted some to try and cheat the system to make themselves look good.

The regional structure turned out to have another critical failing. The regional managers reported directly to the deputy postmaster general, John Mackay. Mackay, however, found that he was spending all his time dealing with labour problems and the whims of the minister of the day.

That left Sinclair as the *éminence grise*, who was really the top dog when it came to operations. Sinclair, however, had no direct authority over the regional managers. If they disagreed, they did not have to do what he told them unless he could get Mackay's signature on the memo.

As the regional structure became entrenched, Ottawa lost more and more control. ''We knew the ultimate in decentralization had been reached when we found out that one region was developing tenders to print its own stamps,'' Sperling once confessed. ''We don't know what denomination they would have been, or whose picture would have been used, but the danger bells had already begun to ring.''

By the time Sperling reached the post office, however, it was too late for warning bells. The influx of new talent, the struggle over mechanization, political interference, the split authority for running the post office, and all the internal feuding had driven many managers over the edge. Overwhelmed by helplessness, management morale had plummeted. A shocking study — locked to this day in the post office's confidential files — was about to reveal the gory results.

By 1974, officials at Treasury Board could tell something was amiss. Postal deficits were climbing far faster than expected, and the budgetary watchdogs wanted to go in and see what might be going wrong. Mackay, however, was already fed up with Treasury Board meddling, and resisted as long as he could.

That wasn't long. To complete a reorganization of staff, he needed Treasury Board authority to hire some new managers. Treasury Board refused to go along until it got Mackay's agreement to a joint study of the organization and pay of postal managers.

The four-man task force was told to see if decentralization was working. A later memo from Mackay expanded the job to include a look at all management jobs down to and including the unionized supervisors of the Association of Postal Officials of Canada. The task force was also supposed to see if the various managers were being paid salaries in line with their duties and responsibilities. The task force held interviews with about 450 postal managers at all levels across the country. It wanted frank opinions, and it got them.

Its report began by noting that the group had felt good about the quality and dedication of postal managers to whom it had talked. Many had locked their careers into the post office because their specialized knowledge was worth little in other federal departments. "As a group, they are highly committed to the post office; many have invested more than a quarter century in mail operations." The comforting comments did not last long.

Several managers talked of feeling besieged by public criticism. They were embarrassed at being seen as a centre of union troubles and falling standards of service. "A number admitted to concealing their places of employment from acquaintances, euphemistically telling enquirers that they are employed by 'the Government of Canada' and avoiding any reference to the post office."

Managers were more than willing to talk about the problems they saw. There were many. At the top of the list, they said, "there had been a failure to provide the Post Office with clear objectives, and stated, in some cases, that a number of services had been initiated because of a recognition that service to the public has a higher priority than matching revenues to cost.'' Those decisions to start costly services were made in spite of Parliament's clear instructions saying that postal service should be good enough to meet the needs of Canadians without subsidies.

When the system of "Management by Objectives" was brought into the post office as part of the Kierans changes in 1970, managers were told that 1975/76 would be the year the post office broke even. Even as the deficit mounted, some line managers felt that breaking even was still important and complained that new money-losing services being thought up by staff officials in Ottawa were undermining the break-even philosophy.

The study group said the lack of postal-rate increases to cope with rising costs had undermined the basic goal of the department. Unless the government made it clear that breaking even was still important, "there is no satisfactory criteria against which to measure the performance of senior management of the Post Office.''

The lack of a clear goal was compounded by a lack of direction from the top. Mackay himself came in for clear and pointed criticism from his managers for spending too much of his time and energy on employee relations and not enough on the department's many other problems.

"This preoccupation, in their view, has resulted in: a clear lack of direction and decisiveness with a corresponding reliance on 'management by consensus'; inadequate follow-up to ensure implementation when decisions are taken; a reluctance to rank priorities which in turn leads to managerial drift; an observed preference to focus on short-term problems to the detriment of longer range planning; an inattention to organizational reporting relationships, particularly in areas of staff relations and public relations; a lack of concern over monthly reports, notably in the case of staff located outside the headquarters area; a failure to hold subordinates accountable for their actions; the absence of a management audit function to ensure consistent adherence to departmental policies; and infrequent visits to field operations.''

It was a devastating list of complaints, but Mackay did not get all the blame. After all, he was already working under his fourth minister, and this too was a major source of discontinuity. Each minister had his own priorities and his own way of working. The deputy had to do most of the necessary hand-holding.

However, the deputy was also the key to a successful decentralized post office, and the study group found clear evidence that decentralization had not worked. The idea in 1970 had been to beef up the regional offices and gradually slim down the Ottawa headquarters from about 1,300 employees to between 400 and 600. The regional offices were supposed to stay lean, adding about 30 staff each.

By 1975, headquarters had in fact grown to some 1,900 employees, while the regional offices had quadrupled in size. Their combined staff had grown by 69 per cent in five years. The growth in the number of managers had been twice as fast as that of postal employees as a whole, and more than twice as fast as the increase in postal revenue.

New jobs were being added to headquarters staff at breakneck speed, mostly in so-called staff rather than in line positions. Line managers move the mail; staff people look after everything from finances to public relations. Some of these jobs had not been thought of when decentralization was planned; others were clearly related to the consultants' other recommendations.

By the hundreds, the new staff members came in. The post office hired managers to handle mechanization, marketing, quality control, industrial engineering, and even language training. Each time, either the post office seemed to need them or the government required them. Yet the post office could not afford to add all these people while politics stopped it from getting more money to pay for them.

What was even more galling to the line managers was the performance of many of these experts. They were the ones suggesting these new services, some of which proved to be outright disasters. The study group found that "no organizational function is more universally criticized by Post Office line managers than marketing. With one exception, the districts view marketing with cynicism bordering on contempt."

Marketing had been one of the big buzz-words of the Kierans era. Sinclair had been handed the marketing title on top of his finance job, but had then hired Garth Campbell from Canadian

National Railways to take over marketing when he moved to the operations slot.

Although marketing produced a flood of ideas, most of them seemed to lose large amounts of money and yet were brought in either without consulting line managers or even over their strenuous protests. The hostility towards marketing people ran through all levels of the post office and reflected a feeling that while the new experts may have known a lot about making a service popular, they knew very little about how the post office works.

Only in Winnipeg was marketing seen to have done something useful. There the regional marketing staff focused on ''productivity selling'', working to persuade large-volume mailers like hydro, phone, and credit-card companies to pre-sort their mail and hand it in when the post office was least busy. That allowed the mail to be handled more efficiently while avoiding the need for overtime or casual labour. In that district, marketing people were seen as helping move the mail.

Elsewhere, marketing divisions trumpeted new, high-profile services such as Postpak, Certified Mail, and Telepost, which were not, and in some cases could not be, money-makers. Certified Mail, a service in which the recipient signs a card which is returned to the sender so that he knows it has been received, lost money with every letter. The study group estimated that the three minutes of a letter-carrier's time, plus the cost of printing and processing the forms involved, cost more than 45 cents a letter, while the charge for the special service was only 40 cents.

The marketing arm also tried to win customer approval by boosting service, even where it made no economic sense. Third- and fourth-class mail, for instance, used to move only when enough had stacked up to fill a truck or a railcar, usually about once a week. The post office decided to improve the service by moving it every day, as often as first-class mail, no matter what the volume. One shipment by piggyback (a truck trailer moved on a railcar) from Kitchener to Regina contained only eight bags of mail, which would have carried stamps worth less than $100 but which cost more than $700 to transport.

All the unused third- and fourth-class space led to other ideas that only made the problem worse. Postpak, the service most often cited by marketing managers as a notable achievement by their division, was also the most consistently and forcefully criticized by line managers, the study group reported.

Postpak was thought up as a low-cost parcel service. Users would send objects that could fit into a one-cubic-foot box that was easy to stack with other such boxes. The customer had to take the box to a post office, and the recipient had to pick it up from another.

These packages didn't fill all the spare space, so the post office started allowing larger packages and offering discounts. Soon, said the study group, special deals between customers and marketing representatives began breaking the rules altogether. Postpak shipments grew to include all sorts of containers and even loose items like tires, ladders, and garbage cans.

The rates were so attractive that Postpak not only took business away from its own higher-priced parcel service, but even convinced some companies they should give up their own shipping operations. Warren Knit Co. of St. Catharines, Ontario, sold its trucks and laid off its drivers when it switched to Postpak.

Supervisors in the St. Catharines post office showed the study group a typical shipment of the company's sweaters to Montreal. One 35-pound box was charged only $3.10; a pair of larger, 55-pound boxes were carried for only $1.10 each: a total of $5.30 to carry 145 pounds of high-value merchandise more than 400 miles. The company would have had to pay $11.85 to send the same package by parcel post, and $10.95 by CN Express.

Postpak rarely even met its transportation costs. A piggyback load of Postpak shipments from Scarborough, Ontario, to Quebec City brought in only $800 in revenue but cost $1,400 to move. Carrying such high-value goods also led to an increased number of thefts, and the resulting insurance claims became ridiculously high compared with the money the post office was taking in.

Even with the low prices, there was still space to spare on the trucks and trains. The word went out from Ottawa setting quotas for increasing Postpak traffic. Accordingly the regional manager in Western Canada decided to stretch the service. He offered Postpak to Woodward's department stores, and, to win their business, sent post office trucks to their loading docks, where their drivers would wait around all day while parcels for delivery to customers were shovelled into them.

It took years for the top managers to discover the problem, let alone its extent, because of confusion between the various branches of the post office. Mackay asked for an audit report on Postpak in March 1972. Three and a half years later, he finally got a report which had been written by three different branches, each of which had reached different conclusions.

This kind of result added to another bone of contention between line and staff managers. The people running postal plants felt that the guys back in headquarters thinking up these strange ideas were grossly overpaid — and the study group found they had a point.

For instance, the study group said the manager of the Toronto post office was classified as a PM-7. His plants, spread over several locations, had 4,150 employees, including 250 supervisors. He had to deal with four unions, including two that were considered very militant. His plants ran three shifts a day, seven days a week. A quarter of all Canadian mail comes from Toronto, and 45 per cent of national mail passes through the city. A typical regional marketing manager with a staff of six had none of those problems and collected the same salary.

The study group found that civil-service salary standards caused real problems when applied to an industrial-style operation. The administrative classifications used in the post office "have been largely developed to describe and measure job differences within a largely middle-management, Ottawa-based, policy-making, administrative group. . . . They fail to effectively discriminate between functional and operational duties and responsibilities within the post office."

The salary structure also tended to persuade ambitious managers to head for Ottawa. The pay rose as jobs moved from plant to district to region to headquarters. The best managers "hop-scotched" out of the plants where their skills were most needed, leaving the least-experienced managers to deal with sensitive problems like labour disputes which could affect the whole system if badly handled.

The pay problems of line managers extended right down to the supervisors on the plant floors. These unionized managers were more upset about pay than about any other issue, because the government's pay policies for managers meant that from time to time they found themselves making less money than the postal workers and letter-carriers under them.

The small divisions between pay classes also made it almost impossible to reward good managers or to hold them accountable for bad decisions. Lower-level managers had to stay ahead of the unions; senior and middle managers had to keep on top of the unionized lower managers. In theory there was money around for merit pay, but it was used up just keeping everyone in line.

The problems with pay and the muddled performance of some of the newcomers in staff jobs had in turn created a burning resentment among many of the old-timers in management. They had come up through the ranks and knew the post office from top to bottom. And yet these new boys from the private sector had been parachuted into dozens of the juiciest jobs, closing off the older managers' chances of promotion.

The newcomers included the deputy—Mackay—all the assistant deputies, two of the four regional general managers, and twenty of the twenty-eight directors of headquarters branches. Many of the old-timers felt the new boys didn't understand how the post office worked and didn't understand the problems faced by the line managers they bossed around. Sinclair says what burned them most was the newcomers' attitude. "It was the new guard with no experience thinking they had all the solutions in the world . . . and the old guard was really a bunch of stupid asses." Their reaction was predictable: "If these guys are so smart, let 'em earn their own money."

The tensions between old and new managers were exacerbated by those between different levels of the organization. Managers in Ottawa said the regions had become too independent. Regional managers said many of those at headquarters still thought in terms of the old post office and handed out orders rather than advice. Those in the district offices considered the regional offices to which they reported as "Xerox machines" that simply got in the way of the flow of information to and from headquarters.

There seemed to be too many memos flying back and forth dealing with trivial items. Postal managers at lower levels complained of a steady demand for information by staff members at the Ottawa and regional headquarters.

One district director told the study group that he had kept track of such memos for three months from April through June 1975, and had collected 112 requests for information about service and delivery, 38 questions on transportation, and 59 demands for data on industrial-engineering matters. In the post offices, managers found that they could not meet all the requests without hurting line operations.

Lack of communication caused further problems. The centralized unions were able to get the results of grievance and arbitration hearings back down to the members of their locals long before such information made its way down the decentralized management ladder.

The bad lines of communication contributed to the confusion over what the post office was doing. Managers found themselves being told to do things without knowing why. This became a particular problem when it came to decisions on labour disputes.

Some managers were simply baffled by some of the decisions on disciplinary measures. Others told the study group that the actions of senior management were "inconsistent or contradictory and suggested appeasement." Lower-level managers felt sold out by their superiors.

A manager in a western city suspended a letter-carrier for three days, with the tacit consent of the union local, after the worker had insisted on claiming overtime regularly for a route that clearly could be done within the usual time. The grievance went to the top level, and two years later, having never been told by senior managers what had happened, the local manager found out through the grapevine that the grievance had been settled by cutting the suspension to half a day and wiping the worker's record clean.

In another case in the Maritimes, a postal driver was arrested and convicted for drunk driving on his own time, and had his licence suspended. His union leaders told him to keep quiet and keep driving at work, but the postmaster found out. Because the driver was behind the wheel illegally, he suspended him for three days. Then, because the union had advised the worker to do what he did, the manager met with the union leaders and suggested that they pay the driver for the time lost. The union agreed to do so, but a grievance was also filed. At the third level it was partly sustained by higher-level managers — with no consultation — and the suspension was reduced to one day.

And one employee sent home by a supervisor for being drunk on the job was seen by witnesses to pick up an iron bar on his way out and smash the window of his supervisor's car. He was charged by police for wilful damage to property but acquitted because he was drunk at the time. He continued to work at the post office.

Even where senior managers tried to get tough, they would find themselves overruled either by their ministers or by adjudicators. Mackay remembers a case in which ten workers behind the counter at a post office got together and figured out how to skim the cash people paid for stamps and get it into their own pockets. But they were caught and suspended. Joe Davidson phoned Mackay in the middle of the night and demanded they be reinstated because the system for checking on the cash was not right.

When Mackay checked the next morning, his officials told him that the workers had systematically been pinching money. Davidson insisted on a meeting, and argued that the system should be good enough to protect employees from their own evil impulses. "These people were absolute crooks," says Mackay, and ten people in collusion could beat any system. The post office fired them, but six months later, when the union appeal reached adjudication, the chairman of the labour relations board argued that the six months' lost work was enough punishment and reinstated the workers.

However, Gordon Sinclair says that in many cases managers' vague feelings of being sold out by their superiors were all too accurate. Because of the union's growing tendency to appeal the decisions of managers and adjudicators to the political level, the top bureaucrats started to second-guess their minister. "When you saw an issue starting to boil, the decision that you had to take was, do you cut your losses now and make a management decision or do you let it go and try to fight it, with the risk that a political decision will be made which would be worse than the decision you could make as management?"

Labour cases became a series of agonizing choices for top managers. But senior officials made the impact on morale worse because they rarely consulted the lower-level managers involved or told them afterwards what they had done and why.

"When you made a decision, then the management underneath you felt sold down the river. They wouldn't understand the political realities," says Sinclair. "If you did decide to cut your losses, you couldn't go out with a printed statement that disclosed why you did it. The best you could do is communicate by word of mouth, which is very imperfect in getting a message like that across. The very senior levels were in a constant dilemma."

Even successful moves to keep a lid on trouble-makers took an agonizingly long time. Corkery remembers the case of the local union president in Sherbrooke, Quebec, a small postal station with about 100 workers. "He was a real S.O.B., a real trouble-maker, and he was just being stupid, too far out, behaving like Montreal in a small town." The word came down: "If he's really that bad, build a discipline case for him, and if he continues not to be moulding, all right, move it up and we'll sign it off as a discharge."

It took two years for managers to count enough infractions to make a case they thought no one could overturn. When it was passed to Corkery, he agreed it was solid, and fired the union leader. "So the guy gets turfed out. The union's first move is to hire him as a business agent at the union office in Montreal." But the post office won its case at adjudication.

It was only then, knowing that the man was gone for good, that his supervisor went to the Sherbrooke postmaster and told him: "You can't believe how delighted my wife is that guy is gone out of this plant. . . . For two years, he and his two goons have been hassling me as I leave to go home . . . one car in front, one car behind, bumping me down the highway."

When asked why he hadn't complained before, the supervisor said Sherbrooke was a small town, and he knew he had to live with the guys who worked for him. "So he tolerates this kind of physical harassment. You don't know what's going on. People just won't say, won't talk, bloody bullying in some cases," Corkery says.

"After a while, you get worn down. If higher-level management isn't going to support you when you get into some of these situations, you tend to back off after a while. You get beaten about the ears for long enough and you just say finally, ah, to hell with it. And to a degree I think this is what happened in Montreal, because most of our ministers came from Montreal, so if the Montreal situation got in trouble, then the minister was down after [the local manager] to settle it, to get the men back to work, bypassing the management system."

Meanwhile, lower-level managers who had seen their superiors consistently reducing penalties started to play the game by applying harsher punishment than was needed, so that after it had been reduced, it would be about right for the offence. "In short, to achieve the proper penalty they believe an offence calls for, managers find it necessary to impose an excessive one in the belief that more senior management will exercise its prerogative and apply a reduction."

Other managers leant the other way. "When the unions started to file grievances in wholesale quantities, these guys were somewhat intimidated, and were loath to take initiatives in the field to improve the environment for fear that it would become a national issue. And in some cases it did," says a Treasury Board official. "It made the job of people in the field extremely difficult. Discipline was uncertain. They couldn't be sure if it would stick. They risked humiliation if it didn't stick."

No matter how managers tried to get around the appeasement approach at the top, they came out looking not only like bastards, but also like people with less influence than the union's representatives. "Many postmasters and middle-level managers consider that the department is much more responsive to its unions than to its managers," the study group noted.

This applied to more than just bad behaviour. One postmaster, for instance, wanted to improve the lighting and relieve the overcrowding in an area of his plant but could not get approval from his superiors. After the union complained about it, the problem got bumped further up the line and action was taken. Once again the union had shown the workers involved that it could get action more effectively than the bosses in the plant could.

To make sure that their study was not biased by relying completely on interviews, the joint task force also hired the Toronto consulting firm of Hay Associates in 1974 to do a "climate analysis report" at the same time. Hay sent out questionnaires to 5,870 postal managers at all levels across the country. The replies were anonymous and mailed directly to the consultants' office.

Managers were asked questions about how clearly they saw the post office's goals and structure, how fast and sensibly decisions were made, how well managers co-operated, how much room they had to use their initiative, whether they felt account- able for their actions, how dynamic and responsive the post office was, and whether they were fairly paid.

"The results of this study clearly and unambiguously indicate that the respondents are very negative about Canada Post. . . . The respondents see no area of Canada Post's climate as being 'average' or positive. Overall, the results have no parallel in Hay's experience," the firm reported.

Hay had plenty of experience in looking at corporate climates. They had already done similar studies for more than seventy organizations in manufacturing, insurance, banking, retail, and services, including major companies such as the Royal Bank, Abitibi Paper, Cominco, and the Canada Mortgage and Housing Corp. They had never seen anything this bad before.

There were only a couple of optimistic notes. For some reason, managers in the Ontario regional headquarters — Jim Corkery's staff — were more positive than the rest, and managers who had joined the post office within the past five years were not nearly as pessimistic as the others.

"Obviously, if Canada Post is to improve, grow and flourish it will require change that is major, pervasive — perhaps even traumatic. The problems are immensely complex, and solutions will be difficult to devise and implement."

The Treasury Board–Post Office task force, in its conclusions, agreed that both studies had proven the need for major changes. On the other hand, it said many of the problems had been caused by the strains of the last reorganization only five years before. Those strains came not so much from the changes as from the way they were carried out.

"First, the recommendations which were acted on at that time were based on the assumption that the department would become a Crown corporation, or a variation thereof. Secondly, the new structure was introduced on a wide scale, over a very short period of time, by a relatively new management team which lacked both governmental and postal experience and which was seen to be unsympathetic to the feelings, aspirations and advice of long-time postal employees."

The study group recommended a variety of measures to clean up the situation. A Crown corporation had advantages, but by this time the bureaucrats had given up on the idea. Their recommendations assumed that the department would continue.

They did say that the post office would have to go to Cabinet and get a better idea of what was expected of it. "It is doubtful whether the department is manageable without a clear and reasonably achievable objective." To make it work, Cabinet would have to not only endorse the objective, but promise to stick to it.

Among the organizational changes suggested, the study group wanted to wipe out the marketing arm. "We all said that was bloody ridiculous, unbelievable, and wouldn't implement it," says Corkery. "It was fundamentally trying to put you back into the service-driven, product-driven organization, stand in line and take what we give you."

The study group also wanted to consolidate the four regions and fifteen districts into seven divisions, knocking out one level of senior management. It also suggested a new job along the lines of a chief operating officer as a number two to the deputy minister. The senior assistant deputy postmaster general, operations, would have the job of running the operational side of the post office, much as Gordon Sinclair was already doing with the same title minus the senior. However, unlike Sinclair, he would have authority over the regions.

Mackay wanted Sinclair to get the senior assistant deputy's job, but it was not to be. In the wake of the report, Mackay's head was itself on the block. Mackay was soon moved to Public Works, while Sinclair became an assistant deputy minister in the Transport Department. The next postmaster general, Jean-Jacques Blais, picked Corkery as his deputy minister.

With Corkery in charge, the post office tried to get its financial house in order while union militancy built to a climax. By 1978, Cabinet approved post office plans to break even within five years.

Then Pierre Trudeau did in a moment what Kierans, Côté, the postal unions, Uberig, and the rest of post office management had tried unsuccessfully for a decade to achieve. The Crown corporation was on its way. Within another five years, most of the newest generation at the top would themselves be out of the post office.

5
Mailed
Fists

■

As they had so many times before,
the men gathered at Montreal's Centre Paul Sauvé at about 6:30
in the morning, piled into cars, and hit the road for Ottawa. After
almost a year of daily treks to Parliament Hill, *"les gars de
Lapalme"* had the art of demonstration down to a science. There
were strict rules for drivers: no drinking. There were strict rules
for the passengers: those who showed up late for the return trip
got left behind. The last car in the convoy, wrote union organizer
Pierre Vadeboncoeur in his book *366 Days and as Long as It
Takes*, was a "mobile garage", equipped with mechanics, tools,
and spare parts to look after any vehicle that broke down along
the way.

When the cars arrived in Ottawa, the men would head for a
small room in the back of Parliament's West Block that had been
set aside for them. There they would eat and warm up a bit
before heading out for their morning march. The signs would
come out, and the procession would start its daily routine. Round
and round Parliament Hill they would walk, sometimes quietly,
sometimes with angry chants. When they had finished twenty or
twenty-five cycles of the Hill, they packed it in for the day. By
1:30 or so, they were heading for home.

By February 2, 1971, the 450 strikers who began marching
the previous April had dwindled to only 150 in the biting winds of
winter. The grinding monotony of the marches, however, was

also getting on the nerves of Canada's political leaders. Shortly after noon, Prime Minister Pierre Trudeau emerged from the Members' door of the House of Commons and got into his limousine to go for lunch. The Lapalme boys shouted their usual catcalls. Their words have been lost in the mists of history, but his have not. The window of the rear door slid down. ''Mangez de la merde,'' Trudeau snarled back. Then the car drove off.

It had not taken long for Trudeau's rose to fade. The romantic bachelor of 1968 would quickly become the tough guy of the October crisis in 1970. The man who preached the ''Just Society'' would become the leader who scorned ''bleeding hearts'' who didn't like to see soldiers in the streets. His quick verbal shot came to symbolize Trudeau's overall attitude to the public, just as the struggle of *les gars de Lapalme* came to symbolize the militancy of Canada's postal workers.

Ironically, the Lapalme boys were not even postal workers in the strict sense, and they did not belong to a postal union. They were affiliated with the Quebec-based Confederation of National Trade Unions (CNTU), and they worked for a private contractor who had the job of collecting mail from Montreal streets and bringing it into the postal stations. Even so, the dispute set the tone for postal conflict in the decade to come, and included all the elements that would contribute to the chaos that followed.

It all started, as so many moves did, innocently enough. Eric Kierans, the dynamic, business-oriented minister Trudeau appointed to run the post office, was determined to cut postal losses. One of his moves was to review the way the post office handed out contracts to private businesses, including those for local transportation in major cities.

For years, the Montreal contract had been handed out each year without tenders on a cost-plus basis, a procedure allowed by the Post Office Act for ''temporary agreements''. In the words of the late Joe Davidson, they were ''a lucrative tool of patronage and political financing''.

Top manager Jim Corkery says the lack of tenders reflected the nature of the job. For many years the Toronto contractor squeezed costs by hiring ex-convicts to drive a fleet of trucks which he ran into the ground, but the workers were tightly controlled and delivered superb service. "Who's going to come in and fight against him? Really what you're doing in renewing the contract with him, you're saying what's a reasonable figure for the next contract and you're really just looking at the price you've got and some sort of escalating factor. And if it's in that sort of ballpark you're saying okay, I'll live with it, because there's nobody around that can compete with it even if you did go to tender."

The multi-million-dollar Montreal contract had stayed with a succession of three companies between 1913 and 1969: Canadian Transfer Co., Senecal Transport, and then Rod Service Ltd. Even the apparent changes didn't mean much. Rod Service started getting the Montreal contract in 1952 after Rodrigue Turcotte took over Senecal and changed the name. After more than half a century of "temporary agreements", many of the workers at Rod Service had worked at the same jobs for years.

Rod Service had already been through a series of nasty labour disputes after workers succeeded in getting a union in 1965. There were strikes in 1966, 1967, 1968, and 1969. Because the government would suspend the contract each time a strike started and get the work done by others, the company found itself in a relatively weak bargaining position. The strikes tended to be short and went well for the union.

In January 1969, after the government said it would cut city mail delivery to five days a week from six, Rod Service decided to give up the contract. Kierans announced that the post office would take over the service itself on March 15, but angry union members started a slowdown. As a result, the contract was transferred to G. Lapalme Inc., which agreed to hire 397 Rod Service employees and assume their labour agreement. Both that and the postal contract were due to expire March 31, 1970.

The real troubles were kicked off on September 24, 1969, when the federal Cabinet met to talk about how to deal with the recurring strikes that were playing havoc with the pick-up and delivery of mail. Kierans says the ministers decided unanimously to hold open tenders for transportation services in the Montreal area. The next day, Kierans wrote a letter to Lapalme and told the company of the decision. The company was invited to bid, but told firmly to bring its employees up to date on the new policy.

The unions refused to help the company in preparing its tender because Lapalme wanted to pay lower wages. Lapalme, in turn, did not submit a bid. On January 30, 1970, the government announced the results. The transportation work in Montreal would be split between four companies: Courrier M. & H. Inc., Moses & Duhamel Inc., H. Lapalme Transport Ltd. (not G. Lapalme), and Menard & Desmarais Inc.

The bidding process did not include any obligation to hire the existing workers. As the end of their contract approached, the Lapalme workers started to vent their anger and frustration through rotating strikes, slowdowns, and outright violence. When they were in a good mood, they simply jammed their trucks into postal loading docks, locked them up, and walked away from them.

The Lapalme boys were a tough union. Their leader, Frank Diterlizzi, was an Italian immigrant who had worked on a farm, in the mines, in a factory making boxcars, as a riveter at Canadair Ltd., and then as a driver for a construction company before buying his own truck.

He was first hired by Rod Service in the late fifties and by 1965 had succeeded in organizing a union. "Dirty Lizzy, they called him," recalls former deputy postmaster general John Mackay, who first met him only three days after becoming the top postal bureaucrat in 1970. "I wouldn't have liked to meet him in a dark alley."

"When the violence started, and they started slashing tires, and burning trucks and the mail, then the government became a very weak government. It didn't do anything about it," says Kierans. "The assistant chief of police in charge of the motorized brigade came to see me in the office of the postmaster in Montreal. And he said, Look, Mr. Minister, we can't keep throwing these people into jail. We catch them red-handed and they're out in an hour. Nobody lays any charges. I started to argue with him, and he said, Wait a minute now, don't blame it on the provincial government. You know that. And I said, Yeah, this is Crown property and it has to be the Attorney General or the Solicitor General in Ottawa. And [Justice minister and Attorney

General John] Turner . . . kept telling me they were going to lay charges, and never laid any charges, and, as a result, people were just destroying Crown property and getting away with it.''

By the beginning of March, Kierans had started hiring new workers to replace those at Lapalme. He also put an embargo on new parcels coming into the Montreal sorting plants because they were already clogged. There was no more room.

''This developed into quite a political storm and got them all nervous,'' says Kierans. At a meeting held on the evening of March 16, the Cabinet decided to back down. They passed an order that told the winners of the bidding process that they would have to hire their drivers from the Lapalme union according to a seniority list drawn up by the CNTU. To make that financially possible for the new contractors, the government would revert to one-year, cost-plus deals, effectively returning to the old way of doing business.

Kierans was livid. Transport minister Don Jamieson came to see Kierans' executive assistant, Richard Gwyn, the next morning to see what he thought. Gwyn was not optimistic about the possibility of changing the decision.

Kierans made his move the next morning, during a meeting of the Priorities and Planning committee, the inner Cabinet to which Kierans did not belong. He sent in a message asking to see Trudeau right away, and Trudeau, sensing a crisis, came out of the meeting.

The Postmaster General wasted no time getting to the point. He had decided to resign, and he tried to hand Trudeau a letter outlining his reasons and making it official. Trudeau refused to take the letter from him. Kierans was adamant. ''I have the instructions and I can't carry them out and that's all there is to it,'' he told the Prime Minister.

''He stayed behind the desk, he wouldn't come near. I said I was sorry, and I left it on his desk and walked out.''

The letter pulled no punches. Kierans said Cabinet's move would ''destroy the tender system as we now know it,'' and cause ''pervasive and enduring'' damage to the economy. And while workers might acquire rights to keep their jobs with a given employer, those rights are not transferable.

''Perhaps they should be, but such a fundamental proposition should come about through appropriate legislation based on principle and not as an 'ad hoc' response to violence. When a union, or any other group, believes that violence will achieve its objectives, then the responsibility of government is to resist and to repudiate that violence. Unless it can be shown that violence won't work, then there will be continual violence.

"As you know, I have all along recognized that the government had a moral obligation to these workers because of their long service and because of the peculiar circumstances of the Montreal mail system. To fulfil that moral obligation, I proposed the assurance of job security for those drivers with more than five years service, as well as ex-gratia payments. However, this is entirely different from the imposed situation now decided on."

While Kierans had enjoyed the challenge of the post office and the communications portfolio that went with it, "I must ask you to accept my resignation as Minister of Communications, effective immediately."

Trudeau was determined not to let Kierans go. He sent Jamieson and Treasury Board president C. M. "Bud" Drury to reason with Kierans, because he knew they would have the best chance of influencing his Postmaster General, but Kierans told them: "No dice."

That afternoon, Kierans broke the news to his senior officials in his Centre Block office on Parliament Hill. They were full of compliments and urged him not to go. He still remembers the shocked look on his assistant's face after they had been ushered out the door. As the door closed behind them, the assistant had heard their first words through the open transom over the door. "After all they said in here about you, you know what they said? One of them asked the deputy postmaster general, do you know who we're going to get?" For the bureacrats, life would go on.

Meanwhile, as Trudeau scrambled for a way to defuse Kierans' resistance, the Prime Minister decided not to show up in the House of Commons for the daily Question Period. Tradition would have forced him to announce the resignation as his first order of business.

Instead, Trudeau spoke with an old friend of Kierans', Judge Carl Goldenberg, who agreed to act as an arbitrator in the Lapalme dispute. At about four o'clock that afternoon, the Prime Minister called Kierans and told him that the previous night's Cabinet decision would be put on hold until Goldenberg reported. Another special Cabinet meeting would be held at five o'clock to reverse the earlier decision. "What the hell can you do? I said all right."

Even so, Trudeau had the last word through his loyal lieutenant Marc Lalonde, then his principal secretary. A week later, Kierans spotted a two-day-old message on his desk from Lalonde and tried to return the call. He wasn't in his office. "Oh, he's over at the Château Laurier," his secretary said. "You can get him at Mr. Goldenberg's room. He's working with Mr. Goldenberg on the report on the post office." Kierans still believes that Lalonde had already determined what would go in the report.

Goldenberg delivered his conclusions to the government on March 25, eight days after being appointed. His report, perhaps the fastest commission of inquiry in federal history, was roughly hammered out on a manual typewriter. His conclusions backed up the Cabinet's original plan to retreat.

Goldenberg said that because of the history of the Montreal contract, the government should have included an obligation to hire the Lapalme employees as part of the tender. "In my opinion, this was a serious omission. Although the post office was not their direct employer, its change of policy would directly affect the livelihood of the Lapalme employees."

Secondly, wrote Goldenberg, the new process for awarding contracts would not do what it was supposed to do: save money and improve service. Only one of the four new companies even existed before the winning bids were chosen. Goldenberg said that "on the basis of contemplated wage rates and the attitude to labour relations disclosed to me, I am of the opinion that they will be unable to fulfil their commitment within the fixed price and, at the same time, maintain industrial peace. Moreover, none has as yet been able to organize properly to commence service on April 1st."

As a result, the commissioner did not back the Cabinet decision to force the new contractors to hire Lapalme employees. Instead, he recommended that the new contracts be cancelled, and that the post office take over all transportation in Montreal and bring the Lapalme employees into the civil service.

The government accepted both recommendations, but did not guarantee jobs for all. Drury also wanted wage cuts to bring the Lapalme workers into line with postal wage rates.

The union refused to accept and began the demonstrations on Parliament Hill that would drag on for a year. The union still wanted the Lapalme boys to keep their jobs, face no reprisals, have their seniority recognized in a distinct unit of workers, and have their grievances handled by their own representatives, not those of the postal unions.

Jobs and pay might have been the coin of bargaining, but the real fight was over union jurisdiction. Kierans says the CNTU (Confederation of National Trade Unions) ''was trying to get a wedge into the public service. It wasn't over money. If the [CNTU] could get their drivers into the public service in the post office, that would represent an enormous victory for them. That's what the strike was all about.''

The Canadian Union of Postal Workers and the Letter Carriers Union of Canada had both initially backed the Lapalme boys, promising not to do any work during the dispute. But after the post office started hiring people to replace the Lapalme workers, CUPW was in a bind. National president Willie Houle endorsed a statement from the Canadian Labour Congress saying that any Lapalme workers hired by the post office would have to join one of the CLC-affiliated postal unions — and give up their ties to the CNTU.

The CNTU, for its part, treated the dispute as a *cause célèbre* for Quebec nationalism. *Les gars de Lapalme* were not in it for the money, but were out on the streets because they wanted to keep their union, a Quebec union. The ploy succeeded only too well. In October 1970 the members of the FLQ (Front de libération du Québec) who kidnapped James Cross made settlement of the Lapalme dispute one of their conditions for the release of the British trade commissioner.

Even though Diterlizzi went on television to tell the kidnappers to leave the Lapalme guys alone because they could take care of themselves, the FLQ connection hurt the image of the Lapalme strikers. It also gave the government an excuse to stall until the kidnappings had been resolved.

The dispute came to a head in early 1971. In January, the post office said it would start offering jobs to individual Lapalme workers in a bid to break their solidarity. In the wake of Trudeau's famous riposte, Diterlizzi showed that he could dish out the insults himself. The federal authorities, he told *Le Devoir*, were "a herd of cows" who were "trying to buy the guys one by one like sheep or prostitutes."

The strain was getting to the men, who had been without work for almost a year. In early February they occupied the CNTU offices to protest its lack of success. After a chaotic week of talks, the CNTU and the Lapalme boys reached an agreement.

On the nineteenth, CNTU executives met with Trudeau for ninety minutes in Ottawa. Trudeau told them he had nothing new to offer them, but would look at any union proposal as long as the former Lapalme workers became part of the civil service and did not take jobs away from those who had replaced them. The CNTU tried another proposal which would turn the Montreal transportation business into a quasi-Crown corporation, but the government was not interested.

In the end, it was another union that finished the affair. The Montreal local of the letter-carriers union, which had agreed to support the Lapalme boys, started signing their replacements as members. It was a graphic example of the LCUC's pragmatism. Since the government had made it clear that the transportation jobs had become part of the post office, it was a matter of laying claim to this entire new category of postal employees.

The government also chose spending as the better part of valour when it came to dealing with the drivers in the rest of the major cities. It decided to bring the drivers into the civil service from the start, and to buy off labour protests. Mackay went directly to Senator Ed Lawson, the national boss of the Teamsters union. The Teamsters represented the workers in only three other cities, but Mackay knew that if he could swing a deal with them, he would have no trouble anywhere else.

"And we negotiated a deal, because the problem was that we could not bring in the Teamsters, obviously, into the government. So we had to lay them off, pay them separation pay, and then hire them separately." In short, the Teamsters agreed to give up their members. In return, their drivers got paid generous settlements for "losing" their jobs, and then were immediately hired by the post office. The LCUC, having made its move in Montreal, picked up the union memberships.

Even though other cities had no unions, they got the same terms as those negotiated by the Teamsters. "It was fairly sweet as far as the employees were concerned." Their new pay was about the same, but they got better pensions and fringe benefits on top of the severance package without any unemployment.

In the end, the post office got what it wanted: city transportation was under its control, both the CNTU and the Teamsters had been kept out of the post office, and the mail was moving again. As a bonus, the conflict had driven a nasty and ultimately permanent wedge between the two biggest postal unions.

But even as the Lapalme conflict fizzled, a new era of militancy was unfolding within the postal workers' union. The government's win had all the triumph of Napoleon's entry into a burning and deserted Moscow. Ahead lay only a decade of ignominious retreat through a never-ending blizzard of public discontent.

6
Stamping
Out Boredom

■

Militancy was no stranger to the
post office. The first union, the Railway Mail Clerks Association,
was formed in 1889, and its first strike came twenty-nine years
later, at the close of the First World War.

That strike was kicked off by what the workers felt were
broken promises of wage hikes and bonuses that had already
been approved by Parliament. Most of the unrest was in Western
Canada, with some support from Toronto and Hamilton, and the
strike lasted about a month.

That did not have nearly the impact of the post office's second
strike in 1924 by the Dominion Postal Clerks Association. The
illegal walkout hit most major cities, but the government reacted
swiftly and firmly.

Strikers in Montreal, Toronto, and Windsor were fired and
replaced. Those in other areas were demoted when they returned
to work. Other civil service organizations argued that the government had been too harsh, and their protests were joined by
those of other groups outside government. Two years later, the
punishments were rescinded. Workers got their jobs back, and
were paid their lost wages.

The anger and frustration lived on for decades. "Among veteran
employees in Canada Post, it is generally considered that the
after-effects of the 1918 and 1924 strikes contributed to the
militancy and employee support of postal associations for many

years afterwards,'' noted a 1981 post office history of labour relations.

The postal workers' Joe Davidson agreed. Every worker who had crossed the picket line was called a ''cuckoo'' by those who had fought on, he said in *Joe Davidson*, his autobiography co-written with John Deverell. New workers in the post office were told who they were by the older union hands. ''Even 35 years later, if you were talking to an older man at your case and the call of 'cuckoo' ran down the aisle, the conversation ceased and from that moment on, the fellow ceased to exist,'' he wrote. Some were rescued by moving them to supervisory and management jobs, but even there the stigma dogged them.

Despite that lasting antagonism, the postal associations were pretty weak for the first half of the century. They had no guaranteed source of money, so all the officers had to fit their union duties into their spare time. And there was no bargaining. Wages were raised when the government so decided, and had nothing to do with what workers thought they deserved.

The lack of union power was combined with a sense of individual discipline and even pride. Many postal employees had got their jobs during the Great Depression, when the post office became a way for the government to help the jobless. The post office held their jobs open when the boys went off to fight in the Second World War, and hence adopted much of the flavour of the military when they came back.

Some long-time employees say the military aspect of postal management has been exaggerated. There were bad eggs in the supervisory basket just as there were among the workers. However, supervisors did have plenty of power by today's labour-relations standards. In many cases, that power was abused.

''The supervisors, with the blessings of their superiors, had sufficient discretionary power to make some lives easy and others unnecessarily difficult,'' wrote Davidson. ''Too many of them used it unwisely, leaving the employees no alternative but to seek, through collective action, more precise rules and the uniform application of them.''

Sometimes friction arose simply because supervisors didn't like being shown up by their underlings. ''I was a night worker,'' says Harry Rowe of his job at the post office in 1951. "Those on days were the aristocrats because most of the mail is handled at nights.

"I was sorting mail and it was not long before I noticed at least 50 letters on my bank sorted in daytime were going to Florida by land instead of airmail. I could see people down there biting their nails waiting for cheques. . . . I drew it to the supervisor's attention and he said to keep a count the following night. There was little change. Then the next night he said it wouldn't happen again. 'We put supervisors on the job.' Well, it wasn't much better; the situation got too hot for me. They were insinuating that I was framing them. So I asked to be moved and I was."

Rowe did not stay in the job long, but later came back one Christmas to work as a casual. In those days, casuals were paid according to the number of pieces of mail they handled, or at least by the number their boss said they had handled. "The underlings in charge requested that you bring in a bottle daily and they would raise the number of parcels credited to you. It was piecework. I didn't stay too long because it was too damn cold."

Union leader Jean-Claude Parrot had his own experience with the insensitivity of postal management early in his career. His father had worked at the post office for decades, but in December 1956 fell sick. When he went to hospital, he was found to have terminal cancer. The doctor figured he had only a few months to live, but did not tell him right away. Post office management, however, found out about the nature of his disease. Before the man even knew he was going to die, the post office sent a letter to his house asking him to retire, his son says.

After twenty-eight years of service, Parrot senior had built up a bank of almost 300 days of unused sick leave — time off he was entitled to take at full pay rather than at the reduced amount he would get as a pension. "It was really my first experience with what kind of management we were facing on the other side. . . . I was really pissed off. My father never saw the letter, but for him, it would have been terrible."

Even in the 1960s, says Corkery, "they were still living in the era when they could crack the whip and expect everybody to stand at attention and do what they were told, and if they didn't they would line them up for a firing squad. Some more than others, but a lot of them, they didn't have to be sergeant-majors, but they had that sort of philosophy.''

None the less, for the first two decades after the Second World War, the post office was full of experienced and competent staff — and they were proud of their skills. In the 1950s, says former manager Gordon Sinclair, the Canadian post office had ''a computer capacity beyond belief'' — all human beings. There were sorters who knew every street in Ottawa or every route in Saskatchewan, and, on the first sort, could divide the mail so finely that it would arrive in Saskatchewan already bundled, almost ready for the letter-carriers. The post office began to break down when it lost that human computing capacity.

The famous railway mail clerks were the cream of the crop. Their roots reach back to the building of the railways as the ties of Confederation. They did get slightly higher pay than the average joes in the sorting plants, but their status was what counted.

''The guys were so proud of what they did that they didn't even have labels on the sorting cases. And that was part of the skill,'' says Corkery. Normally, the cases of pigeonholes in front of each sorter were labelled with the names of the various destinations, but the good sorters, especially the ones on the trains, disdained such aids for the forgetful.

''If you were a railway mail clerk, you got two cents or whatever it was more than the guy in the plant; you got to sleep on the floor of those boxcars but you were not allowed just by pride to label the boxes. So they were clean boxes, and they tested them once a month.''

If the railway clerk scored too low, he could be bounced back to the plants, and if he could hit ninety-nine per cent consistently, he got his next incentive pay raise. ''The pride was built into the system over the years. By negotiation over a period, those things got taken out of the system and disappeared.''

The fact that many workers in the plants and on the streets did have pride in their jobs helped the post office to be efficient. But as the fifties rolled into the sixties, that pride was undermined by the penny-pinching policies of the Diefenbaker government, which used the civil service as its main target for budget-cutting.

Planned wage hikes were cancelled in 1958 and again in 1959. Although postal workers did get a raise of 20 cents an hour in mid-1960, their first in three years, the natives of the plant floors were beginning to get restless.

In 1962, just as the new salary structures were supposed to go into place, the Diefenbaker government imposed another wage freeze. It lasted until the Liberals took over in 1963. Postal workers got another 15 cents an hour after their second three-year wait.

In the end, Lester Pearson's Liberals proved no more sympathetic than Diefenbaker's Conservatives. They were not ready when the next scheduled salary review came around in October 1964, and the increase was put off until the summer of 1965. When it did come, it was a big disappointment — only $360 a year for the clerks, little more than half the amount the union had been seeking.

By the summer of 1965, the post office was ready to explode. "If trade unionism and modernization had begun to come to the post office 10 or 15 years earlier, the whole process of change might have been more rational and orderly, but by the mid-1960s, this was no longer possible," wrote Davidson. "The agenda was supercharged, with major issues overlapping and interconnecting in a way which made conflict and instability at all levels inevitable, both between labour and management and among the employee organizations."

The national leaders of the postal unions had been trying to project a reasonable image during 1964 and 1965, because they wanted to coax favourable recommendations from a parliamentary committee that was looking at new legislation for public-service bargaining. Most of these union leaders felt that no protest over wages should go beyond working to rule. Suddenly they were undermined by two of their locals.

Parrot says a strike vote by the Montreal letter-carriers was the spark. That led the Montreal inside workers to follow suit, and they quickly linked up with the Vancouver local, led by Jim McCall.

Davidson said that Willie Houle and Roger Decarie, the Montreal leaders of the postal workers and the letter-carriers respectively, went to Ottawa in July and demanded that the national executive call a full-scale strike. When they were turned down, they went home and announced a strike anyway, for July 22. Parrot says that a handful of smaller locals, including Windsor, Ontario, and Drummondville, Quebec, were with Vancouver and Montreal at the start, and their leaders began phoning other locals across the country to ask them to join in.

Sentiments within the unions were far from unanimous. In Toronto, Davidson records a stormy meeting of the letter-carriers at which the local officers, who favoured caution, were driven from the stage by a barrage of thrown chairs. Members of the rank and file took charge of the meeting and started organizing pickets.

Leaders of the inside workers also tried to keep matters under control until a formal meeting could be held. That only enraged some of the others, said Davidson. "Brother Towata urged [local secretary] Brother Gould to reconsider his position by applying a stranglehold, and the debate was conducted all the way to the exit with Towata riding Gould piggyback until he was pulled off by a watchful supervisor," he wrote.

At the end of the shift, the night workers joined the letter-carriers on the picket line and turned away their day-shift colleagues. Although local president Al Penney actually crossed the picket line to report for work, a meeting of the local on July 25 overwhelmingly backed the strike and postal plants across Toronto quickly ground to a halt. Other locals quickly joined the strike, until about half of all postal offices and plants were out of operation. Unionized drivers for the private contractors who trucked mail around the major cities refused to cross the picket lines.

The government got court injunctions against union pickets in British Columbia, Quebec, and Ontario, but they had little effect. Other unions and sympathetic groups provided "interested citizens" to form pseudo-picket lines instead. The post office also threatened repeatedly to fire strikers who did not return to work. "We were fired about three or four times during the strike, if not more," says Parrot.

Talks between the unions and the government in Ottawa were in chaos. A judge appointed by the government to take another look at the wage offer recommended an extra $60 a year right away, with a bigger increase to be set within two weeks. The national leaders, who still favoured a settlement, went out to their striking locals to sell the package.

Montreal rejected the new offer. Workers in Toronto followed suit. At least, that's what they did until they heard rumours that Montreal had given up. Then they went back to work, only to find that Montreal was still on strike. By the time the strike wound up in August, postal workers had come up with a 10-percent pay raise. The walkout had never been endorsed by the national union officers.

The union would later tell a conciliation board that while the government's "insultingly low wage increase" was the spark that ignited the strike, the militancy of union members "was the result of years of intolerable working conditions set within an environment rampant with patronage and nepotism. There was no protection from arbitrary measures and favouritism in respect to assignments and staffing was the order of the day."

Parrot says that strike marked the real beginning of militancy in the postal unions. "That's where we started to have our reputation. . . . It was not organized at the national [level]. In fact, they opposed it. We felt they missed the boat completely at the time. They made a lot of mistakes in my opinion. If they had joined the strike, we would probably have had 100 per cent across the country and been a lot stronger." Despite the active opposition of their national leaders, exasperated locals managed to get about 80 per cent of the membership out onto the picket lines, and came up with big gains. Even an unplanned and disorganized strike had worked.

There was another bonus in the form of the Royal Commission on Working Conditions in the Post Office headed by Judge André Montpetit. In the wake of the strike, the judge toured post offices across the country to look at postal plants and talk to workers and managers. His report, with 282 recommendations for improving working conditions, gave the union moral support in public and plenty of ammunition for future battles with management.

The vacillation of the union leadership in 1965 sounded the death-knell for many moderates. At conventions that followed, many were booted out of office and replaced with men who had been leaders in the strike action.

The strike saw the awakening of the Montreal local of the inside workers union, which adopted its new name — the Canadian Union of Postal Workers — at its convention in September 1965. Union dues were raised, and used to hire eight full-time field organizers to help the existing three Ottawa-based top officers. It also set the tone for the first real collective bargaining at the post office under the new Public Service Staff Relations Act, whose rules would prove to be an expensive battleground for the postal struggles of the 1970s.

Meanwhile, the nature of the postal work force was itself undergoing drastic change. Figuratively speaking, at least, the legends of the post office were dying. All the older workers who had joined during the Depression were reaching the point at which they could begin collecting their maximum pension.

Some of those who might have stayed longer changed their minds when faced with the struggle over wages, the changing attitudes of their younger colleagues, and the increasingly frustrating conditions in their workplaces.

Former postmaster general Eric Kierans says that many of their complaints were justified as collective bargaining began. "Six to ten years later they could no longer claim with the same validity that they were exploited, but up to then, we were running the post office literally on their backs. By the time I got there, I must have been signing a hundred retirement letters a day."

"Some of the buildings were thirty years old. They had been built pre-war. They didn't have air conditioning and the volume of mail was growing," says Sinclair. And in Quebec, the children of the Quiet Revolution "infiltrated the whole postal system in the province and gave rise to the almost complete takeover of the union movement in the post office by Quebec labour leaders."

The growth and spread of the Canadian population during the 1960s also meant that postal managers had to change the ways of sorting mail. There were too many destinations, even for the "human computers". Instead of using addresses and street names that could be memorized, the sorting began to be done alphabetically. That made it much easier to train young recruits, but it did little for a worker's pride.

The growth in mail volume took the knowledge out of a sorting job, says Corkery. A sorter used to be recognized as "really something. Then you got to the point where the poor guy couldn't remember which bank sat on which corner. We used to figure that 4,000 points of call was about what they could remember . . . and that's pretty good for a city sorter.

"As you get bigger, you can't do that. . . . Then you're sorting AA, AB, AC, boring as hell, and even worse, because now it's not knowledge, still requiring the judgment call but without the feeling of yeah, I know where that street is, it's in Joe Doakes' box."

It is tough to find people who are happy in a job that requires them to do boring, repetitive work but still forces them to make judgments with each move. Corkery remembers one woman who worked for him on an assembly line in a factory making Christmas bulbs. She had to take four lead wires and plug them together, 1,200 times an hour, day after day. "She wasn't bored stiff, she was a great operator. But she was able — and this is where women seem to be able to do what men can't do — she could separate the physical loading from what was going on with the team around her.

"She never stopped talking for the whole eight hours she was at work. She was the mother hen for the whole team. And she never missed a head, a super operator as far as we were concerned, and she never stopped talking. To her, it was a great job with good pay and nice people to work with, and her mind stayed alert because she could do that."

But in the 1960s good employees were hard to find and harder to keep. There were plenty of jobs around, and if a worker didn't like what he was doing, he soon moved on. The post office could not afford to be picky about who it hired, and, because of the high turnover, was forced to make the sorting process simpler to learn — and therefore even more boring.

Yet the kind of employees it was hiring were a far cry from the proud men of the mail cars. "You'd be amazed if you pulled the records and found out how many Ph.D.s and M.A.s were working for the post office," says Corkery. "It really shook me the last time I looked at it. These characters came into the system out of the sixties, who were really opting out of society, I think, in a lot of cases." The money wasn't bad and there was no responsibility. They were "smart, bright characters, content to be letter-carriers, because they had another life that they wanted to live."

At the same time, many of the old school had moved up to become supervisors and managers. The changing make-up of the work force made it "damned tough for a supervisor . . . who has come up through the ranks, with maybe a public school education but not necessarily, not that sharp or quick or astute."

When faced with a boring job, the more active and inventive minds of the younger generation "have to find their kicks in other ways . . . looking for ways to hassle supervisors just for sheer fun. I wouldn't have been a supervisor at the first level for anything. In this environment, it was really tough. You have to feel for them."

While the advent of contract bargaining did put an end to many of the abuses of power at the lower levels, it also closely bound what supervisors could do. As the work force changed, supervisors found themselves without either carrots or sticks. When they were faced with smart workers who didn't care whether or not they kept their jobs, enforcing discipline became a losing game.

The most graphic account of the resulting "struggle against work" by this new generation can be found in a 1979 book by Walter Johnson called *Trade Unions and the State*. The book includes a fascinating chapter by Peter Taylor, a man who spent nine months working in the post office of the 1970s.

"I really didn't like working at the post office. In fact, I hated it," he begins. "When I applied for the job, they made me write both a memory test and an intelligence test. But in no way did the job require any skill, beyond a basic ability to read. . . . The whole exercise was a holdover from the time when sorting mail required a detailed knowledge of the postal system, and *nobody* seemed to believe in it any more."

He describes in detail the various ploys workers would use: taking unofficial breaks averaging ten minutes every hour, taking days off, leaving early and getting someone else to punch your time-card, and dodging supervisors in the stairwells and wash-rooms. At one point, to protest a supervisor's pursuit of one of their colleagues, Taylor and his fellow workers staged a "shit-in", all deciding to go to the bathroom at the same time. Although it was badly organized, he wrote, about thirty-five of them ended up standing around the washroom waiting for the stalls to clear.

Another tactic was abusing the provision for "court leave" in the contract. This allowed an employee to take a day off with pay for jury duty or if he produced proof that he had "been in court with the purpose of testifying." They found it easy to get a court clerk to state that a person had been an "uncalled witness".

"I found myself working, and at the same time thinking, wishing, pretending I was somewhere else. Dope obviously helped. Like most large factories, lots of people were stoned or drunk much of the time." Every effort was directed at spending less time on the job. "Even now I can vividly remember the pleasure, the sense of relief, that followed my calling in sick. With that phone call I would have gained a free evening."

Because the work was so distasteful, strikes were just holidays. Because workers were in short supply, it made no difference if the strikes were illegal. He admits that the high turnover encouraged their disregard of discipline.

One of the aggravating factors in the feelings of the younger workers was the extent of night work involved in postal sorting. People who have taken a job for the pay cheque and get their satisfaction at home are irritated by working-hours that stop them from getting together with friends who work a normal day.

"Every night all of us used most of these tactics," wrote Taylor. "So much so, that as well as looking like a prison, the post office also resembled a battlefield. Each night was filled with incidents, actions and reactions, all designed to gain an advantage. For us, the aim was more money for less work; the super-visors and management obviously had the opposite goal."

People like Taylor were less interested in doing a good job than they were on building "relationships" in their lives, and night work at the post office contributed nothing to such relation-ships. "In contrast, the struggle against work provided a much better basis for relationships. First, because that was more enjoyable. . . . Second, because we had to do it ourselves — no 'representative' [for example, the union] could do it for us — through them we could exercise some control over ourselves. Third, because all of us engaged to some extent, there was a real feeling of being together against management.

"Caught as we were in a system where our needs came last every time, our struggle against work was the one way we could 'be ourselves', could act on our needs, could affirm our presence and importance. Thus, taking the night off, taking 'unofficial' breaks, talking back, refusing orders, etc., all generated enthusiasm, pleasure and support," Taylor wrote.

Sinclair said he checked the records at one point and found that workers were taking as much unpaid leave as paid leave. Supervisors did not have to grant such leave, but usually did, because if they refused, the worker would just take the day off anyway.

The boredom led to many abuses of the mail as well. In 1979, two former postal workers told the press about the ways postal workers found to make their days more exciting. Ronald Meigh and Stephen Wroblewski, who had worked at the Gateway sorting plant in Toronto during the 1978 Christmas rush, said Christmas gifts broke open every day and workers would often grab items that were exposed.

Those marked fragile would be deliberately thrown around to damage them. "If [a parcel] is marked 'fragile' they call it 'airmail' and just heave it," Meigh told *The Globe and Mail*. Regular workers would tell the temporary ones to slow down. Many would sleep, play cards, smoke marijuana, or drink alcohol when they were supposed to be working.

At times, the new generation's discontent erupted into war. Windshields were smashed. Cars were bumped. Supervisors were threatened and even attacked. One worker would come up to a supervisor and stand on his feet, while another would humiliate him in front of his workers by urinating on him. Some stories can be documented. Others survive only as tales. Certainly, though, supervisors — without training, without support from their superiors, fenced in by contracts, intimidated and outmanoeuvred by those under them — were soon running scared.

The change of generations did not just affect management. The unions, too, had to deal with this fundamental change in the expectations of their members. As a group, they were much more successful in adapting to their changing world than were postal managers and politicians, but they did not all follow the same path.

7
Division
of Labour

■

The action of the Letter Carriers
Union of Canada in signing up the Lapalme replacements was not
the first time it had humiliated the Canadian Union of Postal
Workers. When the Lapalme struggle rolled around, CUPW was
still smarting from its handling by the LCUC in the wake of
Kierans' decision in 1968 to end six-day delivery.

That move meant that as many as one-sixth of the LCUC's
members would lose their jobs. As the letter-carriers felt the
pinch of restraint, they began to express strong interest in merging
with the inside workers. As a first step, CUPW agreed to let
surplus LCUC members keep their seniority ratings if they transferred to jobs in the postal plants and offices.

That was an important concession because of the way seniority was applied to picking people for jobs. Post office practice was
and is that the workers who have been in the unit longest get first
choice when it comes to picking jobs and are first in line for
reserving their vacation periods. Day shifts are more popular
than night shifts; work at the wickets selling stamps to the public
is more pleasant than flipping letters into boxes; and there tends
to be a line-up for favoured vacation slots.

Letter-carriers had lower turnover than inside workers, largely
because walking around town with a bag on one's shoulder was
generally more pleasant than night-shift work in a postal plant.
Carriers stay with the post office longer. When large numbers of

surplus letter-carriers started transferring into jobs in CUPW jurisdiction, they tended to have greater seniority than most of the existing CUPW members, and were quickly able to grab choice shifts and assignments.

Inside workers were furious, but there was little they could do. "Our members were stunned and outraged, and understandably so," said Davidson. "The LCUC had put a fast one over on us and we had nothing to show in return." To complete the humiliation of the CUPW leaders, the merger never went through. Although a referendum in January 1969 showed that members of both unions approved, the LCUC backed out of the deal in a vote at its next national convention.

The LCUC's actions in the Lapalme dispute and its negotiating strategies during the 1970s show a very different approach from the one used by its more notorious brethren in CUPW. In the early days of collective bargaining in the public service, the two unions formed a common front, the Council of Postal Unions, to handle contract talks jointly.

But the leaders of the two unions had sharply different philosophies. In many cases, they also wanted different things from negotiations. The result, when combined with their internal disputes, was an increasingly strained partnership.

"The leaders of the two unions devoted almost as much energy to negotiating with each other as we did to negotiating with the post office," recalled Davidson. The alliance would fall apart in the early 1970s as the more militant CUPW locals flexed their muscles.

The LCUC cultivated a reputation during the 1970s of being a much more reasonable union than the rough, nasty fellows from the inside workers. It is true that they had far fewer strikes, filed a small fraction of the grievances, and yet achieved much the same wages and benefits. In fact, they often wangled slightly higher pay than the inside workers.

Bob McGarry is proud of his record of getting deals without strikes. "We've known how to negotiate and how to take them on. You know that you're not going to get all the things that you want. If you're going to be around for ten years, you set your negotiating style that you're not going to get that this time, but you're going to set up your strategy where it's not quite as hard to get the next time around. We've dealt with that strategy and really dealt with the people at the table to make our arguments more valid. I guess over the years it's been successful. I've sat at the table for the last twelve years as their chief negotiator and we've lost a couple of days.''

Unlike their counterparts in the postal plants, the letter-carriers have always been talkative. They talk to anybody and everybody: stroking, demanding, cajoling, hinting, threatening, joking, or pleading according to the audience and the situation. The letter-carriers don't stand on principle during negotiations. The goal is always to get the best deal possible.

''We simply set up the strategy as to how to go about trying to keep the service, keep the public on our side, keeping the government informed where we were coming from and letting the employer and the membership and the government know where a settlement was. If no one knows where the settlement is going to be, it's all the more difficult. If you hold out with all your demands, as if you're going to strike till your nose bleeds for them all, then nobody's going to move.''

The LCUC's bargaining strategy has also been aided by the very growth of Canada's population. The 1970s were the heyday of urban sprawl in Canada. New suburbs meant new jobs for letter-carriers. The only issue for the union was how much they should be paid. Unlike the inside workers, who were embroiled in questions of technological change and job security, the LCUC leadership did not have to divide its attention.

''I always considered CUPW as somewhat archaic, the nine-teenth-century-type labour group, whereas the letter-carriers and the other couple of unions were not the same,'' says former deputy postmaster general John Mackay. ''They were quite prepared to sit down and talk sense. They weren't impacted to the same point. The other group, all they seemed interested in was causing the problem.''

Corkery felt the same way. ''The union that's the most astute is the letter-carriers. They know how to push it to the wire and then back off. They're just as aggressive, just as abrasive, and just as hard to deal with, but they've got enough common sense

. . . they know how to work [the system], smart enough to scream blue murder and wear you down."

The letter-carriers had no compunction about riding piggyback on the efforts of their CUPW colleagues. The classic pattern of bargaining went like this: LCUC negotiators would go for the best gains in wages and benefits they could get without a strike; they would usually wheedle a little extra for being such reasonable fellows; and they would pick up without much argument whatever improvements in working conditions the inside workers had wrenched from the government in their last dispute.

The LCUC owes much of its success to a unique duo at the top: president Bob McGarry and vice-president Bill Findlay. They have both been around for a long time, a clear sign of their ability to keep their members happy.

The garrulous McGarry joined the post office in Scarborough, Ontario, in 1966. He soon became a shop steward and then a full-time business agent for the union in Metro Toronto. By 1975 he had been elected national president.

Findlay has been unleashing his Scottish burr on management for more than two decades. He became a letter-carrier in Downsview, Ontario, in 1961. Five years later he began a quick rise to the top: shop steward in 1966, local vice-president in 1967, local president in 1968, and general vice-president of the national union in 1969. In 1975 he rose a notch to national executive vice-president.

The two men exhibit sharply contrasting styles as they pursue their common objective. In negotiations, they are like a good cop–bad cop team. McGarry talks endlessly. He never lets himself get pinned down or makes a commitment. "He's the most devious, dishonest individual I've been exposed to in the post office," grumbles one former bureaucrat. "Parrot, he's got integrity. He tells you what he stands for. With McGarry, he's peaches and cream, but he's putting a stiletto in your back."

In the words of one manager: "He talks you up one side of the street and down the other. Then Findlay lets you know when you have a deal." These days, Findlay acts as the wise old man who comes to the rescue to drag hapless managers out of McGarry's verbal quicksand. But he is no fool, and knows plenty about how to rant and rave himself. "Wild Bill", the managers used to call him in the early days before he figured out that being clever got better results than screaming. He learned quickly.

Davidson gives Findlay credit for taking a traditional bugaboo of the unions — work measurement — and turning it into a gold mine for his members.

In 1970 the post office was determined to find a way to make sure letter-carriers did an honest day's work for their pay. It was a tough problem, because it is not easy to supervise an army of people walking around city streets with bags on their shoulders. As a result, managers tried to figure out how much work a carrier should do in a day. Management proposed a series of time-and-motion studies to show how long it took a postman to walk a block, to open a mailbox, to push letters through a slot, to ring twice at someone's door. Each of these "elements" which made up a day's work was assigned a "time value" that said how long that action should take.

Instead of fighting the proposal, Findlay "devoted all his energies to mastering the intricacies of the measurement system and negotiating very favourable 'elemental time values' for each little bit of the letter carrier task, thus limiting the total number of these bits making up a day's work," wrote Davidson.

Even a small change made a big difference to postal costs. In 1971, for instance, the two sides got embroiled in a dispute over the unaddressed advertising flyers delivered by the postman. The letter-carriers wanted to add one minute per day to the time set aside for sorting bundles of admail. The post office said that would mean making all 9,800 routes a little bit smaller, and force it to hire an extra 100 carriers.

The key to exploiting the system lay in persuading management that it was unreasonable to expect a carrier to walk at more than a steady pace. The system also assumed that carriers would stick to the sidewalks and the paths leading to each door. And carriers were allowed time to get to and from the postal station to their assigned walks by public transit.

Once each "walk" had been determined by measuring such things as the length of the route, the ups and downs of the terrain, the number and kind of mailboxes to be filled, and the average volume of mail, it was fixed as eight hours' work. That meant that once the work was done, a letter-carrier could go home and still collect his eight hours' pay. Some chose to saunter through their walks at the measured pace, but others made the most of it.

Ever since that contract was signed, letter-carriers have been able to get off early by walking faster, taking short cuts through alleys or across lawns, driving their own cars to and from their walks instead of taking the bus, and skipping their negotiated breaks and wash-up periods.

A comprehensive audit of the post office by Auditor General Kenneth Dye in 1981 had some sharp words to say about the system. Departmental studies had shown that the majority of postmen were finishing their routes in five to six hours. Some managers say that a really ambitious carrier can finish his route in four. Even union members admit that a six- or seven-hour day is easily achieved.

"For the individual worker, it is a terrific arrangement and will continue to be until management decides to speed things up by challenging the elemental time values in the walk evaluation system," said Davidson.

The good deal was made better when letter-carriers won the right of first refusal on each other's routes. If one letter-carrier falls sick, other carriers at the same postal station have first crack at doing the route — at overtime rates. A postman can wrap up his own route and then take a half or even a full route from one of his colleagues, and still finish within a regular eight-hour day.

Hugh Mullington, a former Treasury Board bureaucrat who also acted as the co-ordinator for a private-sector study of Canada Post Corp. in 1985, said that a postman who really works at it can collect as much as twenty hours' pay — eight for his own route and twelve for a second at time and a half — within a normal working day.

The Auditor General did admit that enforcing the system would not move the mail any faster. "Although letter carriers may not necessarily walk their routes exactly as designed, they are delivering the mail assigned to them each day. Having letter carriers walk their routes as structured would not improve efficiency or result in more mail being delivered.''

Having satisfied their desire for a shorter work week early in the game, the letter-carriers found themselves increasingly at odds with their brothers and sisters in the postal plants, where a revolution was brewing. The first shots were fired at the 1971 CUPW national convention in Calgary. The union leaders had hired trade-union consultant Bill Walsh to put together a new constitution for them, and expected to have it adopted by the convention. The Montreal local, led by Jean-Claude Parrot, Marcel Perrault, and Clement Morel, had other plans.

"We arrived in Calgary only to discover that what we had planned as a quiet and orderly affair was going to be nothing of the sort,'' recalled Davidson, then a national vice-president. "The contingent from Quebec was extremely well-prepared, united and in a very uncompromising frame of mind. . . . the Quebec group fought like a well-drilled team for a program which the rest of the delegates found very disturbing.''

The Montreal group wanted out of the Council of Postal Unions through which they bargained jointly with the letter-carriers; they wanted to take over the letter-carriers' jurisdiction; they wanted to fight for the gains to be had from automation and get rid of all casual labour in the post office; and they wanted the new constitution to include tight control over the way the union was run.

"Although the threat surfaced openly only once or twice on the convention floor, it was apparent that there was a fairly strong separatist inclination among the Quebec delegates, who had been thoroughly unimpressed by the national office's handling of the casual labour issue during the 1970 bargaining, the Lapalme affair and the generally inadequate preparations on the automation issue,'' wrote Davidson.

The rest of the delegates were both surprised and nervous at the extent of the Quebec delegation's goals, and the convention bogged down in a prolonged agony of angry argument. After four days, a meeting of the local leaders was set up. "We told them what we wanted, what compromises we were willing to accept,'' says Parrot. "We told them to study that. They agreed, finally, early in the morning. So the next morning on the convention floor, they passed those things that we wanted, and they adopted the rest of the constitution without anybody even questioning from the floor. So it went smoothly after that."

In the elections that followed, Parrot was voted by acclamation to the newly created job of national chief steward. Six years later he would become president.

Traditional unionists in CUPW would face more surprises in the years ahead. In 1972, Davidson and other union leaders travelled to Montreal for a labour-relations seminar at McGill University. When they arrived, they found that the Montreal local had set up a picket line around the building to protest the participation of Eric Kierans. Davidson was outraged that the local union would pull a stunt like that without telling the national leadership, allowing them to waste union money and look stupid into the bargain.

"In the centre of activities was [local president] Marcel Perrault, quite enjoying our discomfort," wrote Davidson. "Despite my limited knowledge of French, I thought I detected on his lips the unforgettable old Trudeau invitation to eat something unpleasant." When Davidson threatened to discipline Perrault if he didn't withdraw the pickets, "Marcel laughed aloud and replied that the national vice-president sounded like a postmaster. We beat an inglorious retreat back to the hotel, where I argued that to uphold the meagre authority of the national office we had to go back and cross the line. Nobody else could see anything but grief in that proposal, so we bowed the knee and returned to Ottawa."

Jean-Claude Parrot has an unlikely background for a man who would become the public leader of the Quebec militant wing and show himself willing to defy Parliament and go to jail over a contract dispute. Although his father also worked at the post office, "I had no union background, in the sense that I was not born in a family where we were talking union shop at home. . . . I was like most people who got out of school and don't know anything about a union."

Ironically, Parrot says he joined the post office because the pay was so good. "Joining the post office, it was a question of money for me." He had been on the job market for a couple of years already, working at a bank. His father told him of openings at the post office when the work week was reduced to forty hours.

"I didn't intend to work in the post office, because my father was all his life in the post office, and was working on the midnight shift. That was not much attractive to me, but when I saw the wages compared to what I was earning at the bank — it was double — I decided to try it anyway."

He didn't even get involved with the union until 1961, seven years after joining the post office. By then, he had already worked his way onto day shifts as a wicket clerk, with the frustrations of night work and time pressure and strict supervision behind him.

He says he happened to go to a meeting one day set up to talk about problems facing wicket clerks, and became fascinated by the process. "I realized at that stage that we all had the same problems, the same things we wanted to talk about, and I also found it interesting to meet quite a lot of people which I might not meet on a daily basis. It was really, for me, something I realized I wanted to do."

Except for the incident involving his father's cancer, "I never really had anything against or for the post office." He did resent his father's midnight hours, but later found out that he had had the choice of working days but preferred the night-time hours.

The attraction of union meetings was at first simply social. "Then I found out a lot of stuff that was happening, by myself and with the others involved in the union. . . . The attitude of the management of the post office is what made me a union man. I had my own feelings . . . I could be easily affected by what happened to other people. I thought I could do something about that. And I see it as a more interesting thing to do than just working in the post office. To me, it is an interesting job if you really want to put your heart into it. It's very demanding, but it's very interesting."

Over the next five years, he never missed a union meeting. He became a shop steward, and then in 1964 a part-time local officer, and eventually in 1968 a full-time vice-president of the Montreal local. Along the way, social had become socialist.

"The Montreal local has had a lot of influence in the direction that I've taken our union," says Parrot. "Our union went from a national association to a union in the sixties, and then, as a union, developed a very strong orientation, I would say a progressive one. And the Montreal local was part of that. We were very, very strong in what we felt should be included in our constitution, the approach we should take. And we developed locally issues like not socializing with the management to keep the credibility in the membership. . . . It was very strong for us to keep a lot of credibility among the membership. We developed that very strongly at the local level, and obviously over time, we pushed the same kind of approach at the national level.''

The Montreal leaders were not just interested in lining the pockets of their own members at the bargaining table: they wanted to be an example, to show others that the impossible could be achieved.

Parrot says the internal struggle that the Montreal local launched in 1971 reached its climax at the stormy 1974 convention. '''74 is the convention where the true orientation of our union was confronted. That was the last convention before total change in direction took place.''

At that convention, delegates were divided and angry, but the militants carried the day. ''We won in '74 the change in the direction of our union very clearly. And in '77, the convention was the most united convention I ever saw, in the sense that everybody was on the same side, we were thinking the same way. At that stage, the union had definitely decided which direction we were going to take. And after '77 until today, people are strictly playing with words at conventions. . . . There's no real issue of orientation that happens at conventions any more.''

Parrot says that, over the years, the militants have placed in the constitution more and more restrictions on the behaviour of union officers and on the conduct of its locals. To focus the union's resources on its struggles both within the post office and in the wider labour movement, there are strict controls on how its locals can spend their money.

Postal workers used to spend union dues on things like sponsoring kids' hockey teams and holding Christmas parties. One local even took its leftover money at the end of each year and gave it back to its members. ''That doesn't make the union very strong,'' says Parrot. ''We stopped all that completely. We said people pay their dues to be protected by the union, to be defended, so not to use the money for social activities. That was a clear change in direction.'' Locals could send delegates to training seminars and conventions, but not spend their funds on social activities. They could give money to other unions in trouble, but not to local charities.

Communications were vital to the militant strategy. The first part was a matter of bringing union members together; the other half meant cutting them off from contact with management.

Union leaders could not stop managers from publishing bulletins and talking to employees. Instead, they hammered into the heads of their members that managers could not be trusted; only the union was a reliable source of information. ''Always base your strength on the membership,'' says Parrot. ''Get them involved, communicate a lot with the membership.''

For that idea to stick, the militant leaders had to maintain their own credibility. That led to new rules: union members, especially the shop stewards and officers who had to deal with managers officially, were not to have any informal contacts with the bosses. The militants reasoned that if a worker who lost a grievance saw his shop steward and his supervisor having a friendly drink the next day, he might get the idea that the two had cooked up a deal behind his back. That would hurt union credibility.

There must always be at least two union representatives at any meeting. ''We found out in the meetings that we were having in Montreal that we were more effective when we were two, and we adopted that as a rule among ourselves,'' says Parrot. That way, there would be no danger of talk about leaders' selling out their members; there would always be witnesses. ''If you're alone, there's always a question of what has happened there.''

In negotiations, the union decided that under no circumstances would it agree to a ''moratorium of silence'', a deal between the two parties not to talk to anyone outside the negotiating teams during a period of delicate manoeuvring. That decision stemmed from an incident in which the postal minister made a statement in the House of Commons about an offer's being made to the union. ''The membership didn't know anything. The union was caught by surprise. Again the credibility . . . so we passed a resolution to the effect that the union has to communicate with the membership during the whole period of negotations,'' says Parrot.

When the sight of union officers collecting their pay from the union while members were on strike in 1975 drew complaints, the constitution was amended again. Now, when the union is on strike, its officers lose their pay cheques too. Everyone in the union suffers together.

''All these little policies, all together, have developed a direction for our union. We found that our leadership were not following those things, so we put them in the constitution . . . to the point that almost everything that the executive or officer has to do is in the constitution. Even almost the attitude that you have to take,'' says Parrot.

Beneath the surface solidarity with other postal unions, Parrot's feelings about McGarry and his approach to bargaining border on the contemptuous. A question about the letter-carriers' boss brings a stare and a long silence, which breaks down into an angry mutter: ''That guy's only out for himself.''

Ironically, Joe Davidson, the CUPW president during the mid-1970s, was not part of the Montreal-based militant movement, and didn't have much time for many of their dogmatic methods. He was more of an old-style industrial unionist, carved from the same tree as the letter-carriers' Bill Findlay, right down to the Scottish accent. He was quite willing to work out pragmatic deals with management.

Mackay says he was even willing to live with mechanization. ''I think he recognized that we had to do something, but there were some members within his group: just impossible, impossible to deal with on any subject.''

Gordon Sinclair, the head of postal operations during the early 1970s, remembers a deal Davidson made with him. One of his duties after he moved to operations from finance was to take care of all the grievances that had not been resolved at the local or regional level.

He tried to treat them all with appropriate seriousness, but after watching him for a while, Davidson offered him a few private signals to help him in his decisions: If Davidson wrapped up with a very short speech, he expected to lose and wouldn't put up any fuss if Sinclair said no; if the speech were slightly longer, he cared about the outcome, but still expected to be turned down; if he went on at some length, it meant that Davidson really felt the union had a good case and expected Sinclair to give it serious consideration; finally, if Davidson brought the union member involved along with him, it meant that he thought the individual was in the wrong, but the union leader was pleading for mercy.

Sinclair said the informal system worked well for him. Where Davidson said he was serious, Sinclair would take a hard look. He would do his best to grant mercy when Davidson asked, which helped the union leader win points with his members. And, in return, he got off easy in rejecting the rest of the grievances.

That was just the sort of behaviour Parrot's version of union militancy was supposed to end, and yet it was Davidson who gained fame in the public eye as the leader of the postal militants because of a single slip of the tongue. In 1975, with talks dragging their way towards a major strike, Davidson held a press conference to explain the union's position to the public, and, in the process, "wrote my own epitaph and torpedoed the small reservoir of public sympathy for the CUPW."

One reporter asked how Davidson felt about the inconvenience a strike would cause. The union leader replied that workers would be hurting the most during any strike, and added: "I think if the public were fully informed, which is your job, then it would understand what we are doing and support us." After being pressed twice on what he would do if the public were fully informed and still did not support the strike, Davidson snapped the line that immortalized him: "Then to hell with the public."

It did not take Davidson long to realize the extent of his mistake. "Paul Mitchell, our public relations director, turned white and threatened to shoot himself as the journalists headed for the telephones. . . . I now understand why the prime minister avoids hypothetical questions."

New Democratic Party MP John Rodriguez, for many years his party's postal critic, says the unfortunate remark was a turning-point in the union's public support. "Up to that point, the postal union was getting a fair hearing from the public. I think people recognized that there must be a deeper principle here.'' But after the wide play Davidson's statement got in the media, ''you could just see the union support wilting. . . . The public just turned right against the union,'' Rodriguez says. ''The remark stayed with people. Nobody remembers the T-shirts with 'Management sucks' but they remember the remark 'To hell with the public'.''

The new-style militancy in the postal workers did not have room for such off-the-cuff mistakes. They were playing a high-risk, high-gain game, and more than their credibility was at stake whenever they spoke.

But, as the decade unfolded, CUPW's new leaders made few mistakes. They had become a union with a sacred mission, the *mujahedeen* of the mails, determined to win or die trying.

8
The
Militant
Minorities

■

The new militants in the CUPW leadership may have been stubborn, but they were not stupid. They knew full well that to win their larger struggle, they would have to produce results for their members. And to produce results, they would have to build an army out of the rabble that composed the post office's new generation of workers.

"We had to communicate a lot with the membership. We had to discuss with them the problems and explain to them why it would be better to adopt some solutions versus another, get the membership involved a lot in agreeing with principles," issues that individuals might not like, but that they accepted as being good for the union as a whole, says Parrot.

Having convinced its members, the union would then go to the bargaining table with the attitude that the government had to grant its demands because it had such a united and militant group behind it. The idea was to show the government that the economic and political costs of fighting would be greater than those of giving in. A union win at that point not only meant gains for postal workers. It also reinforced the credibility of the union leaders and the idea that militancy pays off.

Demands at the initial stage are always phrased in terms of general policies that are entrenched in the union constitution: receiving the benefits of technological change, getting rid of casuals and cheap labour, banning individual work measurement, pushing for the creation of full-time jobs but still insisting on full benefits for part-timers, and so on. It is tough for family members to fight motherhood demands like that.

For instance, in 1975 the union decided it wanted to get rid of the last vestiges of work measurement. Keeping track of the number of pieces of mail handled by each worker had already been banned for full-time employees. Now the union wanted to protect part-timers too. The union presented it not as an industrial issue, one of more money and less work, but as a social one, a matter of discrimination. It said that 95 per cent of the part-timers were women, and work measurement was leading to sexual harassment by supervisors. Women who were nice to supervisors got easier assignments and credit for work they didn't do. That meant others were unjustly penalized for sorting slower than the average, the union argued.

"We really got the membership to agree that certain things are not novel, and really using their strength to achieve these things all the time. And that required the union to be very active. You cannot wait until the day before the strike and suddenly start to talk about these things. You have to talk about it during the whole period of negotiations," says Parrot.

The intent in taking this principled approach is twofold: to convince the members first that the union's cause is just, and second, that its goals can be achieved, no matter what the apparent obstacles. Parrot admits that this can be a dangerous process, because if it works, it both gives union leaders a strong bargaining mandate and sets up great expectations. If the union leaders do not deliver, they can be in big trouble.

"When we've got our demands and we go into negotiations, we are determined to achieve certain things which are obvious to the other side and obvious to the membership. We create an atmosphere where the membership believes in those things, because the leaders believe in them. They believe they are achievable. That's the way we have broken some ground in the past. At some point in time, the employer can argue whatever he wants, but if you believe you are entitled to that, you know they have to settle that issue in order either to settle the strike or to sign the contract," says Parrot.

The union often takes its case to the public. That is an essential part of its strategy. Getting the best possible results for members means not merely doing its best within the rules, but ruthlessly exploiting any weakness in the structure that upholds those rules.

"The union was like a spoiled child who found out that if he cried loud enough, big daddy would give him candy," says manager Gordon Sinclair. The louder he cried the more candy he got. He feels that this became the union's basic strategy, to escalate every dispute until it became a political problem, "so you would get a political settlement, which was the most advantageous you could possibly strive for. I don't blame the unions. That's smart tactics on their part. Go where you get the best settlement."

Sinclair says the strategy also gave an opening to a small group of extreme militants. Once the success of brinkmanship had been proven, "it got to the point where the union leaders couldn't do anything else but, even if they wanted to do something different, because a very vocal minority of other membership would be accusing them of not doing their job unless they took the dispute into the political forum."

Parrot, though, says he never felt that he was pushed into more extreme action. "I never felt pressured. We were doing the pressuring." Parrot's description of union strategies tallies with Sinclair's view, but it goes much farther. There is no doubt that politicians were exploited, and gave concessions for political reasons that would not otherwise have been made.

And the political level is not the only one the union used in its search for results. "We also have been quite well served by the circumstances under the Public Service Staff Relations Act," says Parrot. That act, which governed all bargaining in the public sector, was itself a major bone of contention. That was because it made many issues non-negotiable. Unions could complain all they wanted, but it was illegal for the management negotiators to agree to a wide range of demands. CUPW saw no reason to let such technicalities get in the way of what its leaders and members had agreed was just and proper.

In 1974, once it had split from the letter-carriers, it started taking the stand that any issue was negotiable. Jacob Finkelman, then chairman of the Public Service Staff Relations Board and the main author of the act, did his best to turn back the CUPW assault.

The weak point in the government's defences turned out to be the conciliation boards that joined the negotiating process if talks broke down. Each side would explain its demands and the arguments supporting them. The board then had to write a report saying how it felt each of the issues should be resolved. It had no power to make the parties agree, but backing from the conciliation board could help to justify one side's position in the public eye. No strike could take place until the conciliator had reported on the offers on the table.

Finkelman had the power to tell a conciliation board what issues it was to consider when presented with a given contract dispute. Parrot says the postal workers would ignore the mandate Finkelman had given the board. "Every time we arrived before a conciliation board, I would tell them, it's nice to say they cannot be included in your mandate, but forget about the wording of the demand, here's the problem. You have to resolve the problem. If you cannot resolve the problem, sorry, but you won't resolve anything.

"So what happened is that the conciliation board ended up recommending things that were not included in their terms of reference, or were trying to settle them during the conciliation process. And sometimes they were successful on issues that supposedly were not on their terms of reference."

Another tactic the union used with conciliators was to make sure that it always provided the precise wording it wanted to see in its contract. "And because the employer was not negotiating, they were not doing it." If the conciliation board agreed with the union position, "the only language they had in their hands was provided by the union, so very often they were using our language in their recommendations. And we ended up having a lot of things in our collective agreement that have been written by us. Obviously it was written to our best advantage," Parrot says.

The union had considerable success in finding sympathy among conciliators and adjudicators. In 1975, Judge Jean Moisan, chairman of the conciliation board during those contract talks, remarked on the union's refusal to acknowledge that not all issues were negotiable. Some items, such as promotion and classification of jobs, were clearly excluded from bargaining, but he chastised the government for refusing to talk about other issues, such as the mileage allowance for the use of a private car on the job, which were governed only by directives from the Treasury Board.

"In any case, we must acknowledge that there is definite merit in the Union's claim that it represents the 'blue collar workers' of the Public Service, and that the work of its members bears more resemblance to that of industry than to that of the public service at large."

Other conciliators and adjudicators were less impressed by union arguments. A dissenting opinion by E. B. Stewart to the report of the conciliation board for the 1972 talks notes that "there does not appear to be any appreciation by the Chairman that his recommendations contravene principles of long standing in the public service in regard to the implementation of job changes and related classification matters. Indeed, I am concerned whether some of these recommendations are within the power of this Board under S. 56(2) and 86(2) of the Public Service Staff Relations Act."

And in upholding the firing of two Toronto workers after a sit-down strike in December 1977, PSSRB vice-chairman David Kates said the union showed "brazen, selfish disregard for the public well-being" at a time when the mails were busiest. He also sharply attacked the credibility of union testimony. "The board has not the slightest misgiving in concluding that the testimony adduced by them was orchestrated . . . in an attempt to mitigate the penalties imposed by the employer."

However, if the neutral third parties did not back the union's position, CUPW negotiators just shifted to the next battlefield and squared off against the politicians. In 1975, for instance, the conciliation board refused to back the union's position on a clause affecting staffing of postal plants, because it felt that it came too close to vital management rights. By the end of the 42-day strike that year, the union had wrested what it wanted from the management team and Postmaster General Bryce Mackasey.

The classic case of political intervention in the bargaining process occurred in 1975. The strike started because Mackasey was fed up with the postal unions and decided to get tough. It ended when he lost his nerve. Once again the militants felt vindicated.

The militant leaders in CUPW found the limits of government tolerance in 1978. This time, the conciliator was far from friendly to the union's aims, and this time the government itself decided to change the rules. The Public Service Staff Relations Act set out two possible routes for settling contract disputes: binding arbitration, and conciliation with the right to strike. The choice of route had to be made by the union before talks began. The rest of the civil service had always chosen arbitration, where both sides send unresolved issues to an independent judge, who tells them what is fair. Once he rules, both sides have to live with his decision. The postal unions had always taken the strike route.

The government passed the Postal Services Continuation Act on October 19, three days after the strike began. It made the strike illegal and said the dispute would be settled by an arbitrator after all. "That's totally unfair," says Parrot. "At that time, I felt we had no choice. We cannot go back simply because on the first day of the strike they decide that it's illegal."

The next day, deputy postmaster general Jim Corkery had a letter hand-delivered to Parrot's office giving him formal notice of the union leader's responsibility to tell his members to obey the law and go back to work. Parrot refused.

A week after the strike began, the post office threatened to fire every worker who stayed out. Because the strike was illegal, they could make the firings stick. "We got a feeling they were going to try it, and get other people to take the jobs," says Parrot. "We could have taken that on too, but it was a little too much. So we decided not to pursue the strike and to go back to work."

The Royal Canadian Mounted Police sealed the decision on October 25 when it raided CUPW offices and then charged Parrot and seven other members of the union's national executive board with breaking the back-to-work law. By the next morning, most members were back at their jobs.

"We warned the union, we warned Jean-Claude before that thing went into law: do not, under any circumstances, get yourself out on a limb,'' says Corkery. But he says the union's lawyers and others were advising Parrot that ''these guys have no guts and nothing will happen.''

The legal process dragged on for months. In May 1979 Parrot was convicted and sentenced to three months in jail and eighteen months' probation, but he appealed. The Supreme Court of Canada eventually refused to allow a final appeal and Parrot went to jail to finish his sentence in early 1980. Some of the others charged pleaded guilty, apologized, and got suspended sentences; other charges were stayed.

The lengthy legal process played havoc with managers' efforts to put the dispute behind them. ''I'm a witness for two years' crucifying some poor guy for what he did two years ago,'' says Corkery. ''That's not the way to solve labour problems, to use the courts, and we know that. . . . But when the government makes that decision and they defy the law, the situation is out of our hands. . . . I'm *persona non grata* at that stage, because I put Jean-Claude in jail. It's my evidence that put him in jail.''

While Parrot says he did not go into the strike expecting to end up in jail, he has no regrets about pushing the government to the limit. ''Some people felt it was a gamble. In my opinion, I always had a lot of faith in the membership, and I felt that if the leadership came out strong, the membership would be there. If you hide, it might be more difficult. So I decided to announce, before they adopted the law, that we were going to defy the law.''

Passing the law did have a shock effect on the rank-and-file union members. One union official, the head of a small fifty-person unit, phoned Parrot the night the law was passed. ''Jean-Claude, you know, if you decide tonight to defy the law, I will be with you. But I want you to know that I'll be alone in my local. The membership of my local will go back to work. I'll probably be the only one on the picket line.''

''Phone me back tomorrow, and we'll talk about it,'' Parrot told him.

''Okay, I will.''

He phoned back the next day. ''You won't believe it! I'm flying! I'm high! Not only nobody went to work, but most of the membership are on the picket line with me!''

"I felt it was quite encouraging to get that phone call," says Parrot. "It was the same all across the country. The membership were really proud of staying together."

Parrot says the union even had some public sympathy in its struggle. People felt that if union members were prepared to go that far and put their liberty on the line by defying Parliament, there must be a real problem that should be solved. "But government and management could not back off. It was obvious they were going to try to slaughter us. They had no choice, they felt. And [Postmaster General Gilles] Lamontagne was the guy to be willing to do it."

The union leaders had pitted their credibility against that of the government. In a struggle like that, there could be only one winner — in the short term. "There may be some attempt to broaden this issue into whether Parliament did a dirty thing to CUPW," said federal prosecutor Douglas Rutherford in his closing address to the jury at Parrot's trial.

"Parliament spoke for you and me when it made this law. It spoke for pensioners; it spoke for businessmen and it spoke for taxpayers across this country who are saying we can't afford more. It spoke to national problems coast to coast, but Parrot spoke for members of the union. When those interests come head to head, only Parliament can prevail. When Parliament can be told to go to heck, we have a thing called anarchy."

While the strike had been ended, militancy in the postal workers union was far from defeated. On the same night they were charged with breaking the law, executive members began planning ways to make sure the same thing did not happen again.

They were particularly upset by the behaviour of the CLC and its then president, Dennis McDermott, who announced publicly that he did not think it was right to defy Parliament. The postal unions were already active in the CLC, and their plans came to fruition two years later at the Congress's 1980 national convention. They persuaded delegates to pass more than twenty resolutions supporting the postal workers and their struggle with the government.

Parrot says they told CLC delegates flatly that if Parliament passed another law to end the next strike, they would defy it again. "And this time, we're not going to go back to work after nine days. You might as well know that. If you want to give us support, give it on the basis that you know that's what we're going to do.'' A chastened McDermott assured them that now they had CLC support for their cause with no strings attached.

CUPW also rolled with the punch at the bargaining table. The government-appointed arbitrator had handed them a settlement they did not like. It included several provisions that made the contract less favourable than earlier deals. The union was determined that these rollbacks would not last long, and when its negotiators went to the bargaining table in 1980, they told the government that, as far as they were concerned, they had simply resumed the talks so abruptly shut off in 1978.

This time they were dealing with André Ouellet, a minister in his second term as postmaster general, who was trying to win their favour as he worked out the structure of a Crown corporation to take over the post office. Parrot says they won back all the rollbacks imposed after the 1978 strike and signed a deal that made them happy, without the need for a strike. Once again militancy had been rewarded. In the following year, on the eve of the Crown corporation's birth, there would be another 42-day strike.

As CUPW has pursued its militant course at the bargaining table, its unabashed support for a new economic and social order has led to persistent speculation that the union is really being run as a front for people with deeper ideological motives, a front for Communists and other left-wing radicals.

There is no doubt that CUPW does harbour individuals with views far more extreme than those of the average union member. "Most of the employees are hard-working, decent people," says Mackay. "They're scared of their own unions. They don't go to meetings." Only a small portion of the members attend union meetings, and "that group determines what happens to the other 80 per cent." Those who might try to object "are ostracized right away by that tough 200."

Some of the extremists have not been shy about either their allegiances or their intentions. For instance, an illegal sit-down strike by a group of coding clerks in Toronto in December 1977 turned into a full-blown strike after nine of those involved were suspended.

Four of them — all shop stewards or members of the local executive—told the press that they were members of the Canadian Party of Labour, a group described as a Communist splinter party with Marxist-Leninist leanings. Peter Liebovitch, Ron Mezwak, Gary Whitehouse, and Lionel Dupuis said their party had several hundred supporters across Canada. Liebovitch said he planned to run for an executive job in the Toronto local at the next elections. The post office succeeded in firing him in February 1978.

The radicals have been visible enough to get under the skin of some prominent people, including the CLC's Dennis McDermott. After denouncing CUPW for seeking ''confrontation for the sake of confrontation'' in the 1978 showdown, he accused a group within the union of trying ''to use the labour movement for ideological ego trips and perpetual obstruction.''

Some of Canada's politicians felt the same way. Postmaster General Gilles Lamontagne vented his frustration one day in 1979 by telling reporters that he could have the post office working efficiently again if he were only allowed to fire 500 people. The trouble with the post office was that civil service rules meant that the department couldn't get rid of its trouble-makers.

''That's a crock,'' says Corkery, his deputy minister at the time. ''You couldn't do that in GE either. In a small company, sure, they can be a little rough with them, but in a big company that's got a conscience and a tough union . . . there used to be a saying at GE that you couldn't fire anybody without the president's approval. And the only way you could fire somebody was you had to rape the president's daughter, and he didn't have a daughter. You had to find other ways — better selection and motivation and all the other tools that you've got to work with.''

Lamontagne's outburst got him into trouble with Opposition MPs who thought he was being unfair to postal workers as a group. But when former prime minister John Diefenbaker asked Trudeau to denounce his minister's statement, he got little satisfaction. ''I cannot vouch for the particular figure of 500,'' the Prime Minister replied, ''but I think even the right honourable gentleman would know that in any group there are some trouble-makers and you can do without those.''

Union officials say the radicals don't dominate the union. Arnold

Gould, president of the Toronto local when Lamontagne made his statement, said the minister was "full of it. . . . Sure there are people who stand up for their rights, but that Gateway plant is not full of radicals. It's full of hard-working people."

There seems to be a difference between the militants who run the union and those who give the union such a reputation on the battlegrounds of plant floors.

August Gonnsen, a doctoral student at the State University of New York at Buffalo, looked at the flood of grievances filed by Canadian postal workers in the late 1970s — some 46,000 between December 1975 and June 1980.

The grievance procedure is a way for workers to complain about violations of their contract. A worker who has a complaint will tell his shop steward, who helps him fill out the grievance form. The complaint is presented first to management within the plant. If the managers on site cannot reach a deal that solves the complaint, the employee can appeal it first to the regional (second) level and then to the national (third) level, where the deputy postmaster general or someone he designates must decide whether or not the contract has been violated. If the union is still dissatisfied, it may be able to take the case to an independent arbitrator for a final and binding decision.

The deluge of postal grievances appears to have begun in the wake of the long strike of 1975. Those negotiations produced an agreement that the post office would give the union an extra copy of grievances. When the department tried to use up its old stock of six-copy forms before spending money to buy new seven-copy ones, the union told its members to grieve. Some 400 individual grievances were filed in one Toronto postal station alone.

Gonnsen made no attempt to study all postal grievances, but chose instead to look at all the complaints filed during 1977 — a year without a major strike — at the Gateway sorting plant outside Toronto. Gateway is the largest plant in the country and was built as part of the mechanization program. Only 316 of the 1,336 CUPW members working at Gateway filed any grievances that year. By then, there was already a large backlog of grievances. The average grievance took 258 days to resolve, and some took more than two years.

Gonnsen found that 70 per cent of the grievances filed referred to issues that had no basis in the contract, and yet 60 per cent of grievances were pushed to the second level and 38 per cent went all the way to the top.

Decisions rarely changed on the way up, because supervisors at the plant level had no authority to interpret the national union contract. "Unless there's a change of information of the basic issue, there really isn't any decision change all the way up," says Corkery.

In the private sector, the costs of an arbitrator are always split equally between the company and the union. Under the Public Service Staff Relations Act, the government bears the full cost of arbitration. CUPW would therefore push cases to arbitration whenever possible.

Gonnsen found that most of the grievances were filed by a very small group of workers within the bargaining unit. Less than one-quarter of the union membership filed any grievances during 1977. Even then, 45 per cent of the grievances were filed by 15 per cent of those who did grieve one or more times, or about 3.5 per cent of the total membership. A small group of 5 per cent of the grievers, or about 1 per cent of the membership, accounted for 28 per cent of all the grievances filed.

Of the 30 per cent of grievances that dealt with legitimate problems, many were upheld. These included pay problems, transfers, safety, management doing union work, and workers who were unable to talk to union stewards about complaints.

Grievances relating to pay were usually upheld, and resolved at the first level. Most of the pay grievances, however, were filed by workers who complained only once, and took no part in the other abuses of the grievance system. There were exceptions, as in the case of the worker who filed a grievance demanding interest on 90 cents' worth of back pay that he had won in an earlier dispute.

Another group of grievances had no basis in the contract but did reflect union objectives. About 12 per cent of the grievances filed were complaints about losing out on the chance to work overtime because there were too many casual workers in the plant. This reflected the union's desire to get rid of casual workers altogether and force management to choose between keeping enough full-time workers on the job to deal with the day-to-day fluctuations in volume, or paying huge overtime bills. The grievance procedure in that case was simply a way of trying to win in one way what the union could not get at the bargaining table.

Another finding of the thesis was that technological change was not a big issue. Only six grievances, less than 1 per cent of the total, dealt with job security, and only eight, or 1.3 per cent, complained about poor working conditions resulting from technological change.

The biggest single category of grievances related to disciplinary measures taken against employees. Discipline in the post office, as in many large organizations, follows several stages. At the beginning, an employee who takes a day off or is often late or refuses to work properly will simply be called for an interview with a superior to talk about his behaviour.

This interview is known as "counselling", and the interview is noted on the employee's file. If an employee goes through several counselling sessions and does not mend his ways, he may be sent a letter of warning, or may even be suspended. These measures will also be entered in a worker's file and kept there for two years. If the employee persists in his ways, eventually he can be fired, but usually not until a large body of evidence has been built up in his file. The standard reaction to any of these disciplinary measures in the post office has been to file a grievance and pursue it as far as possible.

Another response to discipline has been to file a grievance complaining about harassment, discrimination, or violation of civil rights or privacy. Workers have complained about harassment when reminded that a rest period was over and it was time to work again. Such complaints came to 8 per cent of the total.

Because the Gateway plant was new, many employees were transferred to it from other postal plants. This caused another group of complaints, about 7 per cent of the total.

And 30 per cent of the grievances covered a wide range of complaints, including management denial of requests for stools, extra time off, and changes of shift or assignment, as well as disputes over performance during probation and violation of seniority rights.

In many cases, workers and the union stewards who handled their complaints pursued ridiculous points, Gonnsen found. For instance, one employee filed a grievance that he had been bypassed for overtime. He had been on vacation at the time. Another filed a grievance because his pay cheque was not ready for him to pick up on a day he called in sick. A group of seventeen workers filed grievances for the hassle and extra cost of travelling to work after being transferred to Gateway from Terminal A. The hearing found that six of the group actually lived closer to Gateway than to their old plant. All these grievances still went to all three levels.

A mail-handler who was also a shop steward was suspended for insubordination after refusing to handle certain pieces of mail for no good reason. The supervisor then handled the mail, which was getting in the way of other work. The worker filed one grievance to protest the suspension and another over "management working". When the supervisor got some other workers to move in, the first worker filed a third grievance, because they were mail clerks doing a job supposed to be done by mail-handlers like himself. He then filed a fourth grievance for improper action of management and a fifth for discrimination, saying he had been "singled out for duties others refused" and "harassed, intimidated and threatened", probably because he was a union steward.

To Canadians who have now endured two decades of seemingly endless postal conflict, the fact of such abuse on its own is not surprising. What is most interesting about Gonnsen's study is its conclusions about why the individuals involved abused the system.

Gonnsen found that most of the small group in the union which filed the bulk of the grievances had poor work records and complained for very selfish reasons, not out of any sense of union goals. Gonnsen assembled a series of profiles of workers who had used the grievance process.

The most prolific filer was a shop steward who also had an abysmal work record. In the two years prior to 1977, he had been absent 27 times for a total of 117 days without permission and been late 14 times for a total of 20 hours. He was counselled four times, received warning letters twice, and was suspended once.

He filed 17 grievances during 1977, including 6 related to a single incident. The first of these he filed after another worker received an electrical shock from a conveyor belt. He also shut down the whole conveyor line without requesting permission, and was suspended, for which he filed a second grievance. He filed a third because the superintendent of the plant "impeded his investigation"; a fourth, saying that supervisors did not pay enough attention to safety; a fifth, complaining that he didn't have enough time before being counselled; and a sixth, saying he had not been allowed to carry out his duties as a shop steward. All six complaints went right up to the third level and then to adjudication.

Seven of the other 11 grievances he filed that year related to his union duties — lack of grievance forms available, supervisors working, safety, and so on. Five others complain about three counselling sessions he had because of unauthorized absences.

Because most of the grievances he filed related to union objectives, Gonnsen rated him as being active in the union. This case proved to be the exception.

The next worker profiled filed 10 grievances. He too had a lousy work record. He stayed away from work without permission 24 times for a total of 43 days and was late 20 times for a total of 12 hours. He received three counsellings and one letter of warning. He was absent three more times during 1977 and got three more counsellings.

All of his grievances talk about feeling "hassled all the time". In a confrontation with supervisors, he said the bosses at the new Gateway plant were "slave drivers that get people to work all the time," and said that "this place is a dump. It's not like Terminal A where you can take a break and nobody bugs you." He was not apparently active in the union.

Gonnsen's list goes on, listing worker after worker with poor employment records, most filing grievances reflecting their own personal interests and not connected to any activity in the union. Of the group profiled, 70 per cent of the grievers had poor work records. On average, each of them was absent 24 times in 24 months for a total of 43 days, the equivalent of a two-day break every month for two years. Only 23 per cent of the grievances referred to union objectives. Grievers who were active in the union tended to have good work records.

"The present data do not indicate that a political ideology is exerting influence in CUPW, neither among the rank-and-file nor the militant minority, nor do they indicate that the national leadership is pursuing any ideologies which can be identified as political or radical, left wing,'' Gonnsen concluded.

That view is consistent with the writings of Peter Taylor, the man who described so effectively the struggle against boredom by the new generation of postal workers. "On the shop floor, all of us took nights off, took breaks, etc., but we did it more as individuals, rather than in unison,'' he said. "In part this was because we were less visible and therefore less vulnerable when we didn't coordinate our actions too much; in part because each of us preferred to take different nights off, take breaks at different times, etc.

"On the shop floor, our struggles were conducted almost totally outside the union. Of course we would file grievances, but usually they were designed more to hassle management than actually to make any gains. For that, we relied on ourselves and each other.

"During a strike, however, the presence of the union made itself felt. In part that was useful, because if the union supported a strike, then we were in a much stronger position. But the union's prominence during a strike was also a drawback in that they would try to run the show. In this respect, they were just like the supervisors who were always telling us what we could and couldn't do.''

Corkery still feels that militants who were active in the union were behind the abuse. "In 90 per cent of the cases, I would guess they were originated by the steward to foment a particular issue in a particular situation and they'd all sign it because that was what the leadership wanted them to do.''

Even if the flood of grievances did come from bad workers with selfish reasons, the union clearly approved of the trend for its own reasons. Since grievances have to be handled by union stewards and officers, they could have put a lid on the abuse if they had wished.

In any case, the action of filing a grievance is one that brings a worker into the union fold and isolates him from management. It pits the worker against the institution. Plenty of grievances show that workers are not happy and that the system does not work. If the system doesn't work, it should be improved. And the union has no shortage of ideas for improving the system — in its own best interest.

9
Pandora's Postbox

■

No politician has been immune from the demands of Canadian voters for better postal service. Even Lester B. Pearson, the venerable diplomat turned prime minister, discovered early in his political life that world recognition cannot guarantee re-election.

"I was once given a good lesson on this score during a visit to my constituency," Pearson wrote in his memoirs. "I was chattering with some villagers in front of the general store and telling them about a recent visit to Washington, where their member had the honour of signing the North Atlantic Treaty for Canada. It had been a historic occasion and I felt that my listeners had been suitably impressed by my account of it, when one elderly farmer drawled: 'Yes, that was a fine thing you did down there in Washington, a fine thing for Canada, but it won't help you much around here if you don't get us a new post office.'

"Thereafter, I always tried to remember that the United Nations and the village post office were both to be treated seriously. My memory was at least good enough for an Opposition speaker to claim some years later that, if I were elected to Algoma East once again, I would have a dock right around Manitoulin Island and a government-financed stockpile of uranium at Elliot Lake which would top the highest hill."

Pearson did indeed learn his lesson well. John Mackay, the top bureaucrat in the post office when those memoirs were published in the early 1970s, says he decided to check up and see if the village had in fact been given its new post office. It had.

There is nothing new about political influence when it comes to building new post offices. Postal records show that the 1,600 settlers in the new town of Perth in what is now Ontario owe their postal service to the governor general who "interested himself in this settlement and secured the establishment of a post office" for the town. A road had to be cut through the bush from Brockville on Lake Ontario, and the mail was carried from there once every two weeks.

The distribution of post offices across the country bears little relationship to the number of people they serve. "The Ottawa Valley is just dotted with little post offices that were built in the sixties and seventies where really it was more a matter of a public works program than it was a requirement for Canada Post," says former postal president Michael Warren. "And every time you would build one of those things, you would have to staff them — far more expensive. You had this exponential driving up of your long-term costs."

Atlantic Canada is another region well endowed with post offices, and nowhere more so than in the domain of Liberal strongman Allan MacEachen. MacEachen built a reputation as a Cabinet minister under Pierre Trudeau on the strength of his mastery of parliamentary tactics, but the people whose votes let him in to the House of Commons were never far from his thoughts.

Eric Kierans, Trudeau's first postmaster general, remembers spotting areas in MacEachen's riding where rural residents were able to choose between five or six post offices within a radius of two miles. "You can probably see the justification back in 1890 when it was horse-and-buggy. You didn't see the justification now," he says. It was a fascination that would cost Kierans dearly, and turn MacEachen into his fiercest opponent in the Cabinet.

Setting up new post offices is only the beginning of the patronage opportunities. Post offices and plants must be designed and built. Private contractors carry mail by air, by train, and by truck between cities and postal plants. On the rural routes across the country, small businesses use pick-up trucks to run the mail along the byways to and from scattered farms. Smaller rural post offices are run on a part-time basis by outsiders, and the local post office is often part of another business. Within cities, many sub-post offices are run by private businessmen for a fee. Uniforms for postmen must be made, their mailbags stitched together. The red boxes on the corners have to be made in factories; so do the machines in the big postal plants. And the advertising dollars spent to tell Canadians how good their postal service is all flow through private agencies, almost always picked on the basis of political affiliation.

Postal bureaucrats who have endured years of meddling by their elected masters say some of the talk of patronage is over-rated. "On contracts, I didn't see any of that, because fundamentally the politician is now caught in a situation where it's open to audit," says former deputy minister Jim Corkery. "You've gone to tender, and as long as he's under the laws of the province and he meets the criteria that you're calling for, he's got the right kind of trucks, it's pretty tough for you to say this guy and not that guy, politically.

"Selection of advertising agency, yeah, that was a political decision. Selection of construction consultants and architects? Yeah, that was political. And that's through DPW [Department of Public Works]. And that's pretty well understood that that's the way it's done. Even that one isn't that bad, because the consultants and architects I got to do the Toronto one — couldn't fault them, superb people, basically they just happened to be on the list of approved architects that this group was prepared to tender with. So fundamentally what DPW used to do was give the ministers a list of professionals [and say] here's the experts, tell us who you think is next on the list. But I certainly never got a dog because of a political decision."

Similarly, the growth of the civil service and of a bureaucracy to govern the ways bureaucrats got jobs meant a drop in the extent to which post office jobs could be handed out by vote-seeking MPs. There were still plenty of opportunities for patronage, but, generally speaking, the chances for political influence grew larger as the distance from Ottawa increased.

"You would see it in the selection of postmasters in very small communities. They would run a poster and do a rating of candidates. These were not part of the public service," says Corkery.

"Basically the political system would then take a look at those and make sure that who you were looking at were acceptable to the local MP, so there would be some sort of quiet political check. You still had a situation where you would do a boarding first to make sure that the candidates had at least a little bit of brains up here, to scrub out the dogs. I didn't see a great deal of influencing even there, other than the fact that they wanted the right to say yes or no."

Kierans put a stop to the worst of the abuses in the late 1960s. "What used to happen there was that the minister would select the rural postmaster and he would get the names in from the party organizers in that area, and they would send the names and he would select it, and of course he would have one friend then and nine enemies," says John Mackay, his deputy minister. "And when Kierans got in he said, 'I don't want nine enemies, I want ten friends. So from now on, the public service is going to do it.' And when [Jean-Pierre] Côté got back in, he said: 'That's the best thing Kierans could have done. I didn't have the guts to do it.' "

Still, the people who work at the post office never seem to run out of politicians looking for favours. Sometimes they may be impossible to grant. In other cases, the requests are simple enough that the postal manager will go along.

Senior manager Gordon Sinclair remembers receiving a call from Bryce Mackasey during Mackasey's days as postmaster general. There had been a redistribution of mailboxes on the streets of Montreal. One of the boxes that moved had been located right in front of an old folks' home in Mackasey's riding, and he had been getting complaints about its sudden disappearance. Sinclair phoned up the local supervisor, who promised to get a box back in front of the old folks' home by noon. Mackasey was grateful and Sinclair felt that it was a favour granted with little cost.

Political influence becomes more costly when it involves the overall level of postal service. When Eric Kierans cut delivery on most routes from six days a week to five, it was a business decision, a way to keep costs down in an era of expanding addresses. "But they left politically the rural routes for six days," says Corkery. "They get six-day delivery. Why? Because the local newspapers had a deal . . . that they could get delivery through the post office within a range of fifty miles if you were [in a town of] 5,000 or less. And your local press is a pretty powerful animal in a small town. They wanted Saturday delivery, so the MP is going to say, Hey, leave that alone. Don't tamper with that. So this is the saw-off. Cities get five, rurals get six."

For MPs languishing in the back-benches, the post office has provided plenty of ammunition for those seeking profile and glory. It is open to so many kinds of criticism that its critics sometimes shoot themselves.

In November 1978, for instance, Tory MP Walter Dinsdale fired two questions at the Prime Minister. In his first, he complained of waste: Despite the expensive mechanization program, the number of full-time jobs or equivalents at the post office had jumped from 36,000 to 61,500. Then, in a follow-up, he complained that a three-year freeze on expansion of letter-carrier routes to new suburbs had deprived at least 400 Canadians of jobs. "I do not see how this kind of contribution would really be helpful even if it came from a parliamentary committee," Trudeau mocked in reply.

The problems of managing the politics of the post office have been compounded over the years by the people chosen as postal ministers in the Cabinet. "Generally, the postmaster general is an early, training assignment. It certainly wasn't where they put many of their heavyweights," says Corkery. After all, it is a job where there is little to gain and much to lose. A good postmaster general barely gets noticed.

A Blueprint for Change noted that Kierans was the eighth postmaster general to hold office during the six years prior to his appointment on July 7, 1968. William Hamilton had finished a five-year term under Diefenbaker on July 13, 1962. He was followed by Angus MacLean, Ellen Fairclough, Azellus Denis, John Nicholson, René Tremblay, and Jean-Pierre Côté before Kierans arrived. Only Côté had held the job for more than thirteen months.

"The frequency with which Postmasters General are changed — the current minister is the fourth under whom the present deputy has served since 1970 — should also be recognized as a major source of discontinuity in the department,'' noted the 1975 study by the joint Treasury Board–post office task force which exposed the depths to which postal morale had plunged.

"Each new appointee must be indoctrinated and exposed to the complexities of management in the post office. Each, too, brings his own priorities and perspectives to the role and — perhaps most importantly — his own personal approach to union-management relations.

"Moreover, the political prominence of the post office in each community ensures a high degree of Parliamentary and public interest in its operations, the location and scheduling of construction of new post offices, awarding of certain contracts, staffing, service standards, etc., with the result that a significant portion of ministerial time and, consequently, of the deputy's as well, must be dedicated to firefighting."

Sinclair says breaking in new ministers was always annoying for managers. While he was there, they always seemed suspicious of management at first while giving the benefit of the doubt to the unions. Within the first year, the unions would give them grounds to change their minds. "I would become best friend of the minister by the end of his tenure."

Former postmaster general Jean-Jacques Blais says the high turnover made things tough on the ministers as well. The response of the bureaucrats was always tempered by the feeling that the new boss would not be around for long. If a new minister tried to put his own stamp on the post office, the response would be reluctant: "Politicians are dispensable. These guys think that they can reinvent the wheel, and what the hell are they around here for?"

For postal managers, the damage done by political meddling has been less a matter of patronage than of frequent changes in direction, a lack of consistency in the way the post office is run. "That's been the greatest enemy of the post office," says Mackay.

Corkery says politics compounded the problems posed by the multitude of other departments and agencies who had a part in postal decision-making. "What hurts are the political decisions that come at you because of a split structure. This was really why we all wanted to get into a Crown situation, to manage our own affairs. When you're letting your buying process be an open-tender process through another agency who's got different motivations and different reasoning for what they're doing, and when you're letting all your negotiations . . . be done by another group who have got different motivations, it probably is the most critical part of the whole beast. It probably gets you into more difficulties than anything else, because you no longer are managing your affairs.''

Each of those other departments had ministers too, and the decisions at their level had far more impact on matters like contract bargaining than the judgments of postal bureaucrats. ''You might be able to influence the mandate of what they're negotiating, but not very much. You get a government motivation: ministers, the prime minister, Treasury Board, who want a settlement, and they don't want it to be seen as a give-away settlement in terms of dollars. So they'll negotiate very tough on the dollar figure but they will never look at the cost of the management rights on the other side, because who's going to know except the managers of the post office that it was a give-away? We would far rather have paid another one per cent in many cases and retained the right to use casuals, the right to use part-timers and full-timers inter-changeably, but these were all given away by ministers in that final decision, Treasury Board environment.''

The politicians prefer to put the blame on someone else. ''The environment in a post office is like in a shop,'' says former postmaster general André Ouellet. ''The Treasury Board had an approach to white-collar workers that didn't suit at all the mentality, the attitude, and the work force of the post office. And I believe that a lot of the strikes and a lot of the difficulties that existed between 1975 and 1980 have been the responsibility of bad judgment on the part of people at Treasury Board and bad advice given by Treasury Board officials to ministers who were dealing with the post office.''

Corkery, however, says ministers were very much a part of the give-away process. They got involved in contract talks ''quite often — almost every time. I've seen Ouellet right at the table in the final settlement with us out of the room. In that particular case, I think he exceeded the mandate that he was granted, and I suspect he got into a little bit of difficulty, but he got a settlement, and that was his objective. His objective wasn't necessarily the same objective we had.''

Mackay says that in one of the first strikes after collective bargaining began in the 1960s, the union was crumbling and postal officials felt that another three days would give them the settlement they wanted. Then "the political instructions came through to settle. There's a lot that goes on behind the scenes."

That pattern would be repeated over the following decade. Time after time, strikes would be settled and deals made by politicians for political reasons. One disillusioned bureaucrat said that while Treasury Board officials and Cabinet ministers huddled to work out solutions to labour problems, postal managers would wait outside in the corridor, "wondering from which side you were going to be raped."

Corkery says the senior bureaucrats in other departments would also pass on their opinions to their ministers. Postal customers would make their feelings known to their MPs. In the case of a major issue like how to conduct a postal strike, the post office itself had little influence.

"Now you're back into the political system, saying here's what the politician is hearing and he's the shareholder, so some time he's got to make a decision. And at that stage, as you get into a strike, the ones that you think are in favour of hanging tough are lobbying the minister on the side and saying, you've got to settle. Which is what they were doing.

"It's the political pieces that you can't read," says Corkery. "If you could control the mandate yourself . . . that's good. But you've got to recognize the politics of the situation and the union recognizes it too. And they've got you."

10
Signed,
Sealed, Lost

■

In 1968, winning on all fronts looked so easy. Pierre Elliott Trudeau had just swept into office, and the exuberant bachelor prime minister was out to make his mark on Canada. As his new Cabinet met during the summer of 1968, it barely paused to think about the post office.

Eric Kierans had been a last-minute addition to the Cabinet. He had not really expected to be asked, because his belief in strong provincial rights put him at odds with Trudeau's vision of centralized power. On the morning before the Cabinet was to be announced, he had two calls from journalists which confirmed his impressions. One said he even had a list of the new Cabinet, and Kierans' name was not included.

Kierans' father had just died, and Kierans did not get home from the funeral parlour until about 4 p.m. The phone was ringing. It was Trudeau. The prime minister wanted him in the Cabinet after all. Kierans had had no particular interest in the post office until then, but once it was in his charge, he wasted no time.

Even in the first set of negotiations with the postal unions under the Public Service Staff Relations Act, the problems of split authority had become clear. Kierans was quick to discover the other constraints of running the post office. So many people had their fingers in the postal pie that the office of postmaster general was merely ''an honorific position'', Kierans argues, one that had no power and did not really warrant a Cabinet minister.

When the postal workers hit on their tactic of rotating strikes during the spring and summer of 1970, he did not even know about it until he read two stories in an Ottawa paper. One described a one-day shutdown of the Ottawa postal plant. The other predicted that the smaller postal stations in the surrounding areas would close the next day. "I looked at it, and I thought, these guys get two strikes for the price of one." He decided not to let them get away with it.

He called in his top officials. "Why didn't you tell me about this?" He told them that if the union walked out in a given postal plant, the post office was to close all its operations in the region and send the workers home without pay. The next strike was expected to hit Winnipeg, and Kierans ordered all of Manitoba shut down if it did.

"We can't do that," his officials told him.

"What do you mean you can't do that?"

"You haven't got the authority."

"I'm not talking to anybody. I'm the postmaster general. I'm telling you what to do. That's an order," Kierans told them flatly.

"We did it and it was a real row," he recalls. His order hit the headlines. He still remembers the surprised but complacent reaction from CUPW president Willie Houle. "Eric doesn't know that he can't get away with that," was his assessment.

"And he was dead right," says Kierans. Two days later, at the weekly Thursday Cabinet meeting, Trudeau called Kierans on the carpet. He was very upset. When Kierans explained his thinking, Trudeau agreed that it made sense, but he was still angry at being caught by surprise. If Kierans wanted to take that sort of action, he should get authorization first from the Cabinet committee on labour relations, a body on which Kierans did not even have a seat. Even worse for Kierans, the chairman of the committee was MacEachen, then Manpower and Immigration minister, and "he raised holy hell," Kierans says.

He was being told to get committee approval before responding during a dispute in which the mastermind of the union strategy was ordering his walkouts from public phone booths to make sure that management would not get advance word. Kierans says he just kept ordering the regional shutdowns until the committee met a couple of weeks later. By then, the practice was well established.

This need for group approval was foreign to Kierans. As provincial revenue minister in Quebec under Jean Lesage, he was in control of his portfolio. Although Kierans brought in several unpopular measures, Lesage turned away all those with complaints, telling them to talk to Kierans if they wanted a change. In Ottawa, "they saw every minister in Cabinet except me," says Kierans. "You could see them going all around you."

The solution to this kind of split authority seemed obvious to almost all concerned. Great Britain had already decided to change its post office into a Crown corporation. The United States was heading down the same road. When Kierans ran the idea past his Cabinet colleagues that summer, there was a minimum of discussion. "We were the last ones to come around to it, so there was nothing innovative or magical to it. It was something that simply had to be done," he said. "There was no big deal about this thing." In the fall of 1968, a postal Crown corporation was approved.

Kierans had practical reasons for wanting one. He knew that modernizing the postal plants was essential, and that meant getting money. Putting off spending on the post office had been the pattern for years. Kierans had no reason to believe it would change unless the Crown corporation was set up. Once the Department of Finance had given money to a corporation, it would not be as easy to grab it back. Postal management, for the first time, would be able to count on the size of its purse.

In those heady days, he had no problems with his colleagues in the Cabinet. "This was passed. Everybody agreed there should be a Crown corporation. Then the delays started. While the civil service agreed, because it was a new government and they were feeling their own way around, they didn't really want it or weren't able to digest it," Kierans says of the bureaucrats. "So what they did was they came to me and suggested that since the bill wouldn't be ready for another year anyway, how about getting

Peat, Marwick to prepare a report.'' The post office was, after all, the biggest block of federal employees after the armed forces, and the mulling mandarins felt that dropping them out of the family was not a decision to take hastily. Not at all.

Flushed with his easy victory and solid support at the political level, Kierans bowed to the bureaucratic demands for a study. At the time, it seemed like a reasonable idea. The consultants could not help seeing the same problems and solutions as everyone else found obvious, and their report might help to smooth the way for legislation when it was ready for the House.

Kierans hired Peat, Marwick and set them loose. One consulting firm became six, and the original study became a package of fifteen. Their conclusions were as expected, but the minister had found out the real meaning of reports in the bureaucratic mind.

"All Peat, Marwick did and all the management consultants did was go around and ask all the chief engineers and the deputy ministers what they think, a few associated departments, what they think, the unions, what they think about it, and then they submit a report. That's really all that happens except there's a delay of nine months. That was where I made my mistake. I fell for it."

Instead of going to Kierans alone, Peat, Marwick made its report to a committee of seven Cabinet ministers. Kierans was only one member of that group, and the rest "couldn't care less whether you became a Crown corporation or not. And if there were reasons why the [chief bureaucrats] didn't want it to proceed with all due dispatch, they'd take their time." The report was approved, but not until 1970. By then, it was too late.

Too many other events had filled the intervening two years, ones that would abort the fetal Crown corporation almost as soon as it had been conceived. Kierans had managed to get a rough draft for a bill, but the legislation was "nowhere near ready".

During those fateful two years when the post office became the little Crown that couldn't, Kierans did little to endear himself to his Cabinet colleagues, his fellow Members of Parliament, or to the public. He brought a new style to the post office that was blunt and businesslike.

He was personally involved in everything from recruiting new talent to worrying about operating problems. "He was chairman of the board," says his deputy minister, John Mackay. "Kierans was a businessman through and through. He ran it just like a chief executive officer, and he loved every minute of it. He was in every morning at eight, eight-fifteen, and he'd have his troops together and 'By golly, what are you doing today?' type of thing. There was an enthusiasm at the senior levels . . . to do something different and really get this place humming."

The new activist approach caused more than a few palpitations among the complacent. The private-sector imports were ready for it, but Kierans simply could not comprehend the attitude of some old-time postal officials. One meeting with representatives of the CNTU over the Lapalme affair dragged on late into the evening. At 11 p.m., deputy postmaster general Paul Faguy announced that he had to leave to catch a plane to London. He was not only the top postal bureaucrat, but the only one left who spoke French.

"What do you mean, you have to go to London?" asked Kierans.

"There's a meeting of the [International] Postal Union in Geneva, and I'm going over to London and stopping over for a few days. My wife's there and I'm going to meet her for a couple of days and then I'm going to Geneva."

"You're not going anywhere," replied an exasperated Kierans. "I don't care. You've got lots of time. You phone her later in the morning. But you go and cancel your reservations." With postal trucks burning in Montreal, the minister felt that the post office came first. "It wasn't what he was used to."

Kierans later found out that Faguy had gone to Gordon Robertson, the Clerk of the Privy Council, and asked for a transfer to another job because the pressure at the post office was too much. "I found out from Trudeau," who had heard that his deputy minister was leaving. "Everybody knew it except me," says Kierans.

But some of Kierans' moves to fix the post office upset more than his own employees. He saw a need for money, so he raised it. He saw waste, and tried to stop it.

In one fell swoop, Kierans abolished the four-cent rate for local mail. At the same time, he raised the national rate for first-class letters to six cents from five. For local mail, it was a staggering 50-per-cent increase. The public was not amused.

He did more damage to his cause within the party through another move, this one to eliminate many of the smaller rural post offices. Many of these, created in response to political pressures, brought in far less revenue than they cost to maintain, and many seemed so close together that they could easily be eliminated.

Some parts of the country took the closings — about 1,000 in all — more calmly than others. Kierans says they were more than justified. In some cases, geography had changed, leaving towns stripped of the schools and shops and dentists and doctors that had made them centres for communities in the past. A crossroads with a general store could not support a post office — not financially, at least. One store, he says, sold only $80 worth of stamps in a year, and yet the post office was spending $1,900 to keep it open.

Even within the post office, some officials felt that he went too far. "I can remember asking for the analysis on which this decision was based, which wasn't terribly complete," says then postal finance chief Gordon Sinclair. He looked at the estimates and challenged the projected savings. "I think this program's for the birds. I don't think you're going to save that much money," he told Faguy.

Even so, he says about half the closings were warranted by any standard. "There were a number of them that should have been closed down. A post office with an annual rental of $19, yes, there's a basis for closing that down. . . . There was a lot of that kind of stuff, post offices 300 yards apart. That kind of stuff was legitimate and long overdue, and it was a housecleaning and tidying up that certainly needed to be done."

But the abrupt way the closings were handled "alienated every rural MP in the House of Commons," says Sinclair, and that in turn doomed Kierans' chances of getting a bill setting up a Crown corporation through Parliament. Kierans concedes that the decision hurt him in the caucus, but in Cabinet, "the only person that was really upset was MacEachen. MacEachen was always a thorn in my side and it was mainly because of this. Allan was a politician to his fingertips.''

Kierans managed to get under the skin of Cabinet members in other ways. ''I'm convinced that they felt that Kierans was too non-political, wasn't astute enough in how to handle some of these very tricky situations on labour relations, and also because he was constantly talking about the post office, at all the Cabinet meetings,'' says Mackay. He pushed too hard and asked for ''too much too fast. . . . He kept on talking about all the problems of the post office, and there were a lot of problems, but he magnified them and every time he got into Cabinet meetings, it was always Eric Kierans and the post office. And nobody really thought that the post office was that terrible and that bad and that much of a problem.''

Even though Cabinet might not have been too upset at the rural post office closings, ''there was no way he was going to get Cabinet support to move into a Crown corporation at that stage, because it would be a very controversial issue.'' The debate on any postal bill would be sure to tie up business in the House for months, and there were plenty of other problems on the government's agenda.

Even so, Kierans might have been able to win the argument if he had not carried his blunt approach into other issues facing the government. One of his officials at the time says the very strength of his principles became his undoing. ''Being so, he became a very poor politician. I think he would admit that. Eric did what he thought was right, irrespective of what the political consequences might be. He also took his job as a Cabinet minister very seriously. Any proposal that was put before Cabinet, he felt it was his duty to express an opinion on that, not as postmaster general, but as a member of Cabinet. He had a very highly tuned, analytical mind, and there were occasions when I think he destroyed some of the propositions of some of his colleagues, and in doing so, got to the point where a number of them owed him one.

''I suspect it got to the point where there were enough of them looking for a way to put a knife in Kierans' back that eventually they were successful, and one of the ways they were successful was preventing him from obtaining Crown-corporation status. My belief is that it failed in the '69-'70 period primarily because of that.''

Mackay says Kierans took his duties as a minister so seriously that he would send his own officials — even those within the post office — off to do reports on matters ranging from agriculture to eliminating railway branch lines on the prairie railroads. If they objected, Kierans would tell them: '' 'You're in the transportation business. Find somebody and give me a report on it.' I would spend hours working on this,'' Mackay says.

''I remember attending a meeting one day, and he ran circles around [Energy minister Joe] Greene. He was the minister responsible for putting through this case to his Cabinet colleagues, and Kierans knew far more about it than he did, and just tore it to shreds. You'd sit there and cringe because you could see the hatred on Greene's face. You'd think, if he's looking for support from his colleagues for a Crown corporation or whatever, he's not going to get it.''

Kierans says he and a handful of others were active in all Cabinet debates, but the rest hardly talked at all. During his term, he tangled with several, including Edgar Benson, Jean-Luc Pepin, and Joe Greene. ''You'd start talking to them and they'd look at you and think: 'Why the hell doesn't he deliver the mail instead of criticizing?' '' Kierans once told Mackay that Cabinet members started to take the attitude that ''If Kierans is in favour of it, it must be politically wrong.''

''I'll never forget that,'' says Mackay. ''He was right. He always looked at things from a very financial point of view, whether it was in the interests of the economy of the country. He would have done that in any party. That was just Kierans.''

''I don't think I ever saw him make what I would call a political decision,'' says Sinclair. He remembers being in a meeting with Kierans where the minister's executive assistant, Richard Gwyn, was trying to defend his boss and smooth over a political wrangle. Kierans leaned over and muttered: ''Richard's trying to look after my political backside. But I really don't give a damn.''

Kierans showed the strength of his principles when he resigned, or tried to resign, during the Lapalme affair. That time, his drastic action was enough to force Trudeau to work out a compromise deal, but by the following summer, everyone seemed tired of him.

The crunch came in July, when the Trudeau Cabinet regularly met to discuss strategy for the fall session of Parliament. The big topic in the summer of 1970 was tax reform, and once again Kierans was disappointed that his colleagues were reluctant to go ahead with what he felt was serious reform. "I was really the only minister interested in tax reform as such, and the others were thinking of political stresses and strains. I was very frustrated at the end of July," he recalls.

The real frustration was about to begin. On the day of the last meeting, Kierans asked to see Trudeau in private. Trudeau told him to come along and complimented him on his performance during the tax-reform debate. But Kierans had something else on his mind.

Kierans had seen media reports that he was going to be dumped from the post office and handed the more important Manpower and Immigration portfolio in a Cabinet shuffle expected in August. "He was really surprised. He said, 'I didn't know that. Where'd you get that?' " Just in case, though, Kierans told him that he wanted to stay in the post office. And if he was moved, Kierans added, would Trudeau please make sure that the handful of top men he had brought into the post office, including Mackay and Sinclair, were looked after properly? "I've made commitments to these people. These people are first class."

"First of all, I don't intend to move you," said Trudeau. "I'm just absolutely pleased . . . that you want to stay. You can look after them yourself."

All that changed a week later. He asked Kierans to lunch at his official residence at 24 Sussex Drive. The Prime Minister was having second thoughts about the plans for a Crown corporation.

Trudeau felt that if the government tabled post office legislation in September as planned, it would tie up the House all fall. Kierans agreed that, because MPs always want to get involved in any debate over the post office, the Prime Minister's assessment was probably right. "They all pull a letter out of their pockets, even the best of them . . . that was eight days late."

Trudeau, however, had a pile of other bills that he was anxious to get through the House, and asked Kierans to let the Crown corporation go for a while.

It was the last straw for Kierans, who said that without a Crown corporation to give it direction, "nothing's going to happen to the post office. It's still going to run along in the same old inefficient way." Sensing his disappointment, Trudeau quickly offered him a better post — Manpower and Immigration — the very job that Kierans had said he was worried about getting only days earlier.

"It was very funny, and he had the grace to smile a little," says Kierans. Realizing his mistake, Trudeau proffered four other posts, but Kierans wasn't interested. At the very least he wanted to hang on to his job as minister of Communications, and that is what he kept. The title of postmaster general went back to Kierans' predecessor in that job, Jean-Pierre Côté.

"After that, I walked away from the post office and never looked back," says Kierans. Even now, he won't talk about what happened to the post office afterwards, and he paid no attention to the format of the Crown corporation that was created more than a decade later. He had pushed for his vision of postal salvation. He lost. "The thing was just set aside. It's like the original Reciprocity Bill. The Americans approved it in 1911, but we never got around to it."

From then on, the idea of a Crown corporation to run the post office gradually faded away as Trudeau appointed as postmasters general a series of men who either cared less than he did or were actively opposed to the Crown corporation.

Côté shared Kierans' sense of where the post office should go, "but they were two entirely different men," says Sinclair. "Kierans was very much the hard-driving executive type, and Côté was much more laid back, very quiet; [you] never knew exactly what he was thinking. He would work behind the scenes with his colleagues.

"He was a very astute politician. He knew what was possible politically and what was not possible politically. His way of getting things done was to talk quietly to some of his colleagues, so before he ever went near Cabinet, or Cabinet committee, he already had seven or eight people who would support his position." If he didn't have a majority before the meeting he was close. "He always went with a sure thing, or he didn't go.

"Jean-Pierre wasn't a manager per se. He expected his officials to manage the place properly. His job was the political job, our job was the managerial job, and he expected that if there was going to be a management judgment that was going to have political implications, he expected to be consulted thoroughly on the matter, and that no decisions would be taken until we had his views. He very seldom gave orders, but on many subjects we would get to know what his views were, and would temper our judgment."

Côté, a dental-technician-turned-politician, agreed that the government should create a Crown corporation to run the post office. He spent much time studying other countries' efforts to do the same thing. Sinclair remembers travelling with him to study the new United States Postal Service in Washington, to Great Britain to look at their recently-set-up Crown corporation, and to France and West Germany to pick up their ideas on running the post office.

"But he knew he wouldn't implement it. He knew he was only there for a short period of time. I don't know why he knew that, but he did. So he just kept quiet. So we just carried on with the Kierans momentum and the momentum of the people who had been brought in. . . . He was very much for the Crown corporation, but he was the last of the ministers that I'm aware of." He worked hard on the idea, and Sinclair still believes that if he had stayed around longer, he might well have soothed the antagonism of rural MPs enough to get their approval for the Crown corporation.

In his own understated way, Côté was equally effective in dealing with his fellow politicians and with troublesome postal unions. "You couldn't help but like the guy, a great sense of quiet humour."

Mackay was introduced to Côté's sense of humour and his sense of the practical problems of the post office in 1970, when Kierans asked him to move to Ottawa and become deputy minister. People being considered for top-level appointments like that

were first checked out by a handful of ministers. Trudeau wanted
to meet him and felt he should see a couple of other ministers,
including at least one French Canadian.

The government handed that assignment to Côté, then minister of National Revenue and a man who had already been
postmaster general before Kierans. That struck Mackay as a
reasonable choice, and he arranged an appointment a few days
later at Côté's office in the Revenue department's headquarters,
a foreboding, almost medieval castle, across the Rideau Canal
and round the corner from Parliament Hill.

"In those days it was very dark inside and I was feeling a little
nervous. I walk in to this great big room and there's one secretary sitting there, and I introduced myself and she said, 'Oh yes,
yes, yes, just a minute.' She goes in and comes out and says, 'Mr.
Côté will see you now,' " recalls Mackay.

"It was a very dark room and he's sitting in the corner. He
stood up, he didn't come around the table, but we shook hands
over the table. He said, 'Sit down.' So I sat down. And waited.
And I waited. And he looked at me. Never said a thing. And after,
it seemed like three or four minutes — it seemed like three or
four hours — he said to me: 'What are you here for?' I looked at
him, absolutely astonished," and stumbled through an explanation
of what he thought the arrangement was supposed to be.

"And he said, 'Oh, you're here to see me.' And I said, 'Yes.'
'Well, why would you even be interested,' he said, 'why would
you even be interested in the post office?' I said, 'Well, at the
moment I work there.' It was a whole series of that type of
question."

"And, my gosh, I thought, 'What a strange interview this is!'
I thought: 'I must have bombed out, I must have looked stupid.'
And then I thought to myself, 'The man himself must be stupid. . . .' " Despite his confusion, Mackay passed all the tests,
and a few weeks later found himself the top bureaucrat in the
post office.

"First guy I get a phone call from is Côté. 'Did you think that
was an unusual interview?' he said. 'I wanted to see how you
would react, because when you're dealing with the unions, you
have to say nothing, and wait for them to speak. You have to

learn that very quickly.' We've grown to like one another ever since then. A tremendously simple guy, but my God, clever,'' says Mackay.

Sinclair says Côté was determined that there was never going to be a strike at the post office while he was there, not even an illegal one if he could help it. He was aided in that goal by circumstances: Kierans wrapped up a long-term deal just before Côté took over. Nevertheless, Côté showed his style in the way he dealt with the Lapalme affair, laying it to rest at last and then getting a deal with the Teamsters that allowed a trouble-free transfer of city trucking in other centres from the private contractors back to the post office.

Mackay says Côté's strategy was a matter of playing for time and making a few minor moves when he thought the time was right. ''He had sort of an inner sense about union strategy and union thinking. When I was touching base with him about the negotiations, I didn't have to explain the way they thought,'' says Mackay.

''Côté was easy to deal with. It would have been much more difficult to deal with Kierans, because Kierans would say: 'How much is it going to cost me? That's too goddamn much. It doesn't matter how much it is, it's too much.' He would have found it difficult to solve politically. He found that [Lapalme] problem difficult to solve in Montreal. It hurt him. . . . He couldn't understand why they didn't put the government first and Canada first and their feelings second.''

Mackay makes no secret of his admiration for Côté's way of operating. He got his first chance to see Côté in action not long after the disconcerting interview in the Revenue Canada headquarters. By then, the Lapalme boys were in town, trying desperately to reach a deal.

''I was trying to negotiate something and I didn't speak French very well in those days, and a lot of it was in French. And Côté was sitting there and I'm sitting here and about five union leaders from CNTU are sitting there — the Lapalme boys — all big fellows, you know. And Côté's got his glasses off and he's got a little screwdriver and he's working on his glasses, and I think he said about five words in that whole meeting.''

The union leaders did most of the talking, berating the government for its unfair treatment and demanding a better deal. Côté's response was simple: " 'A decision was made. There's no point going over that again.' So they would say the same thing over again and he would not say anything. And they would say: 'You're not saying anything.' And he would say: 'Well, I've said what I said five minutes ago. There's no point saying it again.' And he would carry on with his glasses. His technique was that the less you say, the less trouble you can get into. That technique has worked. I've done it myself," says Mackay.

Then again, Mackay had good reason to appreciate Côté's way of operating. The minister used the same sort of tactics to protect his officials from Opposition politicians. Mackay had urgent need of that protection during the outcry over the government's decision to buy machines for the post office from his old company. He had written Côté to warn him of the problem, and made sure that the minister dealt with any quotes on the tenders for the machines.

"Côté knew it was going to come up. It was inevitable, but I had never been exposed to that type of questioning. . . . There was this parrying that went on. 'You can't ask him the question directly, you have to ask me as the minister, and I will ask him, I will ask my deputy minister, first of all I'll decide whether it's an appropriate question. If it's an appropriate question, then I will ask him the question.' It took them an hour to work all that out of a two-hour session. It was all part of the game."

"The first question was, 'How many shares do you have in ITT?' So when the question was asked, Côté thought about it for a few moments and said, 'I think that's an appropriate question. How many shares have you got?' and I said, 'None at all.' So he turned round and said, 'None at all.' And this went on for an hour, and I was sitting there absolutely exasperated on one hand and amazed and appalled on the other hand. Welcome to Ottawa. Anything after that was absolutely tame."

Within the postal plants, however, the dispute over mechanization was heating up. Côté's successor as postmaster general after the 1972 election was André Ouellet, a man who would later have a profound influence on the structure of the Crown corporation.

In the early 1970s, however, he was still an ambitious young politician on the way up, the kind of person who was often assigned as postmaster general. It was his first Cabinet assignment. Although Ouellet became the Crown corporation's creator almost a decade later, he made no effort to push the idea in his first term as postmaster general. He agreed that it had benefits, both political and practical, but he was one of those who disagreed violently with Kierans and his ways. "The things he did just antagonized everybody, and he wasn't there long enough to do anything about it." Ouellet and other MPs feared that the corporation would be imbued with Kierans' spirit: business first, politics second.

The Lapalme affair was one sore point. "This was a very bad situation that instead of getting resolved was getting worse and worse." During the seemingly endless marches around Parliament Hill by the Lapalme boys, "I was one who said publicly that sometimes, coming on the Hill, rather than going to my office, I felt I should go and picket and walk with these people on the Hill, which made a few people very furious," says Ouellet. "But I got the job of postmaster general after the election. I never did walk on the Hill, but what I was saying was something that I deeply felt. I felt that these people were unjustly treated, and that the government should rectify the situation."

He felt the same way about Kierans' moves to close rural post offices, because the post office, in his mind, was very much a matter of public service rather than of making money. "In a small town, the mail is a social ritual. All paths lead to the post office," he said in a 1973 speech. "The post office brings everybody together. It binds the community. It's a unifying force. It gives the community and each person a sense of identity. That's why I don't hesitate to tell you that the massive closing of post offices a few years ago was a regrettable error."

For Ouellet, a postal deficit was to be expected; it was the expense of providing a service. "The post office learned from that," he continued. "It learned something about efficiency. It counts, but it's not the only thing that counts. The quickest way to get downstairs, after all, is to jump out the window — but it's not always the most sensible way."

He carried a similar attitude into negotiations with the postal unions. The problem, as he saw it, was that postal contract talks were constrained by the Public Service Staff Relations Act and by Treasury Board's dominance at the bargaining table. "I worked for a good nine to twelve months to learn the post office, get acquainted with the union leaders, and to try to establish a feeling of better understanding and trust that I felt was essential."

He shared Côté's desire to avoid a postal strike during his tenure, but unlike Côté, Ouellet was not favoured by the timing of his appointment. On the day he was sworn in, the letter-carriers and the postal workers reached a legal strike position in what turned out to be their last try at joint bargaining through the Council of Postal Unions.

The fledgling minister immediately set out on a cross-country tour of postal plants with his deputy, Mackay, to talk to his field managers and get a feel for the sentiments on the plant floors. "I felt that the employees didn't really want to strike, but the leadership wanted a strike," was his conclusion. "I told the leadership that I'd met hundreds of employees and not a single one had told me privately that they wanted to strike."

Jean-Claude Parrot was quick to show Ouellet his vision of proper style in post office labour relations. Mackay remembers their first meeting in Montreal. "In comes Parrot, and Ouellet, being a sociable guy, liked to shake everybody's hand. Parrot walked right past it and didn't even acknowledge he was there. It was a strange sort of phenomenon because Ouellet didn't know what to do with his hand."

Nevertheless, with Ouellet moving in to take charge of the negotiations, the government and the unions reached a deal without a walkout. As his term continued, Ouellet hoped that his attitude toward mechanization would help to keep the peace.

His feelings echoed the recommendations of the consultants in *A Blueprint for Change*. "They say if you're lucky enough to get to work without being hit by a machine, you find that one has taken your job," he joked in a 1974 speech. "I understand this viewpoint. I'm not losing sight of job security. Our new union contract assures it. We expect these changes to pay for themselves in about nine years — but not at the expense of our employees."

The new machines, he argued, would make the mail faster and more efficient. That in turn would mean that the post office could win back lost business and attract new business, and that would mean it could not only keep safe its existing jobs, but go out and hire even more postal workers. He would still be making the same argument eight years later as the Crown corporation took shape.

"There is another change we're going to make. We're going to take the drudgery out of his job. We're going to make it a safer, cleaner job, a more pleasant job. In creating change, we have to think of people. A government's goal is the people's welfare. . . . Change is just a means to this end."

This was the beginning of Ouellet's struggle with Treasury Board bureaucrats which would reach a dramatic climax in the post office's dying days as a federal department. Ouellet wanted to get the workers to accept mechanization as a way of making their lives easier and more pleasant. Treasury Board was interested only in classifying the new coding jobs at the level it thought right: the lowest wages the post office paid.

Despite Ouellet's sympathy for the union position, his patience ran out in 1974. He agreed with the managers in the Montreal plant that the T-shirts being worn by workers protesting the postal code went too far. He approved the management's move to suspend and then fire workers who continued to wear the shirts after being warned not to.

Their defiance spilled over into the illegal strike that spread across the country, forced union president Jim McCall to resign, and brought the dispute over the classification of coding clerks to a head. Ouellet, who had hoped to avoid strikes while he was postmaster general, had to deal with his first. His solution was the appointment of special mediator Eric Taylor, who came up with the unofficial PO-2⅝ classification that was the first step in bypassing the Treasury Board rules.

As Trudeau dissolved his minority government in 1974, Ouellet headed off to the hustings with a sense of regret. He says he was hoping to stay on as postmaster general. The Liberals won the election, but Trudeau had another job in mind for him.

During his short term, the dream of a Crown corporation had

finally slid from limbo into oblivion. Practical politics had taken over, and in that sense, Ouellet had been able to keep the lid on. But in the post office pressure-cooker, that lid was under increasing strain and the vessel itself was beginning to crack. Under his successor, Bryce Mackasey, it would blow apart.

11
The Great Conciliator

∎

"I was offered several portfolios, including Industry, Trade and Commerce, but I asked for the post office," says Bryce Mackasey. "I surprised everybody by saying, 'Give me the post office and I'll straighten it out for you.' Straighten it out didn't necessarily mean being hard-line on the unions. . . . I saw the visible effects of sloppy, shoddy mail delivery and the impact it had on the less fortunate. I didn't see much logic for it, and it stayed in my head."

Mackasey today remains an enigma, still clouded with impenetrable billows of blarney. In him lie the best and the worst of the populist politician: one senses a genuine concern for the common man, but one that is tempered by an overriding concern for appearances. Looking good is the ultimate key to success.

And his record suggests another internal conflict. For all his concern about the welfare of others and the role of government in promoting that welfare, his own fine sense of self-interest has never been far below the surface. He says he wanted to get the post office because during the election campaign he had been struck by the hardship imposed on pensioners when their monthly cheques came late, but one cannot forget how he made his own pension the first order of business after getting a short-lived patronage appointment as chairman of Air Canada in 1979.

His philosophical passions and his overriding desire to be liked and admired were to prove a devastating combination when he was placed in charge of the post office.

Mackasey says he felt that his experience as Labour minister, when he had managed to reach settlements without strikes in more than a dozen major disputes, was just what the post office needed. Those who worked for him agree that he thought of himself as a true friend of labour, the great conciliator, a man who would have no trouble getting to the root of postal workers' discontent and coming up with a solution because he knew more about solving labour problems than the Treasury Board bureaucrats did.

He took charge as the wrangling over mechanization reached a peak, and at first he was sure he could ease the tensions by injecting the right attitude into the post office. "We didn't do much for people in the first industrial revolution and we're still suffering the social consequences. In this one, I think the government should lead. We should be socially responsible. If we can't, who can? I think the government of Canada should be Canada's best employer," he said in a speech as he opened the brand-new, highly mechanized postal plant in Calgary in October 1974. "This means we should try to structure jobs to give people a sense of personal worth. Ensure that employees have purchasing power to meet their needs. Try to develop teamwork. Find ways to break monotony. If all our managers would be as concerned with employees as with machines, a lot of union-management tension would disappear."

His deputy minister, Mackay, remembers a ceremony to unveil a new stamp held shortly after Mackasey took office. The post office had managed to gather together a good crowd for the event, which took place next to the cafeteria building behind the Ottawa postal headquarters. Ouellet and Côté were there, and so were a couple of others who had been postmasters general at one time or another.

"And here's Bryce Mackasey, he's got a prepared text, I'm glad to be the new postmaster general type of thing, and I'm happy to announce this, whatever it was. He stood up, and set aside his prepared text, and goes on about labour relations, and how part of it must be management's fault, and most of the people there were management. Côté was sitting next to me, and he says: 'Give him a week, he'll change his tune.' "

A couple of days later, Mackasey had his first meeting with the three top leaders of the postal workers union. Until then, Mackay recalls, he had been telling his top managers: "I don't understand why you people have labour-relations problems. You know that's why the Prime Minister put me in here, to solve these labour-relations problems."

"I said, 'Bryce, see for yourself. I'm not going to tell you my feelings about their personalities.' Well, he met them, and it lasted five minutes. They all walked out of his office. He got annoyed as hell," and came out muttering about how could he see how there was a management problem in the post office if his top people didn't warn him about how the unions behaved with ministers.

Undeterred at first, Mackasey let it be known to the unions that his door was always open to them if they had a problem. A Treasury Board official at the time says it was an invitation they couldn't refuse. "He was going around and doing his very best to woo the unions, particularly the CUPW, and made it clear that he had an open door, and that the unions should feel free to consult him on any problems. It gave rise to some bizarre circumstances. It involved, for instance, unions getting turned down in grievances in the field and calling him and getting a decision reversed."

CUPW was always alert to ways of beating the system, and Mackasey's attitude fitted perfectly with their strategy of escalating disputes to the political level, to win from him what they could not get from management.

At times, the ministerial interference reached ridiculous extremes. The devastating 1975 report on managerial morale documented one such case in St. John's, Newfoundland. The postmaster in charge of the plant had to come in late one evening to deal with complaints from the local CUPW president that casual labour was being used to handle what he felt were preferred jobs that should have gone to union workers. The postmaster decided that the facts did not support the complaint, and refused to make the changes demanded by the union.

"As a result, the local president and vice-president addressed the employees present and urged them to walk out. They did so, forcing operations to cease,'' the report said. The two union leaders had incited similar illegal walkouts before, and the postmaster decided he had had enough. The next day, after clearing his proposed action with district and regional management, the postmaster suspended both union leaders for five days.

After the suspensions were imposed, word came down from Ottawa, insisting that the decision be changed and the suspensions lifted. The postmaster, incensed, refused to change his mind and told his superiors that if his original decision was not upheld, he himself would walk out in protest. When the suspensions were lifted, he refused to report for work.

The letter-carriers then walked out in support of the postmaster, and supervisors scheduled a meeting to talk about following suit. The media got wind of the dispute, and that finally provoked another change of heart. ''The headquarters decision was then rereversed, and the suspensions reimposed thereby allowing the postmaster to return to his office,'' the report noted. Only by setting up his own one-man picket line, taking the dispute to the public and therefore political level himself, was the manager able to counter the union's penchant for using politicians to overturn management decisions.

And in public, at least, Mackasey maintained his philosophy that the government should be a ''good'' employer, doing everything it could to make sure its jobs were as pleasant and well-paid as possible. Financial performance was not in the picture. Labour peace was.

''Well, if we can't make the job better, perhaps we should build in compensation: shorter hours, a pleasant workplace, good pay,'' he told the Canadian Direct Mail Association in May 1975. ''Let's not design an unpleasant job that doesn't call for thought, and then put a low price tag on it because it's mindless. Why should the guys with the most pleasant jobs, like you and me, get the most pay? There's a growing feeling that people should be paid for what they put up with.''

But his top officials say that after a while Mackasey lost patience with CUPW, and turned into a tough guy. Mackay, who complains bitterly about flip-flops by postal ministers who kept interfering with disciplinary actions, says Mackasey was actually very consistent if the law was broken. "He was very tough on illegal acts like vandalism at the post office and not giving in to it."

He also had a flair for the dramatic, as he showed during one illegal strike in Montreal. "That was a bad episode. That's when they locked in all the supervisors. They were all huddled on the sixth floor in a room. They phoned me from there," says Mackasey. The minister, who was about to set off for a black-tie dinner, stormed into the plant in his tuxedo and ordered the rebellious workers back to their jobs.

"You won't find many ministers willing to do that. When they didn't go back to work, he called the police in," says Mackay.

And his operations chief, Gordon Sinclair, remembers with a kind of glee the one time that Mackasey set him loose. The illegal Montreal strike had caused a huge backlog in the plant, millions of pieces of mail that would have taken weeks to clear up without extraordinary measures. When Mackasey asked for advice, Sinclair promised to get it moved fast if the minister gave him unlimited clearance to hire casuals and fire union members who caused trouble.

When Mackasey gave him the go-ahead, "we arranged to get a bunch of kids from school, from university." Sinclair knew that the Montreal local, already inflamed by the passions of the illegal strike, would not take an invasion by casuals lying down. Sure enough, according to union leader Davidson, the Montreal local reacted by forming a gauntlet at the entrance every time the casuals were spotted on the way in, and blowing whistles at them until they retreated.

For a few days the casuals went away. Then postal management sprang its response. Sinclair says the post office hired its very own "goon squad" of off-duty Montreal policemen, all big tough guys, to provide security inside the plant, and then brought in 1,200 casuals all at once to start digging into the mountain of mail.

On the first day, he says, "there was almost a riot." But the security squad would simply grab hold of any worker who started to cause trouble, drag him to a side door, and throw him out. Outside, the Montreal riot squad was waiting. Three days later the disruptions were down to a minimum.

With the main plant under control, Sinclair toured all the smaller plants in the regions, where workers were still off the job. He knew they could see what had happened at the central terminal, and his message to managers was blunt: If the guys weren't back to work in ten minutes, fire them. With 300 of their members already under suspension, including 90 in danger of dismissal, Perrault and his Montreal executive called off their actions and yelled for help from Ottawa.

In 1974, Lou Murphy of Toronto and leaders of other locals around the country had been willing to walk out illegally as well to back up their brothers and sisters in Montreal. By the next spring, when they were asked to do it again, they were still feeling the after-effects of the stormy 1974 union convention, and seemed to feel that this time the Quebec militants would have to live with the consequences of their actions. The national executive called for a work-to-rule campaign, but, in Davidson's words, the response was "pathetic".

Sinclair says the post office fought every one of the suspensions through adjudication. In the end, some workers were reinstated and others had their suspensions reduced, but the post office managed to fire almost 30 union members and make suspensions stick for others.

The debacle put added pressure on the militants in the postal workers union to produce results as they headed into their contract talks. The pressure was already high, because 1975 was the first time that the postal workers negotiated on their own rather than jointly with the letter-carriers. The Council of Postal Unions had been broken up because CUPW leaders had different goals from those of the letter-carriers. Their implicit promise to the postal workers was that they would negotiate a better deal alone than they would have wrested from the government in partnership with the LCUC.

The letter-carriers, however, were already at the bargaining table when Mackasey became minister. They reached a deal with the government in 1975 without a strike. The deal gave postmen a big raise, one that boosted their pay cheques well above the average wage in both the civil service and the private sector. It gave Mackasey his first settlement without a strike. Both sides were happy.

"It was a very generous settlement for the letter-carriers," says Mackasey, generous enough that he found himself with a fight in Cabinet to win their approval for it. "It wasn't all that easy within Cabinet, but I got their support." While Treasury Board president Jean Chrétien would normally have been doing the bargaining, "I think they were very glad to hand it over to me."

As far as the minister was concerned, the deal with the LCUC also set the pattern for the talks with the inside workers. "The strategy of getting the letter-carriers settled made all the sense in the world." The split between the two unions was still recent, and Mackasey saw no reason to treat them differently. "The pattern of the letter-carriers should have set the stage for the other union. Once I had the letter-carriers in place, there was no way that the inside workers could expect legally or logically to create a differential. . . . There was no bloody way I could, even if I was inclined to, give Parrot's group more than the letter-carriers. That had been signed, sealed, and delivered."

Parrot, for his part, was eager to put the frustrations of joint bargaining behind him. "We finally got out of this Council [of Postal Unions] and really did our homework. The minute we started negotiating on our own, it made a big, big difference."

He was not overly concerned with the basic wage rate as long as it matched that of the letter-carriers. But he did want more money for his members in other ways. The key demands were for bigger premiums, extra wages paid on top of the base rate for shifts done at night or on weekends. Since most postal sorting is done at night, better premiums were just as good as a higher base wage to inside workers, and this had been one of the big stumbling-blocks as long as the letter-carriers, who work days, had been tied up in the same contract talks.

CUPW began its pre-bargaining offensive by reviving the idea of a Crown corporation. Since the Public Service Staff Relations Act prevented the union from negotiating many items that bothered it, the postal workers demanded that the post office be turned into a Crown corporation. Mackasey thought a Crown corporation was a silly idea. "I never supported the concept. If there's going to be any agency of government where you've got to take the public good [into account], it's got to be the post office, more than any one I can think of. You've got to run at a deficit," he says.

He would soon put his beliefs into practice when the postal workers made their final bid to control the spread of technological change in the post office that had begun with the Kierans mechanization program. As more machines were bought and new buildings put up to contain them, postal workers decided that they must get a strong clause into the contract that would allow them to have a say in what and how many machines would be installed. They wanted to avoid any repeat of the struggle over classifying the coding clerks.

On that score, they had little to worry about. Mackasey had been minister of Labour when he brought in changes to the Canada Labour Code in 1973 that made technological change a legal bargaining issue in the private sector. The Public Service Staff Relations Act prevented such bargaining in the civil service. That didn't bother Bryce Mackasey. His deputy, Mackay, says that his boss's attitude was that "the law is the law and if the law's an ass, you change the law." Mackasey wasted no time in putting technological change on the bargaining table.

"On the question of technological change, there was no problem," says Mackasey. "I gave that away, and gladly gave it away. I thought in principle it makes sense. And I naively perhaps hoped that by so doing, that they would have bargained in good faith and come up with a settlement."

Davidson said that Mackasey made his first move at a late-night session in the minister's office on the seventh floor of the Confederation Building, across Bank Street on Parliament Hill's west side. One evening in September 1975 he phoned NDP MP John Rodriguez in his office downstairs on the third floor, and asked him to set up a private meeting with Davidson, one that would exclude Parrot. "I've got a proposal to make to him," Rodriguez says Mackasey told him.

Rodriguez was doubtful, feeling that if the minister had a proposal to make, he should stick it on the bargaining table, but he agreed to call Davidson, and the union leader, after talking things over with his negotiating committee, figured they might learn something worth while. His only condition was that

Rodriguez accompany him to the meeting, to prevent any chance of under-the-table dealings.

Rodriguez says Davidson came over at 9:30 or 10 p.m. and the two went upstairs to meet Mackasey. During the meeting, Rodriguez says Mackasey reached into his jacket pocket and pulled out a piece of paper, saying: "I've got a solution." It was essentially a photocopy of the regulations on technological change under the Canada Labour Code, the same rules that Mackasey had authored as Labour minister. Now he was offering to let the post office negotiate technological change in the same way. "I'm putting it on the table."

The New Democrat MP says Davidson was non-committal, and questioned whether the union could trust Mackasey's word that the clause would be included in violation of the Public Service Staff Relations Act. Rodriguez said Mackasey then offered: "I'll sign it right here."

Davidson's autobiography says that when the union leader asked how Mackasey could sign something that violated the PSSRA, the minister declared: "Forget about the act. I'm the minister, and if I sign it that's the way it will be."

Mackasey, for his part, says he does not remember ever negotiating with Davidson, whom he considered to be no more than the union's public-relations figurehead. "I never had any meetings with Joe Davidson, at any time. He didn't attend any of the [bargaining] meetings." He says he did sometimes meet Davidson away from the negotiating table. Of the meeting with Davidson and Rodriguez, he says: "Could be. I don't recall it, but that isn't to say it didn't happen. . . . I have absolutely no recollection of that at all."

Davidson wrote that Mackasey offered drinks all round as the meeting began, and although the union leader turned him down, the minister continued to drink throughout the meeting, which lasted until the wee hours of the morning: Rodriguez says about two o'clock, Davidson, three o'clock. Rodriguez confirmed that Davidson abstained, and said he joined the minister for one round, but then left Mackasey to pour for himself. By the time the meeting ended, he says, Davidson had to help the minister downstairs, but no one else saw the two public enemies with their arms round each other. Davidson wrote that he drove Mackasey home "and poured him out at the doorstep of his apartment." The union leader said it was the only private meeting he ever had with Mackasey. His deputy minister, Mackay, says he never heard about any meeting between the two men.

There is no doubt, however, that Mackasey did put technological change on the bargaining table in spite of the rules of the PSSRA. Mackasey says he made his proposal formally on the afternoon of Sunday, October 20. "That was something I conceded. I didn't even bargain. I made it abundantly clear on Sunday afternoon that it made sense that the union be brought in to negotiating the impact of technology. It was a breakthrough for the union, but it was not very hard to achieve because I was philosophically dedicated to it."

By the time October rolled around, the battle for the hearts and minds of the Canadian public was well under way. Mackasey made plenty of ground in the early running by ridiculing some of the union demands: cutting the work week from 40 hours to 30 hours while still being paid for 40, and at the same time adding a pay increase of $3.26 an hour to the existing postal clerk's wage of $4.59 an hour.

His task was made easier by the legal wage controls of the Anti-Inflation Act, which came into effect October 14. Because the inside workers failed to reach a quick deal, even matching the raise won by the letter-carriers would break the law.

Mackasey's successor as postmaster general, Jean-Jacques Blais, was still an anonymous back-bench MP at the time, and remembers the belligerent mood of the Members of Parliament in the Liberal caucus at the time. As a group, they pretty much reflected public opinion, and "public opinion was very anti-union, and 'Give it to them, Bryce', sort of thing, which was basically the position that caucus took. That's why the strike lasted so long, because, you know, 'Give 'em the guns, the sons of bitches deserve it, let's bury them for once and we'll take the pain now for the long-term gain,' which in my view was a completely immature and unacceptable position to take." Blais, however, remained the loyal party follower and defended the government's position throughout the strike.

Sensing the political mood, the bureaucrats had done their own homework in preparation for a strike. Gordon Sinclair says they did "a fair amount of missionary work" with the big postal customers. "You people have been crying for us to control costs, to gain control of the union," the postal officials told them. They asked customers whether they would like the dispute settled on the basis of the unions' demands, and have the costs of that settlement passed on to postal users. "They said: 'Hell no!' They'd had enough at that point, and felt that it was time to go to the wall. So the large customers at worst took a very neutral position and at best supported the government stance in dealing with the unions at the time of the '75 strike."

Postal officials knew that their biggest problem would be dealing with the so-called social mail: the pension cheques and the baby bonuses and the unemployment insurance payments. Complaints about pensioners or children starving because their federal lifeline had been cut would be sure to have the politicians howling for a settlement at any cost in short order. They worked out ways to get those cheques delivered during a strike.

Throughout the negotiations that fall, Mackasey remained convinced that he could work out a deal. Having decided to give in on the union's major demand for protection from technological change, "I frankly didn't expect a strike. I couldn't see any logic for one. . . . What turned me off in that strike was that the big issue was technological change. I had conceded that to the union the very first time we met. So it no longer became an issue for the union to rally around."

But despite Mackasey's first personal visit to the bargaining table with his offer on the eve of the strike, the union began its walkout, starting with the midnight shift that night. "I could have got angry with the methods they were using" after the rejection of his efforts on technological change, says Mackasey, "but it really became a public-relations battle, and somewhere along the line the union workers turned my way."

It was a battle the minister soon felt he was winning. "I like to think I did it because I was fair. I didn't destroy the union. I didn't belabour Davidson. I took him on because he was their public-relations man. He wasn't their negotiator. . . . With the experience I had, I understand that much of it is showmanship on both sides.''

The minister who only six months earlier had still been preaching the government's duty to be a ''good'' employer and offer lots of money for unpleasant jobs began singing another tune. Instead, he complained about how much power the union had in relation to the government.

''The government has no dollar control, no motivator, no regulator,'' he said in a speech to the Ottawa Rotary Club on November 24. ''The government can say it's got a billion-dollar deficit and it won't shade the union's demands by a cent; they know the government isn't about to go broke. Union representatives know they won't be fired no matter what they do. Most important, they know how much damage a strike in a vital service inflicts. And the government often has no counter-leverage except loss of pay — and this can often be held down by 'selective' or 'rotating' strikes.''

Davidson's 'Then to hell with the public' crack had already shredded much of the public sympathy for the union, and Mackasey feels he gained the edge for good with a successful debate on public television in Toronto. By then, ordinary members of the union were worried about more than their public image. For the first two weeks of the strike, they had gone without any pay, as usual. Then, for the first time, the postal workers opened the locks on their $1.2-million strike fund. But even with strike pay of only $40 a week per member, the fund was exhausted within two more weeks. ''After that, we didn't have any more. The last two weeks of the strike, we didn't have any strike pay,'' says Parrot.

As the strike dragged on into November, some workers lost heart. In the West, local leaders put pressure on the union to settle, but held. As the strike pay ran out, some locals, including Toronto, took new strike votes. Parrot says the Toronto leadership was weak, but the shop stewards were strongly militant and the local voted to stay out by a whisker.

Mackasey chose that strike to accuse the union leaders of unnecessarily prolonging the strike by collecting their regular pay from the union while their members on the picket lines did without. He poured on the pressure after four weeks of the strike by unsealing all the mailboxes and sending the trucks round the streets to clear them. Mackasey had himself filmed dropping a letter into a mailbox. "There was nothing in the trucks. It was just a show they were making," says Parrot.

But with the strike fund exhausted, the union was running out of time. "The government, if it had let it go on much longer, would have ended up with a broken union, because about 2,000 or 3,000 employees had come back," says Mackay. Parrot disputes the numbers, but admits that there were defections. He says that perhaps 500 people across the country went back to work, but were spread so thinly that no work got done.

"It was sort of pathetic to see them going from door to door in Parliament," says Mackasey. "They couldn't get any support even from their traditional supporters. But I got no pleasure out of that. I wanted it over with. But I wasn't prepared to concede any more to get it."

Sinclair remembers taking a break in a suite at the Lord Elgin Hotel one day during the strike. He was in the main room, while Mackasey was lying down in one of the bedrooms. Suddenly a messenger rushed in and handed a note to Mackasey. He looked at it, and then had it handed out to Sinclair. The note read: "I want a settlement now. Give them everything they want. [signed] Pierre Elliott Trudeau."

"And I stormed into his bedroom, and he kept a straight face for a moment and then he burst out laughing." The mischievous minister had arranged to have the fake note delivered to him. "I guess this was his way of relieving the tension a little bit. I must admit it did break the tension, because we all had a good laugh about it," says Sinclair.

But Mackasey himself was desperate to get a deal. "I was conscious of Christmas coming up. I knew small business had been uncharacteristically co-operative on this thing." And, above all, he prided himself on his record as Labour minister in settling strikes.

Mackay says the minister also argued that the government could not afford to destroy CUPW, because the Teamsters were trying to sign up postal workers as members at the time, and that union would be an even tougher adversary.

Mackasey had already ousted the chief negotiator from the

Treasury Board. "Mackasey was not convinced that he was capable, because he didn't come up with a collective agreement," says Mackay. "So he said, 'I'm going to take over the negotiations.' I said, 'Bryce, you can't do that, because there's nowhere for us to go now. There has to be somebody in the back room that we can confer with. . . .' "

Even his own bureaucrats, always chafing under Treasury Board's dominant role, did not want the minister right at the bargaining table. If the ultimate authority on one side is at the table, there can be no excuse to adjourn a meeting for consultations; it puts on immediate pressure to accept or reject proposals that come up, and even casual musings by the minister could be taken as binding commitments by the union side. As a compromise, Mackay was forced to join the bargaining team, even though he knew little about the details of the contract. And to satisfy Mackasey's desire to be on hand, the bureaucrats installed a camp-cot in a room just around the corner from the negotiating room on the twentieth floor of the Bell Canada building.

Parrot says that with a completely new management team at the table, some deals were struck. Management agreed to make concessions on the critical staffing clause, always perilously close to the question of management's right to decide how many people it needs when to do what jobs.

But, with most of the items settled, the talks stalled. As the days passed, it became increasingly clear that the union was willing to fall apart before it gave in, and that prospect was too much for Mackasey to bear. "Bryce Mackasey sensed that the union was beaten, and the union was about to fall apart, and Mackasey didn't want to have it on his hands that he'd broken a union," says Sinclair. "He hated that union with a passion. And he hated the leadership of it with a passion. But he would not allow himself to have broken the union as an institution."

"Frankly, I moved in and settled rather than see them humiliated," says Mackasey. "I was very, very angry, and the temptation to hang it on them was there, but I never had to go to Parliament once in my career as minister of Labour to resolve an issue. Never once did Parliament, when I was there, order men back to work, and I was determined they would never do it."

On the other side of the table, Parrot called on Shirley Carr of the Canadian Labour Congress for help. The CLC was as eager as Mackasey to prevent the disintegration of one of its largest and most powerful unions, and suggested a way of bypassing the stalled talks.

To help him out, Mackasey had already called on Bernard Wilson, his old deputy minister at the Department of Labour, who by then had retired from the civil service. Mackasey says he hired him on contract for those negotiations, to act as "a very good counterbalance to the advice I might get from my own team, because I was in uncharted waters." Mackasey told Wilson to work with Carr.

Away from the pressures of the bargaining table, Wilson and Carr tried to clarify the issues and piece together the elements of a deal that Mackasey might be able to sell to Cabinet and that Carr could persuade the CUPW leadership to accept. "That was really unofficial," says Parrot. "Nobody really knew about those meetings."

The two finally reached an agreement and the two sides went back to the bargaining table. "But what happened at the table was that the agreement was not the same one on both sides," says Parrot. "We told Shirley Carr, 'We told you, they're always like that.' " He says Wilson agreed with Carr's interpretation, but management said the union's proposal at the table did not match the agreement.

The two sides were not far apart by then, and Mackasey was growing impatient. "Everybody wanted it over, and I gave them certain concessions to bring it over so they could save their face in public," he says. "It didn't matter to me, there was no reward to me to just be prepared to destroy them or humiliate them. I set out to get a collective agreement. You don't get collective agreements by confrontation."

"Bryce Mackasey kept on wanting to make sure that we wrapped it up before the eleven o'clock news," says Mackay, then acting as the chief negotiator. "By about nine o'clock it was just about all sorted out, and we sent a message to Bryce, and a note came back, 'Make sure it's before the eleven o'clock news, and let me know when you're ready, because I want to come in and shake their hands.' "

Then the talks bogged down over the wording and proper translation of a handful of minor clauses, including leave for injury on duty, a change in the rules for part-timers,and an extra pay boost for the mail-handlers, the lowest-paid category.

Mackay, on the management side, argued that the intent was clear, but Parrot wanted to have his contract language accepted before he would initial the clause. "What a way to negotiate. There was none of this business of acceptance in principle," grumbles Mackay.

Finally, Mackasey couldn't wait any longer. At about half past ten, Mackasey charged into the meeting. Mackay describes the subsequent conversation:

"I understand it's finished," said Mackasey.

"No, it's not finished yet," replies Parrot.

"Why not?"

Mackasey's bureaucrats told him what they were arguing about. Mackasey dismissed their quibbling. "We're all decent gentlemen, we're honourable gentlemen, surely we've got the intent, why don't we just shake hands now and initial the clause?"

"I will never trust management," said Parrot.

Finally, Carr took Parrot outside for a few minutes. When they came back in, the two sides had found a word that satisfied both of them.

Then, just as Parrot was about to sign off the last clauses, he stopped. In 1972, the Council of Postal Unions had agreed to include a "no strike, no lockout" clause in the contract, which prohibits either side from using that weapon to resolve disputes during the life of the contract. Although the law makes similar provisions, putting the clause directly in the contract makes it much easier for managers to suspend or fire workers who go on an illegal strike.

Parrot says acceptance of the clause had been a bone of contention not only between the letter-carriers and the postal workers during their joint bargaining, but between the militants and the moderates in CUPW. "Even within our own union, we were quite pissed off about what happened." After Mackasey had arrived and the two sides had settled their wording problems, they sat down and started initialling each clause to make the deal formal.

"Suddenly I say, Article 43, no strikes," says Parrot. "We never agreed to that. We don't want that in the collective agreement."

"If you don't want it, you won't have it. It's in the act anyway," Mackasey replied.

"He took the thing, and tore it all apart," says Parrot. "All the people on his side look at him, and if their eyes had been guns, he would have been dead right away. They were pissed off. He felt, what the hell, it's in the act anyway, but they wanted it in the collective agreement. So that's the way we got rid of it. We never got it back."

"It was five to eleven, and all these press people were outside," says Mackay. "I went over to shake Jean-Claude's hand, and he wouldn't shake it." His officials say Mackasey, although he had only been there in the latter stages, made sure he looked suitably haggard and mussed, and then walked out the door to tell the waiting cameras how he had saved the day and reached a deal with the union.

The union still refused to sign the agreement as a whole and therefore give up their right to go back on strike until it won the stamp of approval from the Anti-Inflation Board. Mackasey says he had to go to bat for the union in Cabinet. "Nobody said it was fair, but arbitrarily here's the date [that wage and price controls went into effect]. Do we break it in full view of the public, and if we break it there, what about other unions in other jurisdictions?" The board grumbled, but Cabinet overruled its objections and agreed to violate the wage controls it had approved less than two months earlier.

Postal officials still argue that, because the union had its back against the wall, it was forced to accept a bad deal. "The union paid a price for the settlement," says Sinclair. "It was not a good one for them."

A senior Treasury Board official takes a different view. "In the case of the '75 strike, there were a lot of people crossing picket lines, there was a lot of muttering about the union, and it was in deep trouble. Mackasey dictated a settlement and they got benefits that they wanted, but more important, that the leadership could hold up to the rank and file and say, look, we were out, but, look what we got for you. They got re-elected, naturally, and militancy was perpetuated.''

Parrot also thinks he got a good deal. The union may have edged close to disaster by raising high expectations, ''but we signed a damned good collective agreement in '75.'' He says that while the basic wage increase may have been no larger than that won by the letter-carriers, the union won breakthroughs in several areas that mattered only to the inside workers. The wage premium for evening shifts went from an extra 15 cents an hour to 40 cents, and extra bonuses were added for weekend work. There were tighter rules on management's use of casual labour, a final ban on the measurement of any individual's work, even for part-timers, and a host of improvements to less visible contract clauses. ''We made a breakthrough in those areas, which we were not capable of making before.''

And, of course, there was the technological-change clause. On paper, at least, it was unusually strong. It defined technological change as any form of new equipment or new methods of work that affected one or more workers. It required the post office to eliminate any adverse effects on workers resulting from such changes. And the post office had to tell the union what it planned at least ninety days ahead of time.

When union members voted on the deal, they approved it by only 52 per cent. But while no one knows for sure how close the union came to breaking, its leadership emerged with credibility intact. Parrot, who had led the bargaining team, would take over as president of the union in 1977.

12
Countdown
to Crown

∎

Thud! The familiar red mailbox rocks to the impact of a booted foot swinging in from the side. Thwack! It shudders as a different foot thumps into it from the opposite side. Crunch! It teeters gracefully as a third assailant boots it from the rear, and then it flops with a despairing crash to the ground.

As a television image, no words were needed. In one short sequence, it portrayed the beleaguered post office, and silently asked watchers: If everyone does nothing but attack the post office, how will it ever stay on its feet? "The battered mailbox was my idea," says former postmaster general Jean-Jacques Blais, leaning back in his modest law office on the top floor of a Sparks Street office building in Ottawa.

When Blais was offered the chance to become postmaster general in 1976, he did not complain. "As you can imagine, as a back-bencher, coming in to Cabinet was really the important step, and basically when the question arose as to my being invited to Cabinet, that was the major preoccupation. The question as to which job would be offered . . . was not of the same import."

In any case, Blais figured the post office looked like an interesting challenge. It suited both his small-business background and his training as a labour lawyer. He was also intrigued by its potential to expand into the field of telecommunications. For an ambitious young MP, it had other advantages as well.

"I identified the post office as being a relatively junior ministry, which has some challenges and which offered some opportunity and some profile. . . . It was great politically, because I could get to go any place in the country. And I could do politics at the same time. So basically it was ideal, and I loved it."

But he took charge of the post office just after the longest strike in its history. The unions were angrier than ever and managerial morale had dived into a chasm. "So when I came into the place, I mean everybody was licking wounds. There was a great deal of blood on the floor, there was a great deal of acrimony, animosity, mistrust."

He received the usual greeting from the postal workers union during his first meeting with Davidson and Parrot, whose attitude he describes as one of "complete and utter bellicosity". When they came into his office, he offered them coffee.

"No, minister, we will not accept coffee," they replied.

"Is it because you don't drink coffee?" Blais asked.

"Oh yes, we like it well enough," Davidson said.

"But why don't you have it?" pursued a bemused Blais.

"We don't fraternize with the bosses," Parrot insisted.

"Basically that was the attitude, and I was told very early on by Parrot that if I thought like Mackasey that I was going to destroy the union, that I'd better consider that the post office would be destroyed before the union. Those were the signals that I got," Blais says.

His reaction was simple. "What you have to do is re-establish trust. The whole of my period there, if there was one mission, it was to re-establish trust in that department." The advertising campaign with the toppling mailbox was part of that effort.

"In fact, I was naive enough to think that if I went in there and really concentrated my efforts we could do things. One example: as soon as I came in, rotating strikes started all over. The issue was the question of implementation of technological changes." The concessions Mackasey had made a year earlier had now moved to the plant floor.

Although the clause in the new contract seemed to cover almost everything, managers had come up with an argument to get themselves off the hook. If a change they were considering did not actually involve a new piece of equipment that had not been used before anywhere in the post office, they said it was not a matter of technological change. Since most of the machines in the mechanization program were already in use in many plants, their introduction in other plants should not suddenly be subject to consultations.

When Blais arrived, the postal workers were conducting a series of rotating strikes across the country, hitting a plant in one city one day and a plant somewhere else the next. "And of course, my officials advised me, 'Minister, these are not technological changes, and they do not come within the terms of the contract.' I accepted the advice of my officials," who also suggested that as a rookie in both the post office and the Cabinet, he had to show that he could be tough.

He backed management at first, but then decided to look at the contracts for himself. "I read the contract, I looked at the circumstances that were at issue, and I said: 'There's no question in my mind. These are technological changes. That's the whole purpose of the consultation, to deal with concerns amongst the workers and the union of the impact of whatever measure you're going to be introducing. And therefore that consultation should take place right away, because they are going to be affected downstream.' Well, there was resistance, but once the arguments were advanced, my officials accepted." Blais told the union that consultations would start, and the rotating strikes ended. "I was very pleased with that and it gave me some credibility with the unions."

To get a better feel for his new charge, Blais began travelling from coast to coast visiting post offices. Even if he was on other business, he would stop by any small post office he passed for a chat. And he held regular meetings with all the unions except CUPW. To meet inside workers, he just went into the plants and talked to members there. The union accepted that, because any discussions were public that way.

Even so, Blais's attempts to get spontaneous reactions from postal workers tended to be frustrated by the union's long ears. "Lo and behold, my presence in that particular post office was known to the workers as a result of CUPW intelligence before the local postmaster had knowledge of my coming around. The intelligence the CUPW had in terms of being able to disseminate information was superior. They knew what was going on at the post office at all levels.''

He was not impressed by some of the sights he saw during his tours. During one Western swing, a union member complained about the observation galleries, the rooms hidden behind postal plant walls from where post office security men kept an eye on workers to make sure they were not stealing from the mail. Workers never liked being spied on, and their complaints redoubled when the post office began to consider using television cameras as well. Blais agreed with the workers' feelings about monitoring. It did not fit his plans for rebuilding trust, and when video monitoring became an issue, he prevented cameras from being used except for keeping an eye on machines.

Blais's soulmate in the search for trust and reason was John Paré, the latest addition to the senior ranks of postal managers as assistant deputy postmaster general for personnel. Paré wanted to build more connections between workers and managers. He set up a new communications system that fed information out to workers and brought their responses back to senior managers. He also helped Blais organize seminars for middle and senior managers across the country. But Paré's greatest concern was for those at the bottom of the postal pyramid. ''He came in with the view that the workers really mattered. Paré wanted the people at the bottom to know he cared,'' says Blais.

The minister was offended by some of the careless decisions being made when new machines were brought in. ''Everybody was really technology-crazed you know.'' Blais particularly remembers one time when managers were eager to show off a new parcel-sorting machine, where workers sat on a chair attached to one side while handling parcels and adding the postal code.

''And I looked at the seat, and I sat down, and I was down here, you see,'' slicing his arm across his upper chest to show the level at which parcels would move past him. ''How do you adjust this thing?'' he asked.

''Oh, minister, that's one of the problems. You can't adjust them,'' came the reply.

"What do you mean you can't adjust them? You can't adjust the goddamn seat? Everybody's supposed to be the same size?" he exploded. "That typified the sort of insensitivity to the human dimension."

So deep was the rift between union and management that Blais says the high point of his term in office was getting a phone call from the Calgary president of the postal workers. The Calgary plant, one of those built from scratch during the mechanization program, was having troubles, and Blais was about to go for a visit. Despite the union's strict directives that no union member should meet managers or ministers individually except on the plant floor, the Calgary official said: "Minister, I want to see you when you're in Calgary."

"On the floor?" Blais asked.

"No, in private."

"That was the beginning," says Blais. "I just thought that was super. And we had the meeting. It was a good meeting, a constructive meeting, and it had nothing to do with him personally."

Not everyone in management agreed with the approach favoured by Blais and Paré, and the personnel chief ran into troubles with his colleagues. "He was soft," says Blais. "The problem was that when he dealt with officials at his level, you could see that he was getting frustrated at all turns. I guess he was afraid of communicating with me to too great an extent because he was afraid that maybe I had become a prisoner of the others."

Blais also liked some of the other top managers like Larry Sperling, the man in charge of marketing, whose attitude Blais says was more one of: "Let's get the bastards to do the work that they're supposed to do, and after that we'll talk turkey with them." People like that felt that pleas for sympathy and co-operation like the battered-mailbox ad campaign were wasted effort. "For Sperling, that was just a pile of shit," says Blais.

Whether he agreed with them or not, Blais spent much more time than most of his predecessors dealing with the nuts and bolts of running the department. He was astounded that, after the years and dollars spent on the mechanization program, the optical character-readers could only read twenty-five per cent of the mail. Everything else still had to pass through a coding desk or be handled manually.

While there was never any question of putting the mechanization program on hold, Blais says he did want to raise the level of consultation with the unions, because he was afraid that any more shocks to the system might result in a complete collapse.

That fear also prompted him to try and heal the growing splits between the post office's regional kingdoms, whose leaders, the powerful regional general managers, had become steadily more independent since the decentralized structure was set up under Kierans.

Mechanization had succeeded in speeding up the processing of mail within each plant, but the movement between plants, and especially between regions, left much to be desired. Even when the new plants were being built, the regional managers sometimes refused to follow the scripts they had been given.

The main plant in Montreal, for instance, was supposed to follow the same design as the new building in Toronto. The outer shell followed the same design, but then the Montreal regional manager changed his mind about the internal layout. "At that point, they said, Screw you, Toronto, we're not going to take your crap. We're going to have our own crap. Because they had the same shell, they had to rearrange the insides in order to accommodate the new equipment at substantial cost increases."

Blais insisted on sitting in on the monthly meetings of the regional general managers in Ottawa. The first time he tried it, he says they got into a flap because they couldn't figure out where he should sit. Blais didn't care if they were embarrassed or uncomfortable, especially after one incident during his travels.

He was touring one of the smaller sorting plants in Campbellton, New Brunswick, when he noticed a large bag of mail sitting underneath one of the sorting machines.

"What's that?" he asked.

"Oh, that's the Montreal bag," came a defiant reply. "It's aging properly."

Blais could not believe the disdain shown by managers for their colleagues in another part of the country. "Anything that was going to Montreal had to be 'aged' before it got sent off."

There were other surprises in store for the rookie minister. The leading mandarins in Ottawa had taken careful note of the conclusions of the joint Treasury Board–post office study of management morale and pay levels. As a result of that report's stunning conclusions, a shadowy group of senior officials gathered and decided that Mackay had to be removed as deputy minister. In the normal manner of the civil service when dealing with high-level bureaucrats, Mackay would be sent to another job.

Blais says he does not even remember being told about the study. He could see the problems with morale for himself, but he has no memory of being bothered with the gory details of the task-force conclusions. And he liked Mackay and planned to keep him as deputy minister.

Blais arrived at the post office in September 1976, and in November he got a phone call from his colleague Judd Buchanan, the minister of Public Works.

"J.J., tell me something about this guy Mackay," Buchanan asked.

"Nice guy, good administrator, I like him, he's personable, he's very helpful to me, etc., etc., etc., he knows the post office," replied Blais, giving Buchanan a general rundown on his deputy. "Why do you want to know?"

"Oh, don't you know? They're giving him to me."

"You're out of your cotton-pickin' tree. Nobody's told me about that."

An outraged Blais called Michael Pitfield, the Clerk of the Privy Council, and asked him, "What the hell's coming off?" He asked Mackay to stay, because he thought the two of them were starting to make some headway in turning the post office around. But it was no use.

Blais then had to fight off two efforts by the mandarinate to choose Mackay's successor. One was from Treasury Board, the very body that Blais felt did not understand the post office's needs in negotiation. Blais wanted to promote from within, and he liked the look of Jim Corkery, the former CGE executive who was running the Ontario region.

"We didn't need any more upsetting, we didn't need any more upheavals within the shop, we needed a steady course, we needed stability, we needed people who knew what [was] going on, and the big problem had been in the recent past that all sorts of outsiders had been inserted. . . . So they didn't want any more of that, and I supported that wholeheartedly.''

Corkery, who now had lots of post office experience to add to his private-sector background, fitted in perfectly with Blais's interest in making the post office run better rather than worrying about broader policies.

Blais says he was responsible for several changes, from small stuff like following the banks' lead in setting up a single queue for all wickets in post offices to the start of the post office's own courier service. Blais figured that the post office was really a telecommunications company rather than a transportation service. He felt managers were stuck in the rut of an obsolete mind-set that involved moving only hard goods. The number of letters moving through the post office had levelled off at about six billion a year, and Blais felt that only by going head-to-head with the couriers and the parcel companies could the post office regain some growth in its revenues.

Even so, Blais did not see Priority Post as just another courier service, taking goods from one place and sending them to another. He felt that Canada's failure to follow Europe in linking the telephone and mail services into a single department had let many postal managers fall asleep at the switch. They were not on the leading edge of technology and they knew it.

Blais wanted to see much more electronic use made of the post office's network. For instance, he thought post offices across the country should be used for electronic funds transfers. That would allow people to send money electronically between post offices. The government could send out its social cheques electronically and either print them or cash them at a person's nearest post office. They would be set up with machines like the now familiar electronic tellers used by the banks.

Blais also wanted the nation-wide network of post offices to be used as one-stop shopping and information centres for federal programs. The postmaster would not just worry about the mail, but be trained so he could tell small businesses how to get grants and help individuals having problems with federal services.

"The big concern that I had, coming from rural Canada, was that there would be a time when the post offices at the local level would be shut down because they couldn't be justified any more. I felt that if there were other services that the post office could render, it would justify its presence, even if you had to provide courses for the postmaster," or had to set up extra kiosks relating to government services. Later, Blais became minister of Supply and Services, where he funded development of the Telidon system. He thought post offices would be great places to put computer terminals with access to federal data bases.

He also tried to raise more money by selling more stamps to collectors and offering related products like stationery. The response he found to that move contained a lesson for the managers of the Crown corporation a few years later. "The reaction was that the small-businessmen came to me and said, 'You're competing with me. You're selling envelopes. I'm selling envelopes. What the hell business have you got selling envelopes?' " However, Blais could see little opposition to his thoughts on electronic funds transfer, because the banks were already beginning to close smaller rural branches and consolidate their own rural networks.

Despite his interest in moving the post office into a more aggressive, commercial approach and into expanding its lines of business, Blais never accepted the idea of a Crown corporation.

"There was a lot of discussion while I was there, but I stifled it. I didn't believe in it. I thought that, and I still do, I think it's a waste. I think it's a government department, and no matter how you try to create a Crown corporation, you're still going to be susceptible to political intervention. It's in the nature of the beast. And so long as you've got credit that you need or monies from the government, parliamentarians are going to be involved with it. The Crown corporation, all it did was created the impression of *renouveau* which was completely fictitious."

Blais, like many other postal ministers, never got the chance to fulfil his ideas. On January 27, 1978, Francis Fox was forced to resign as solicitor general after admitting he had forged a man's signature on a hospital admission form to let his wife, Fox's mistress, get an abortion. Trudeau asked Blais to fill the vacancy.

Blais said he would really like to stay at the post office, but Trudeau just looked at him and said: "You don't want to stay there forever, do you?"

Blais moved on. He was then replaced by a veteran politician but House of Commons rookie, Gilles Lamontagne. Lamontagne had been mayor of Quebec City, and when the death of a local MP left a vacancy, he easily won the by-election that followed. Since Quebec had traditionally had a member in Cabinet, Lamontagne was first made minister without portfolio. "He doesn't have a clue how to operate in the House. . . . Then the Fox situation developed, so there was a musical chairs, Fox gets turfed out, and two weeks later, he's moved from minister without portfolio to postmaster general," says his deputy minister, Jim Corkery.

He liked to keep close tabs on his responsibilities. "As mayor, he had a police and fire band on his radio. So, in the evenings he would cruise around, and if he heard a police call, he would race to the scene and then check and see how long it took the cops to arrive, and the same with fire. It didn't matter what hour of the night. It was one of his kicks, I guess," says a senior official. "When he went to the post office, he believed that he could do the same thing, come into the post office in the middle of the night and see how things were going."

But the tight control that worked well in the mayor's office was far from enough to let Lamontagne survive the daily savagery of the House of Commons during Question Period, and he knew nothing at first about the post office. On top of the usual problems with shuffling Cabinet members in the middle of a parliamentary session when they have no time to learn their new jobs, Lamontagne took over the post office right in the middle of stalled contract talks that would lead to another nation-wide strike.

"He's now accountable to the House for the post office, right in the labour dispute. He hasn't a ruddy clue, he has trouble with the language, and I don't speak French," says Corkery, which made the job of explaining the post office and its strange ways even tougher. "He had a short fuse anyway, so he was frustrated, and trying to defend what's going on in the House when they were after him. . . . When they realize you're uncomfortable, they're out with the knives. So he was having an ungodly time for the period he was there. I think he was mighty glad to get out of it."

As the labour dispute came to a head, Lamontagne seemed determined to avoid drastic measures. As Mackasey had done before him, Lamontagne tried to wage a public-relations battle, talking with workers and with customers in an effort to place the government on the side of truth and reason. "We will try to avoid an escalatory situation of power struggling," he told the House of Commons in April. "It is not a question of who is the strongest. When one talks about leadership, there are all kinds of leadership. . . . Hitler was a leader, but that is not the kind of leadership we believe in, and I do not think Canadians do either."

Others in government were determined not to allow a repeat of 1975, where the initial resolve to be tough had wasted away during a long strike and resulted in the minister's intervening personally to reach a deal.

Corkery says that while Lamontagne may have been a member of the Cabinet when it decided to bring in legislation to stop the postal strike, he was still operating in the dark. "He didn't know the business, he didn't know the politics. But you can't blame Lamontagne, because what was happening, he couldn't fight back. He doesn't have a base to argue from, so what's happening is he's in a situation where others are making decisions around him."

The Prime Minister and his bureaucratic advisors in the Privy Council Office, other Cabinet ministers and their deputy ministers, the members of the Liberal caucus, the Treasury Board, and postal officials all had their own ideas of how hard to push. Corkery says the post office was not demanding legislation to stop a strike, but said, "We don't see any other alternative but to go the court route to order them back to work if you want them back to work."

As the contract dispute moved toward its climax, the idea of a Crown corporation was creeping back onto the table. Opposition MPs began promoting the idea in the House of Commons, but Lamontagne remained sceptical. "Both the United Kingdom and the United States have moved in the direction of Crown corporations for their post offices. Neither country seems to have solved its problems. They have experienced greater rate increases and larger deficits even than Canada,'' he said in May.

Although he did appoint a three-man task force to look at the different kinds of Crown corporations that might be set up, he remained unconvinced in June. ''This has been tried in the United States, and after seven years it is a mess. Are we to copy them now? . . . I do not believe that even if we convert the post office into a Crown corporation we will settle all our problems.''

Less than two months later, Prime Minister Trudeau made the decision for him. The Bonn summit meeting of the leaders of the seven major industrialized countries had brought an agreement that government spending must be cut. Trudeau figured that one way to cut spending would be to shove a quarter of all federal civil servants into a Crown corporation, where they would no longer show up on the books.

Despite the fact that no one in the bureaucracy, least of all those working on the study of options, had done any work to prepare for the actual formation of a corporation for the post office, Lamontagne had a bill ready for the House by December. It included the infamous ''secretariat'', which would remain a unit of the bureaucracy and effectively continue to allow the minister to control all important decisions of the Crown corporation. Coming so soon after the strike and the criminal charges against union leaders, labour's response was less than enthusiastic despite its earlier urgings.

More meetings were planned in order to explain the bill to union leaders and to listen to their views. Lamontagne also planned to get advice and reaction from major postal users. These meetings would all take place before the House got down to detailed discussion of the bill.

But the legislation was destined to die on the order paper as Trudeau called an election in the spring of 1979. The Liberals lost, and the new postmaster general, John Fraser, had to take a look at the pieces of the puzzle that had been left to him.

Fraser asked his officials to set up meetings between the government and the Canadian Labour Congress to review the Liberal bill. He wanted to find out what changes both sides might want to make, to identify compromises where possible and set out the differences that remained.

A group of three senior officials from the post office, the Department of Labour, and the Privy Council Office met with CLC vice-president Shirley Carr and representatives of the postal unions affiliated with the CLC. Bob Rapley, the assistant deputy postmaster general for corporate affairs, and personnel chief John Paré also held meetings with the smaller postal unions which did not work under the CLC umbrella.

Fraser, however, was allowed little time to hear their conclusions. In December, his government's first budget went down to defeat. Trudeau and the Liberals were back in power with a majority.

Trudeau turned to Ouellet to go back to the post office portfolio and get the Crown corporation off the ground. Ouellet says he was tagged for the job almost by accident. Aside from having been postmaster general before, he had also stepped in as acting Labour minister in 1979, and been part of the government's talks with the CLC in the days just before the election. He was told to get the job done, and then he would get a better Cabinet post. "Frankly, I thought it was a three-month affair."

But all was not well at the post office. Contract talks were bogged down again. The contract imposed by the arbitrator under the 1978 back-to-work bill ran out on December 31, 1979. The postal workers union held its first meeting with the government in November and presented its list of 98 initial demands.

The CUPW shopping list included the deletion of all clauses and rollbacks inserted by the arbitrator in 1978. That imposed deal allowed the post office to monitor workers by closed-circuit television and to measure the speed at which postal workers did their jobs. Until 1978, the post office could test postal workers' abilities off the job, but was not allowed to measure their performance on the job in groups of less than ten.

As it began the 1980 talks, the union also wanted total job protection, with no layoffs or contracting out, and compulsory union membership for those working in the plants. It asked for complete protection against inflation, and a shorter work week. And as an incentive to speed up the grievance process, it wanted the post office to pay major financial penalties whenever it failed to meet rigid time limits for resolving grievances.

The leftovers from the 1978 confrontation plagued the talks in other ways, too. Jean-Claude Parrot's attempts to appeal his conviction finally ran out. In early 1980 he went to jail to serve the rest of his sentence. "The prospect of a quick settlement following conciliation is also remote in view of their chief spokesman, J. C. Parrot, being imprisoned," the post office told Ouellet in a confidential briefing paper.

Ouellet, however, was determined not to let disagreements with labour stop him from doing his job: getting the Crown corporation off the ground. The meetings at CLC headquarters to win union approval for every clause of the Crown corporation legislation were only the beginning.

He also bent over backwards to apologize for the mistakes of the past, including those of the mechanization program which he himself had helped to direct. "Ten years later, I can appreciate that the post office did what had to be done because it could not stand in the way of progress," he told the House of Commons as he introduced the much-modified Crown corporation bill, now numbered C-42, on July 17, 1980. "But I can also say that the implementation procedure was very wrong and resulted in a decade of unrest in the post office."

Ouellet was determined not to let labour unrest derail the Crown corporation. At the same time as he was seeking labour's clause-by-clause approval for the legislation, the government agreed to take the contract talks out of Treasury Board's hands and put Ouellet in charge as part of the build-up towards a Crown corporation. Ouellet did not want bureaucrats he didn't control in a position to cause an irreparable breach between the government and the unions at such a critical time.

In the process, officials who worked at Treasury Board and in the post office say that Ouellet gave away far more than he had to in his efforts to reach a peaceful deal. Ouellet says he did what was necessary to clinch the contract, but admits that he did exceed the mandate he had been given by the federal Cabinet.

Having got his deal with CUPW, he then had to wrest more money from Cabinet to make it possible. It was not easy. "I got it by literally arm-twisting," says Ouellet. "I had more or less to plead, kneeling in front of Allan MacEachen, who was minister of Finance, to get a deal that I felt was acceptable to avoid a strike."

The clause that clinched the deal and also pushed him over his spending limit was the one that finally gave the union its shorter work week by allowing a half-hour paid lunch, to be included in the eight-hour day. The union argued that the concession would cost nothing because the break would refresh workers. They would work harder during the rest of the time and therefore process just as many letters as before. They promised in writing that productivity would not fall, and Ouellet accepted.

Michael Warren, when he came on board a year later, was less than impressed by what he saw. "Ouellet said, 'Fine, but you have to give me a commitment that it will cost nothing, because productivity will not fall.' " The commitment, however, was "very broadly worded," says Warren. "My understanding was that later, when Treasury Board found out that this was the deal, they couldn't believe it. There were a lot of hard feelings for some time, and it didn't stop there."

Trudeau, suspicious of the union's good faith, ordered Corkery to monitor the productivity in the plants on a monthly basis to see if the union was living up to its commitment. Corkery could not find much evidence of productivity falling, but he was short of good information because of the restrictions on measuring the output of individual workers.

Warren says he found himself paying the price for the deal after the Crown corporation. All of a sudden, productivity seemed to be dropping in the corporation's early months. "What we found was happening was that not long after the reporting to Trudeau had stopped, the productivity began to fall apart," he says. The real cost came to some $20 million a year. "This was not a cheap item. It was also symbolically one that certainly showed that the unions could walk away with an awful lot."

The union was delighted with the deal. "It was probably the best breakthrough in gains we made without a strike. And we took away all the rollbacks they imposed on us after the '78 strike. The things we lost, they were all brought back," says Parrot.

Ouellet might have been justified in paying a higher price for the 1980 agreement if he had not made another mistake. He settled for a short-term contract. "We never expected that the Conservatives, who were so mad at losing the election, would filibuster every damn piece of legislation coming before Parliament," he says. After all Ouellet's work, the post office legislation certainly had the support of the unions. It was also supported by the New Democratic Party, and Ouellet thought that since Fraser, the Tory postal critic, was in favour of it, the Conservatives would also go along.

But the Conservatives proved less than co-operative. It took months of debate in the House of Commons just to get the bill into committee, where it would be picked apart clause by clause. A small group of Tory MPs, including John Gamble, Bill Kempling, Don Blenkarn, and Sinclair Stevens, called witnesses and raised a multitude of objections. "In those days, [Conservative Leader Joe] Clark didn't control his party and it was all over the map," says Ouellet.

Ouellet gives credit to Fraser for playing a moderating role. At times, he says, Fraser even got into arguments with fellow Conservatives in committee. Ouellet says he was willing to listen to serious concerns, but told Fraser flatly that "I'm not going to compromise the agreement I have given to the unions."

Eventually the Crown corporation bill was passed, but in the meantime, the contract that Ouellet had hammered out in 1980 had run out. "It took so long to get the legislation that then we were involved in another round of negotiations, and they just took it away from me," says Ouellet. "The hilarious thing is, we had hired Michael Warren to take over the Crown corporation and we were in the process of hiring people. . . . Both Warren and I were on the sidelines. We had nothing to say in the second round. Treasury Board put us out."

Warren was not exactly upset at being left out. It was not yet his show. But Parrot also tried to get the future president involved in the talks. "Just before the strike was called, Parrot called me and said: 'I'm formally asking you to come into these negotiations,' " says Warren.

"So I said I would get back to him, and I think for a fleeting moment Ouellet thought that he had an opportunity to re-enter the fray here and to take charge again of the negotiations and pull off a win. But the Treasury Board was having none of that, and they tried to secure and maintain a very firm hand over this thing. . . . I got back to Parrot and said, 'I have no mandate and I can't get one. When we get a Crown corporation, then we'll be dealing together.' That's the way it was left.''

Partly because Ouellet exceeded his mandate in 1980 and partly because it was flexing its muscles in other arenas such as the troublesome talks with air traffic controllers, Treasury Board took a much tougher line than Ouellet or the union wanted to see. With Treasury Board back in the driver's seat, Don Johnston became the lead minister for the contract talks. This time he was the rookie minister, a well-known tax lawyer on the right wing of the Liberal Party, first elected in a by-election in 1978 and now settling into his first Cabinet post.

''The record of costly settlements convinced me that the negotiations should be re-assumed by the Treasury Board,'' Johnston wrote in his 1986 book, *Up the Hill*. ''Post office workers had previously won levels of benefits far in excess of other departments by holding the public hostage until negotiators caved in. Once again, the demands of Mr. Parrot for higher wages, reduced hours, vacation benefits and so on, were out of the question. I determined to take a hard but fair position.''

''He's the guy who said 'No' to everything and took the hard line and all that, so we ended up with a 42-day strike and ended up with what we could have had without a strike,'' says Parrot. ''He wanted to show Ouellet how to negotiate. He did not show anything. The strategy was bad.''

''He had in his pocket what I thought was an ace, an agreement that we gave him in Cabinet,'' says Ouellet. That ace was permission to give the union a clause on paid maternity leave, something that they were seeking and that had never before been granted in the public service. If talks came down to an impasse, that could be used as a deal-clincher in the same way as the paid lunch of the 1980 talks.

Under the law, pregnant workers can collect unemployment insurance during their unpaid maternity leave. The clause won by CUPW in 1981 said that the post office would supplement those UI benefits, so that pregnant women on leave would collect

93 per cent of their salaries for their entire leave, including the first two weeks, which are not covered by unemployment insurance. The union said maternity benefits were one of the main reasons for the strike, and trumpeted the clause in the contract, after mediation by Judge Allan Gold, as a major gain from its willingness to endure on the picket lines.

Johnston said he saw realistic maternity leave as the way of the future, and offered the clause to the union before the strike even began. CUPW says that is misleading. The government was willing to offer paid maternity leave, but at first wanted to top up UI payments to no more than two-thirds of a worker's salary. By the time Judge Gold intervened during the strike, the government offer stood at 75 per cent, and, at the end, the two sides split the difference between the government's offer of 90 per cent and the union's demand of 95 per cent.

Ouellet, on the other hand, says Johnston gave away too much too soon, and should not even have given in on the principle of paid maternity leave until the negotiations reached an impasse. "Poor Don just fumbled the damned ball. For CUPW, it was a major, major victory, and he gave them this right at the very first meeting. They said thank you very much and they grabbed it and put it in their pockets and pretended it was not important at all."

A six-week strike was not the way Michael Warren wanted Canada Post Corp. to begin life. Labour problems, however, would not be his first problems as the Crown corporation's president. By the time he gained control of the levers of labour relations, he was already embroiled in the first of his fights with the politicians.

13
Crown
Duels

■

"I really didn't go looking for it. It came looking for me," says Michael Warren, leaning back behind a massive and ornate wooden desk. It is more than a year since he left his vast panelled domain in the northwest corner of Canada Post Corp.'s Sir Alexander Campbell Building in Ottawa. His office is smaller now, but it is full of antiques in dark woods, carven elegance that evokes an earlier, simpler age of tycoons and fat cigars.

He seems happier, more relaxed. Becoming a father again has eased the strains of a second wedding marred by television cameras seeking details of his sudden resignation. The wiry frame that seemed so tightly controlled while he tried to manipulate the forces surrounding the mail now slouches a bit. His words come out more naturally, less like the perpetual sales pitch of his Canada Post presidency.

It is October 16, 1986, the fifth anniversary of the birth of the Crown corporation. The new boardroom at Canadian Investors Corporation Debentures Ltd., a small collection of high-profile money managers and venture capitalists, is still being finished. Guests have to tread on plywood flooring in their trek from the elevator rather than on the plush carpets that will undoubtedly follow. Warren seems delighted with this capitalist perch: he points out the side window, looking down onto the squat headquarters of financier Conrad Black at 10 Toronto Street next door. He has sunk into the obscurity of institutional money management with the same relief as he shows folding himself into his new chair. He has been almost invisible since the hectic days of his departure.

He is comfortable in his new present, and has to be coaxed into reliving the past. He prefers to walk away from it and forget, to get on with something new. And as the talk begins to focus on those trying four years as head of Canada Post Corp., it is clear that the old habits remain. The words come more slowly and precisely, protecting an image with the same care he shows in making sure the coffee cups will not stain the inlaid desk-top.

"I was a logical person for the job, and when it first was raised with me, I thought, this makes some sense." He had spent about fifteen years as a public-sector prodigy, becoming a deputy minister in the Ontario government at the age of thirty-two. He served in three departments as deputy and then resigned as deputy minister of housing after a series of run-ins with municipal politicians opposed to public housing in their towns. He went on to become chief general manager of the Toronto Transit Commission and, in his latter days in Toronto, head of a troubled Canadian National Exhibition.

"In a way, the Toronto Transit Commission was a more successful, smaller version of Canada Post. We were delivering services to millions of people, we were very visible, and we had to deal with political agendas, and you had to actually make something work properly at the same time. It was the same sort of business." When Warren arrived at the TTC in 1975, ridership was declining, it had a large and growing deficit, and it had just been through a long strike.

"It was a turnaround situation. Five or six years later, ridership was up, we had a financial formula in place with the province and Metro that was working pretty well, the TTC was sort of back in partnership on land-use planning with Metro, we financially were in much better shape. . . . On the whole, we tapped into a new ethic in the community, that transit was good." Other factors, like the oil crisis, helped the transit commission along. Labour relations continued to be a problem.

In early 1981, a head-hunting firm asked if he would be interested in the post office. "This was just another one of those feelers at a time when people sensed that I was ready to move on.'' The process wound its usual way from the recruiting firm to the people at Privy Council Office, the nerve centre of the bureaucracy in Ottawa.

''I then started to say, What do you want to do with Canada Post? Because I have always had a feeling that your best chances for success are if you put the strategy first and then sort out the staffing and the structure and a variety of other things second. So, what do you want to do? What are your priorities? What do you want to accomplish?

''I asked for it all to be put on a single piece of paper. I thought that at the level we were discussing this, that the government's . . . objectives for a new Crown corporation ought to be capable of being put on one piece of paper.''

That sort of definition was vital to Warren's decision, because he felt it was ''a job which probably could not be done, but maybe, under the right conditions, you might pull it off. So it was extremely important to have a clear understanding with the shareholder. So at least on this one, let's have the shareholder and the president, who's supposed to go out and do this thing, agreed on what winning is and what winning isn't, and put it in writing. To some extent that was a novel idea.''

Warren spent early February shuttling back and forth between morning management meetings for the CNE in Toronto and afternoon talks about the post office at the PCO in Ottawa's Langevin Block. Then came the formal interviews of Warren and the handful of other candidates for the top job.

These interviews were held in the dignified surroundings of the official government guest-house, across Sussex Drive from the Prime Minister's house and near the gateway to Rideau Hall, the abode of the Governor General. Each of the potential postal bosses met a select group of influential mandarins, including Jack Manion, head of the Treasury Board, and John Mackay, the former deputy postmaster general, who was then at Public Works. ''It was all very nice, with gins and tonics, and maids and butlers. It was literally a fireside chat . . . I was asked a number of different questions in a very civil way about my background, and what I thought about Canada Post, and how I thought I might be able to help them. It was a traditional senior-level interview.''

A couple of weeks later, toward the end of February, he was told he was on a short list. The next step was to meet Ouellet. Warren figured that no understanding he might reach with the Privy Council Office would mean anything unless the postal minister agreed.

"I had at least two, maybe three, meetings with Ouellet, and we talked about Canada Post in some detail. We focused a lot on the labour-relations aspects of things, because the negotiations with CUPW were under way. But he also wanted to know whether I understood how governments work, and whether or not, in addition to being a well-known and competent public manager, whether I was a flexible fellow who could understand the problems of government. . . ."

Warren had plenty of experience with the need to bend to the huffs and puffs of political wolves, but he wanted Canada Post to be as much of a stand-alone business as possible. "I said to him very clearly that I thought one of the major problems with Canada Post was that it had been used as a political [tool], one of the big patronage places in government, and that had to stop. If one of the things that they expected of me was that the deficit would be reduced substantially and quickly, then we couldn't have deficit reduction and continued patronage. Ouellet didn't at that stage see a major problem with that."

Warren knew that Ouellet could have a decisive impact that went beyond the words of the legislation. "I always believed that beyond the written rules and the institutional framework and so on, there is also something which is called the force of personality, and that can make an enormous difference in terms of what rules are adhered to and which aren't."

He did have a few worries about the bill. For instance, it required the federal Cabinet to approve the hiring of all vice-presidents of Canada Post. But Ouellet told Warren that "because this was such an enormous transition . . . he felt it was appropriate that some things be staged. So at the time I accepted that with some reluctance. Later, it became a bit of a sore point."

For the moment, Ouellet was satisfied that Warren could do the job, and Warren felt Ouellet would let him do it. The next step was a dinner meeting with top civil servant Michael Pitfield.

They huddled in a corner of the luxurious main dining-room of Ottawa's Four Seasons Hotel. They started late, and were the last customers to leave. Warren almost missed his plane back to Toronto.

The two men spent part of the time dealing with the mandate question: what Canada Post and Warren were supposed to do. The rest of the night they dealt with pay and the perks that would go with the job. Pitfield was satisfied with the talk, and suggested that the next step should be an interview with the Prime Minister himself.

Trudeau and Warren met one afternoon in the Prime Minister's parliamentary office. The conversation was more philosophical than practical. "I mentioned to the Prime Minister that I felt it was really important that the government be clear on what they want to accomplish, and it would be important that we were all on the same wavelength. He didn't disagree with it, but he didn't comment on that. We ended up for some reason getting into some long esoteric discussion about the Quebec labour movement. . . . What caught his imagination was the question of how would he have dealt with Parrot and CUPW and the union situation . . . how would he and how would I handle this element, because it is very destructive, potentially one of the most difficult of the really big issues at Canada Post."

At that point, the ball was in Warren's court. The government wanted him. He had to decide if the challenge and the pay made the inevitable headaches worth while. Despite the price-tag — about $180,000, give or take a few stamps — he was not completely happy with the pay package, especially the pension clause. As he wrestled with the choice, he talked with friends in Toronto, including Metro chairman Paul Godfrey and Julian Porter, his chairman at the Toronto Transit Commission.

He got mixed advice. They felt there was little chance of success, but the move to a Crown had created some momentum. On balance, "maybe if you went and tried it, you wouldn't lose a whole lot, and even if you failed to turn it around, there's an experience there and there's probably something that you might benefit from for the rest of your career." Others felt that the post office was a career-wrecker, judging by the mauling that ministers and deputies had received in the past. "I decided to take it in the final analysis because I felt it was a challenge that could benefit from some of the skills that I had. And I felt the government was serious about a number of things."

Before he accepted, though, he made sure that he had his concise marching orders. The one-page mandate was not complicated. "There's no great mystery to it. What I drew from that were the three objectives of the corporation that I set up very early in its life and tried to externalize and internalize. One was service: that the service of the corporation had to be improved, in terms of reliability, and the level of service in relation to the price. And the next one was that we had improve the human relationships within the post office, and that meant a whole host of things. And the third one was that Canada Post was clearly to become financially self-sufficient within a specific period of time. . . . That's where I got service, people, and money, the three themes that I played out. There's no hidden agenda or anything."

He started work on April 1, with the ambiguous title of "special advisor to the postmaster general". From April until June he worked only part-time, splitting his work week between Canada Post, the Transit Commission, and the Canadian National Exhibition. Then, as the contract talks with the postal workers fell apart, his work began in earnest.

The pile of issues to be worked out by proclamation day stacked higher than the mailbags in Montreal after an illegal strike. The post office did not even know which of its buildings it would own at first. After much haggling, it settled on a formula by which buildings that were more than half occupied by the post office would be transferred to the Crown corporation; the rest would remain in the hands of the Department of Public Works.

The key to a successful launch of Canada Post Corp., however, was not accounting. Michael Warren needed people. The Crown corporation had many jobs to do that had never been handled by the postal department. He needed people to handle labour negotiations under the new rules of the Canada Labour Code. He needed people to maintain the postal plants and office space that the corporation would take over from Public Works. He needed financial officers to keep the corporation on track towards break-even. He needed people to help him to keep the public, the politicians, and the unions in a good frame of mind. And, of course, he needed people to make the mail move better.

The post office already had plenty of managers. Before Warren could go recruiting too many new managers, he had to decide what to do with the old ones. He liked what he saw of the managers in charge of moving the mail. As he listened to their proposals at Gray Rocks that spring, it was clear that some of them really knew their business. He picked up on several of their ideas for quick improvements in service.

But he was not happy with the overall picture. And the uncertainty hanging over everyone's head meant Warren had to be careful whom he asked for advice as he forded the white-water creek of transition.

"At the TTC, I could walk around on some stones. I knew after only a few months that there were five or six solid stones, so you could go from one stone to the other. There was a lot of deep water in between them, but you could go from one stone to another with relative safety. . . . But at Canada Post, you were immediately walking around knee-deep and the stones were down three feet below the water and you were lucky to find some of those."

The old structural problems of government reared their heads. Treasury Board had always looked with suspicion on postal figures, thinking that they had been fudged. Warren says they were not really fudged; postal managers just did not have the basic information to start with. Many of the numbers they needed to make proper reports and projections were stored in the filing cabinets of other departments. When Warren started asking basic questions during the planning process, he found that postal managers often could not give him answers.

Stewart Cooke, the man he hired as executive vice-president for personnel and labour relations, says many of the public-service managers had trouble adjusting. "You'd wonder why nothing was happening. You'd push, and shit, they all had their shoes nailed to the floor. It took me about three months to realize that what I was asking people to do was initiate things, and they were not used to that. They were used to responding. And a lot of people couldn't cope with that.''

John Paré, the booster of industrial democracy who had been brought in only five years earlier, was soon on his way out. Warren decided that ''it would be a good idea for John to seek some other challenges. He'd been in the midst of a lot of the labour negotiations in the previous years and had given it a very good try, but had built up some relationships with the unions that would be tough for him to change.''

Larry Sperling, the assistant deputy postmaster general for marketing who came to the post office in 1975 from Consumer's Distributing and IBM, was asked to stick around. Warren felt he had the right ideas, but had never been given the chance to carry them out. ''He had a marketing operation, the feet of which had never really touched the ground in the system. It was all there, and all the right words were there and the brochures were there and the strategies were there, but nobody'd ever let the feet touch the ground and really get it going.''

He picked Georges Clermont, a vice-president at forest-industry giant CIP Inc., as his vice-president corporate and legal services, and recruited Elisabeth Kriegler, an economist then working as director-general of the broadcasting and social policy branch at the Department of Communications, as Canada Post's vice-president for corporate planning. ''We were certainly being pressed to include women in our top fifteen or so. We had almost hired a woman in two other jobs; frankly they were tough, you would get a good woman and she was so much in demand in the corporate community that either we couldn't afford her or she thought, 'Why choose Canada Post?' In Elisabeth's case, I think we got a very good person, but it was the result of deliberately going out and finding a competent woman who could come in and who had management skills.''

The key to the whole management structure lay in the three goals of Warren's mandate: money, people, and service. The top management group would consist of three executive vice-presidents, one for finance, one for personnel and labour relations, and one for operations. The latter would act as the chief operating officer, Warren's number two.

When some of the existing managers started getting the message that they would not be moving up into the major slots of the new structure, they packed their bags. Part of the deal in setting up the Crown corporation was that officials who preferred to remain bureaucrats had the chance to move into other federal departments instead.

Recruiting talent to fill the new jobs as well as the old proved more difficult than expected. Warren himself only recruited the top group of twenty or so executives. He interviewed the people selected for many of the other jobs to make sure he approved, but, by and large, the three executive vice-presidents were responsible for filling out their own shops.

Cooke got a graphic feel for the interest in Canada Post on his first day at the office. "I came in, and there were 3,500 files, in round numbers, 3,500 letters or applications that had been written to Warren, people who wanted to come and work. And on those 3,500 files, each one of them said: Thank you very much for your letter, and so on. My new executive vice-president, Stewart Cooke, will be here in the first part of January and he will be in touch with you."

"It was a very clear mandate at that time, and a fresh one," says Warren. "That was exciting to a certain kind of executive." Despite the obvious interest, however, Warren faced several restraints in his recruiting efforts, including the reluctance of some people in the business world to work in what they still saw as a quasi-government organization. Some took a look and then walked away.

The salaries Warren could offer were not the best. "You had to come in and see this as an exciting opportunity to do something with a big, visible organization that nobody else had been able to do, to compensate for the fact that the salaries were at the low end of the competitive scale." And because the vice-presidents were all appointed by Cabinet, all the federal rules on conflict of interest applied. On top of leaving the private sector and taking worse pay, the prospective postal executive had to worry about putting his stocks and investments into a blind trust.

But Warren says his biggest problem was the very prominence of the post office in a political sense. "When you hire twenty vice-presidents for a new Crown corporation, people watch to see who's being hired and what their background is. That's got lots of visibility. How many women did you hire? How many francophones? What's the ratio? How competent are they and where did they come from?''

The politics of hiring were only part of dealing with the broader question of patronage. "When you start ordering trucks by the thousands, and you do build some facilities, people start to watch you. Some of it is just saying, We're going to do what we did before, we're just changing the rules. It's merit now. So an MP gets put off, and goes up to the minister and says: Tell Warren to change the rules. And then Ouellet will say, Gee, I've had ten of these in the last two weeks, can't we do it some other way? And you've got to be careful of that because the minister responsible still controls your access to Cabinet, controls who's going to support what you need in terms of other tough decisions. So there is a lot of practical politics that go on between the president and the minister.''

The Liberal government of the day was very keen to get a good number of francophones and women into key positions. Because Cabinet had to pass judgment on the vice-presidential selections, Ouellet could effectively block Warren's choices if he did not like them. "I had about two and a half years of delicate stick-handling to try to find people who would be prepared to accept these things and who were almost sequentially the right linguistic background, [and] because the chairman was franco-phone, the president an anglophone, then the emphasis on the chief operating officer would be that he probably should be francophone and then maybe one of the three executive vice-presidents should be francophone.''

Warren says that Ouellet, as an influential Quebec minister, was very sensitive to such issues, as was Trudeau. "I had no great problems with that except that it really made it difficult. I mean, trying to build a hierarchy of a new corporation on the run, where you're trying to get rid of some of the deadwood, find new wood, and also deliver the mail every day with these kinds of hiring conditions, it made it very tricky.''

The most delicate juggling act involved choosing the three executive vice-presidents. Warren had little choice but to pick them all at once, "because I really had to pay attention to this francophone-anglophone mix, and I also had to pay attention to the mix and chemistry of these people."

The resulting team was made up of three men. André Lizotte, the president of Nordair Ltd., a regional airline in Quebec, became executive vice-president for operations and chief operating officer, nominally Warren's second in command. Ken Harry, the senior vice-president and chief financial officer at Consumers' Gas Co. from 1973 to 1980 and then a consultant, was appointed executive vice-president for finance and administration. And Stewart Cooke, an energetic executive from Canadian National Railways, joined the post office as the third executive vice-president in charge of labour relations and personnel.

Lizotte was not Warren's first choice. "What we ended up with were negotiated packages of candidates," he says. "When you get up to the pinnacle of this, for the three top jobs, the three best people were anglophones. And I was an anglophone. This was Ottawa, and this was the Liberals in 1982, and francophone participation was very important. So then you start saying, Well, who is the best francophone in those three jobs on your candidate list. Probably Lizotte was. . . . I ended up getting Cooke and Harry and Lizotte. Lizotte was not the prime candidate."

Lizotte himself had to be coaxed into joining the post office. He liked his job at Nordair, where he had a good relationship with his employees. The government had pledged to sell off Air Canada's stake in the airline, and Lizotte led a group of employees who wanted either to buy it themselves or to make sure it fell into friendly hands. "I wanted to stay at Nordair to defend our group."

"Lizotte was the type of guy who knows everyone who works for him," says one of his colleagues. "André epitomized Nordair: he could pinch every stewardess's ass."

When Ouellet asked him to join the post office, Lizotte turned him down. Ouellet went for help, and Lizotte received a phone call from Pierre Trudeau. Any executive faced with an offer to move to another city thinks hard about the choice before accepting. "Now if the Prime Minister calls, you do a hell of a lot more thinking," says Lizotte.

A job offer became more of a call to patriotic duty. "He invited me to go up there. When the Prime Minister of Canada calls you, I don't care if he's wearing a blue tie or a red tie. You stand up and salute. . . . Prime Minister Trudeau was a pretty good salesman. He did it on the phone and then I made up my mind within a week or so.''

The manner of his recruitment tied in with Lizotte's feelings about the nature of the job. ''When I did go to the post office, I assumed my function was to do something for Canada.'' What Canada needed, he felt, was a post office that would be a good place to work at, one that would encourage employees to work against the competition rather than each other, and that could bring in enough money to cover its costs, so it would not be a financial burden on taxpayers. ''I accepted that as a personal mission.''

The transition from being the boss of a smaller company to being number two in a large one, however, proved tough. Warren's choice of management structure proved tougher. ''My decision was that we would have the three EVPs, who would really have equal status,'' says Warren. The chief operating officer ''would be equal to the others but a little more equal. But his more than equal status had to be won by performance.''

''Warren had a style. He appointed three musketeers,'' says Lizotte, ''and then Warren and Cooke or Warren and Harry would make decisions without my being involved. And then afterwards I was told that this is what we were going to do. It was very difficult.'' Unlike their literary counterparts, Canada Post's three musketeers would spend more time duelling with each other than with their common enemies.

Warren says there was too much to do in the early days to waste time on turf wars. ''I mean, everybody was just over their heads anyway, and throwing each other lifelines and hoping like hell you could get in to work the next day, because you just got home at two in the morning.''

''There was enough work for everybody, so we didn't have that problem,'' says Cooke. ''There was almost twenty-four hours a day, seven days a week togetherness. There was a structure set up that put all the key people together. I don't think there was ever one day that there was not at least one three- or four-hour session with a variety of subjects. We had no other way to do it.''

But Lizotte says he could tell within a month of his arrival that he had a serious problem with the way Warren ran the company. ''My relations with Warren had had it up to there after six months. I tried to stick it out for another year or so.''

As each of the top three built their management teams, there were arguments about who reported to whom. Lizotte felt that the staff people in the regional offices working in areas such as finance and labour relations should report to him through the operations structure. ''I became the arbitrator in many cases: who was responsible for transportation or pricing,'' says Warren's executive assistant, Jonathan Goldbloom.

What chafed at the top end was that Cooke and Harry not only controlled their own shops, but always had Warren's ear any time they disagreed with one of Lizotte's decisions. ''Lizotte had a lot of problems with that,'' says Warren. ''At first it was okay, but after a while he had trouble making that work.''

Harry and Cooke were busily hiring people from outside to handle jobs at the post office which it had never before done for itself. But as they went on hiring binges, Lizotte was being told to cut back, to get rid of people in order to save money. He felt that the new hiring in jobs that were not crucial to moving the mail and getting new business made no sense while the corporation was still losing so much money. ''You were moving from the right column to the left column. I was dead against that, and I used to fight that with the CEO and I was not getting his support.''

He had inherited a good group. ''I walked in there, and I assessed the people in operations and marketing, people who were under me. I noticed some very high-quality managers that had been there for quite a while. I pulled in from the outside very few people within that group. They were people who knew how to move the mail, and that was our basic mission: Move the mail. They knew how to do it and I had confidence in them.'' When he abolished the old structure, replacing the four regions and fifteen districts with nine new geographic divisions, eight of the nine people he picked to head the divisions were long-time postal managers.

Lizotte had no problems with the idea of slimming the post office payroll, but he felt there were plenty of good people in the operations group who could have been loaned or transferred into the new jobs in personnel and finance and done them well. "It used to make me very mad to see that. If you're going to chop PYs [person-years: a full-time job or equivalent in part-time positions], then you've gotta chop PYs right across the board. Until you break even, you don't add PYs."

Lizotte became the spokesman for his managers in operations. "I was going through hell for months with my vice-presidents because PYs were being cut in my department, in my area, and being increased in others. Those guys were looking at me and saying, 'What the hell are you going to do about it, Lizotte?' I had to fight for my people."

But because Harry and Cooke could make their proposals directly to Warren, Lizotte found himself walking into Warren's office with the decisions already made. Cooke says it was all part of his job. "I was clearly responsible for personnel and labour relations and organizational change. And I reported to Warren."

"You can have the vice-president finance responsible to you. That's no problem," says Lizotte. "But, by the same token, you've gotta be in a position to say, 'Goddamn it, COO [chief operating officer], I disagree with this,' when the door's closed." If the two top executives disagree, they should hash out their differences over a squash game or during a quiet weekend and not in front of other executives. Lizotte says he never got that chance.

"I think that Cooke and Harry in their own way did a hell of a nice selling job on Warren. I was unable to do a selling job on Warren. I was too busy moving the mail. . . . I did not go there to sell myself to the president. I went there to try and do a job. . . . I was not the type to sell myself to the boss. I prefer to sell myself to the vice-presidents and managers and employees that are responsible to me.

"I used to run up the wall. I used to get into discussions with Warren, and it never resolved anything, so that's one of the reasons that Warren and I agreed to disagree. And I left."

Warren says it was Lizotte's problems with the decision-making structure that eventually led to his departure. Warren had set up the three executive vice-presidents as equals because that was the way he wanted it. It gave Warren more direct control over the company. Where Lizotte's role was concerned, "the organization chart was very clear. And he knew that he would be working with two others, that this was not a COO position where two other executive vice-presidents reported to him."

Warren believes that Lizotte's main problem was that he felt he needed more control to do his job on the operations side. But the former postal president feels he could not have attracted people like Cooke and Harry to the other top jobs if he had not been willing to give them the freedom that they had to run their own domains. "I would not have been able to get a first rate EVP on either side of him. They want to be able to have a piece of the policy-making process."

Ron Lang, the Canadian Labour Congress official who sat on Warren's board of directors, said the arrangement "placed Lizotte in a goddamned untenable position in being chief operating officer. He couldn't move. They didn't get along with André Lizotte, he was a hard-nosed son of a bitch, but he was honest, he was straightforward, and he knew exactly what needed to be done. He was another guy, if he gave his word to the unions, it was done, no ifs, ands, or buts.

"Any time they didn't like what was going on, they made an end run around André Lizotte and went right straight through to Warren. And pretty soon the wedge between Warren and Lizotte was like that, and Ken Harry and Cooke were playing on it just like a fine fiddle," says Lang.

"To me, he was the guy for the goddamned job. He was the guy, in my opinion, that ought to have been sitting where Warren was sitting. Warren was a manipulator. Lizotte was too honest, straight up by far. But I think in the end it would have proved out that he was the guy who could have done the job."

Warren says that Lizotte seemed to take a slower approach to change than Harry and Cooke. The chief executive, however, didn't pay too much attention. "I had other things going on as well. You couldn't spend an enormous amount of time holding hands, because everybody was very busy.''

Lizotte says he was happy with the performance on the service end. He, like Ouellet, believed that success for the post office could only come through expanded business. He pushed hard in areas such as Priority Post, the post office courier service. Canada Post decided to ''take over'' the courier business in one city at a time, starting with Ottawa and moving on to other centres. Priority Post became the fastest-growing courier service in the country — a project in which managers and the letter-carriers union worked together.

Warren, however, figures that Canada Post may have lost as much as a year in pursuing the service leg of its three-way goal. He did not expect much during the first year when everyone was floundering, but kept emphasizing financial performance and good relations as the corporation matured. ''I was responsible for the overall balancing act, so I would say that that was a mistake . . . not have it pushed to demonstrate that the operating thrust of the business was correct, very solid.''

Warren admits that he has to take some of the blame as the person responsible for the whole show. ''I wasn't seeing that the operational end of the business was not coming to terms as aggressively and correctly with issues of interfacing of the plants, what was happening in the plants, the productivity associated with moving the mail, the computer applications for mail flow, and so on, the linking of the whole country to make it a single production line. That sort of stuff was not as much front and centre as a lot of other things.''

Warren says his decision to accept Lizotte was one of the biggest mistakes he made during his term as president. The two men simply did not match. ''I accept responsibility for that because I was the one hiring. We moved quickly to replace him, but the new person had to come in and start from scratch. . . . There are some students of that four-year period who say that that was the biggest single problem that we had. We lost two years, not because Lizotte was that bad as an executive or anything, but because the focus at that level in the operating end was not as sharp and tight and immediate as it needed to be.''

Lizotte says his mistake was not gritting his teeth and carrying on the fight. He admits that "fifty per cent of the reason Warren and I didn't make out was because of me. Maybe my approach with Warren was wrong. . . . Definitely Warren and I just did not see eye to eye. The chemistry between Warren and Lizotte was not good." With a little more support from his president, he thinks he might still be there.

"I'm never going to say that Warren was not a good president. He had a style that I did not like, and I had a style that he did not like. . . . I did not leave by saying bad things about Warren. I just left." That careful balance of competence and personality that Warren had sought for his top team simply wasn't there. Lizotte left for a short-lived posting as president of the national sports pool corporation before making his way back into the airline industry.

There were other casualties among the newcomers. The most spectacular crash was André Duval, who was hired from Hydro Quebec to come and put together a computerized management information system. MIS had been a buzz-word since the Kierans era, but had never really been created. In essence, the idea was to use computers to keep track of the mail system and its supporting elements. If it worked properly, managers would be able easily to tap into everything from the state of the mail system at any moment to the costs and benefits of individual contract clauses during labour negotiations.

"He got there, he was there for six months, and basically got ill. He was already sixty-one. He came back, but never really recovered, and part of the reason he got ill I think was just the enormous, unbelievable kind of challenge. The stress was just incredible on some of those guys. . . . In the MIS area, this guy's up to his waist, trying to find the stones to stand on."

Whether by chance or not, the casualties seemed to be largely francophone. At one point, the intended ratio of 25 per cent French-speaking managers dropped substantially. Warren was worried, but only for political reasons.

"It's great to talk about it in theory. I basically support it, but I think that that imposition on us, a requirement for basically 25 per cent of the executives to be francophones, when you're trying to build something quickly in response to a crisis situation at the post office, didn't help us at all. It didn't help with the main issues. And because the government held the approval card, it became a necessity and made it very, very difficult. We had a number of situations where we didn't end up with the best people in the right jobs.''

When Warren went shopping for a new chief operating officer to replace Lizotte, he got someone he liked and someone who could not only accept but thrive in Warren's structure. Don Lander had spent years as an auto executive with Chrysler Corp., and he knew how to handle a tough union in an industrial setting. Nearing retirement, he was looking for one last challenge to cap his career. He took a chance on auto-industry renegade John DeLorean, and accepted the job of running the DeLorean Motors auto factory in Belfast, Northern Ireland. When that venture collapsed, Lander was on the street again, looking for something interesting.

He is just what Warren wanted, a nuts-and-bolts executive who shuns publicity and does exactly what he is told by his superiors. On the other hand, he does not hesitate to be tough, even brutal, with those who work with him and for him. He would run the company well, but would not challenge Warren's authority.

Lander was not one to fret over whether a divisional manager was directly under him in a table of organization or not. ''Lander knew what the real issues were,'' says Warren. ''The key to the COO's job, as it was structured then, was to be able to know enough about how to take the organization in the right direction with the support of the people around him. . . . To Don's credit, he very quickly ended up becoming the number two guy in the corporation because of his leadership skills and his ability to diagnose large organizations like that. We very quickly, within three or four months, resolved some of these lists of what we were calling structural issues.''

''Lander was good at manipulating Harry and Cooke. Lizotte was not,'' said another of his colleagues more succinctly.

But if Lander's arrival in 1984 finally settled the internal feuding among top executives of Canada Post, it had not seen the end of the carnage on a different level. Warren and Ouellet had begun tangling over the chairman and members of the board of directors even before the corporation was created, and the skirmishing of 1982 erupted into full-scale war in 1983. The boardroom became a far bloodier battlefield than the executive suites of the eighth and ninth floors of the Sir Alexander Campbell Building.

14
Board
Games

■

Warren had a pretty clear idea of the kind of person he wanted as chairman of the board. Since Warren was chief executive officer, the chairman's duties would focus on keeping the board in line. He would not stick his nose into the day-to-day operations, but would, in the best private-sector tradition, back up management in its dealings with the shareholder. Warren wanted a businessman for the job, one who would only work part-time, but be there when needed to give the president extra clout when dealing with the politicians.

André Ouellet had other ideas. He didn't want a chairman who would try to exert a strong control over Warren. On that subject they agreed. Ouellet criticizes the results of later Conservative appointments as Crown corporation chairmen of people like Ron Huntington at Canada Ports Corp. and Lawrence Hanigan at Via Rail Canada Inc., who he feels tried to take over the lead role from their presidents.

But the Liberals were determined to keep a close eye on Canada Post, and that meant getting a full-time chairman. "We used to have only part-time chairmen who came in and were told by the president, We're doing this, that and that, and that's it. The guy comes once every three months and doesn't know what's going on, so the government insisted, and that was government policy, that every Crown corporation from now on was to have a permanent chairman who would be able to be there, and look at the interests of the corporation. Obviously at the same time [he would] make sure that this corporation was not putting the government in deep trouble,'' says Ouellet.

"So I told Warren, You're going to have a chairman that is not going to second-guess you, he's not going to put his nose into your day-to-day activities. He's going to look at the overall policies and report to the government. That's his job. He's going to be our eyes." Keeping tabs on Warren for the corporation's political masters was a far cry from the private-sector model, but it was very much a full-time job if the chairman was to have any hope of knowing everything that was going on in such a large and complex company.

It also meant that the government would inevitably pick someone it trusted to put politics ahead of management. Warren had accepted the fact that because he was English-speaking, the chairman would have to be francophone, but he was still pushing for a part-time businessman. He wanted Guy St. Pierre, a former Liberal Cabinet minister in the Quebec government under Robert Bourassa who went on to become president of Ogilvie Mills Ltd. But he was not available, and by the fall of 1981, Warren and Ouellet had not been able to agree on a name. The corporation had to have a chairman by proclamation day, October 16.

Then Ouellet put forward the name of René Marin, a judge whom he had already appointed in 1980 to head a commission of inquiry into the security and investigation services of the post office, which had become another sore point with the unions during Ouellet's negotiations with the CLC over the Crown corporation. Marin says he got to know Ouellet in the mid-1970s, while heading an inquiry into the Royal Canadian Mounted Police, and insists that the appointment was not a partisan one. "I have no allegiance to anyone to this date."

Warren says that when Ouellet suggested Marin, he went to have lunch with the judge, and was not impressed. He told the minister that he would still prefer a francophone businessman. But with no time left for looking, the government went ahead and picked Marin. Ouellet told Warren not to worry. Marin "would work out and wouldn't bother you," says Warren.

That, at least, proved to be the case. Marin was assigned responsibility for some of the non-controversial jobs. He looked after new stamp issues and took care of the postal museum program. He also took care of the hundreds of appeals from publishers who had been turned down in bids for second-class mailing privileges. "I would never trespass on his turf," says Marin, but would push the president to follow the government's wishes. "It's the obligation of the chairman to make sure that he who pays has a say."

When Warren had a problem with Ouellet, he usually argued his case himself, and the arguments were sometimes loud. "I had set-tos with Ouellet," says Warren. "We had a couple of shouting matches over the phone that were really something, and a couple in his office, where his secretary came running in to see if we were all right. But we also had lunch once a week and kind of liked each other."

Ouellet never minded Marin's sometimes invisible role when Warren got upset. "I think he was a very strong president, and he argued strenuously for his point of view all the time. I accepted this, and I never had any problems with this. In fact, when I hired him, he asked me: 'Are you going to run the show, or am I the one?' And I said, 'You're the one, and I'm going to get the hell out. I have the ultimate confidence in you and you're going to do it. But you're not going to be alone. It's impossible.' "

Ouellet argues that Marin was in fact the right kind of chairman for Warren. "If we would have picked up another Warren type, it would have been turmoil. Another alternative was Ray Hession [a career bureaucrat who was then president of Canada Mortgage and Housing Corp.], but Ray Hession was very much an executive officer at the CMHC, so was not really suitable for that. There would have been a clash. It would not have lasted a month, Hession and Warren."

The struggle over the choice of a chairman, however, was only the beginning of the battle of the board. The board of directors of a Crown corporation lies at the pivotal point of its dual identity as an agent of the government and a business in its own right. Choosing members for such a board is always tricky. The government often wants some related civil servants involved. It certainly wants the board to reflect Canada's cultural and regional make-up. Interest groups affected by the corporation are always clamouring for places. And the government never forgets that appointments to Crown corporation boards are handy rewards for faithful backers of the party in power.

"To his credit, Ouellet worked with me on that and shared some of the process," says Warren, but the post office's high profile made the choices tough. "This got very complicated. So we had names coming up from the regional mechanisms that had been set up across the country, the Liberal Party, and the government, and we had names coming out of the centre, and there was the business list."

Much negotiation followed, some between Warren and Ouellet, some between Ouellet and his political colleagues. Warren argued that at least three or four of the nine board members other than the chairman and himself should be solid business people.

He was partly successful. The first board included well-known names like George Cohon, president of McDonald's Restaurants of Canada Ltd., and Derek Oland, president of Moosehead Breweries Ltd., the Maritime beer-maker which had made its brew one of the leading imports in the United States market.

Warren says Cohon did a first-rate job during his three-year term, while Oland "turned out to be just a superb board member. Derek was one of those very solid guys who does his homework. He's got a set of values, and just is one of the rudders. He worked out very well." The president was also happy with a couple of other choices, including Moose Jaw, Saskatchewan, insurance broker Frank Reidy, who brought a small- and medium-sized-business outlook to the board.

Cohon and Oland are even praised by Warren's opponents on the board. "You can say what you want about George Cohon — he's anti-union and wants to operate union-free, but the son of a bitch, when it comes down to a vote, what he thinks is right and what he thinks is wrong, he'll drop down on the right side, the one with a bit of social conscience," says former board member Ron Lang of the Canadian Labour Congress. Oland and Cohon, he says, are "two good, competent, solid people, who said what they thought and many times voted with me against the rest of the board."

Other appointments, however, were recognizably political. The most prominent was Lynda Sorensen, a Liberal politician from the Northwest Territories who was also the region's representative on the board of the Consumers' Association of Canada. Warren says Sorensen was competent enough, but was undoubtedly following a political agenda at the same time.

Ouellet said her appointment was not simply partisan. "She was an outspoken woman, highly involved in consumer activities, speaking on behalf of the remote areas of the country. Yes, she happened to be a Liberal, active in Liberal circles, but I was as much impressed by her credentials [in terms of] involvement in consumer matters and a spokesman for the north."

Ouellet insists that the directors as a group formed "a top-notch board, and certainly not a board that could have been accused of being a partisan political board. . . . I always insisted on having top prominent people qualified for the job, instead of Joe Blow who happened to be president of a Liberal association or something like that."

The former postal minister says he planned to divide the eleven-person board this way: a chairman, the president, three business people, three labour representatives, and three members to speak for the public at large and its various interests in the post office.

Lang says Ouellet offered to have labour representatives on the board in the latter stages of the negotiations over the Crown corporation bill, and simply asked them how many members they would like: two, three, or even four. Ouellet says he always had three in mind.

"Eventually we sawed it off at two, but even that was a very big decision and had a lot of implications," says Warren. The postal unions themselves were not united on whether to seek representation on the board, and, as a result, the first members were picked from the labour movement at large. One was Henri Lorrain, honorary president of the Canadian Paperworkers Union, and the other was Lang from the CLC, who was used to working closely with the postal unions. Warren was not happy.

"We had on our backs already lousy service, a huge deficit, bad labour relations, far too many people, a system of plants where nobody quite knew how they worked, and you're trying to get a board of directors who will be a plus. And you find out that part of the deal — and I wasn't blind to it, I was told before accepting the job that they wanted to have some labour representation on the board — but you end up with this experiment from day one of labour participation, which makes a difference."

With members of the labour movement sitting on the board, Warren had to work out rules on keeping board discussions confidential, which led to labour complaints that the other board members didn't trust them. "That, in my view, had a profound effect on the board."

For Warren, the real blow came in the summer of 1983. Lorrain was one of the board members who had accepted appointment for two years rather than three, so that the government would be able to stagger future appointments rather than replacing the entire board at once. As Lorrain's term ran out, Warren found out that Ouellet was thinking of appointing to the board Bob McGarry, the president of the letter-carriers union.

"Ouellet didn't tell me about it for a while, and finally he just sheepishly introduced this thing, and said, I think we ought to give some thought to it. I said, For Christ's sake, we've got enough trouble without getting Bob McGarry on the board, and this was going to be two, because Lang was going to be stepping off, and they were going to put McGarry on and one other and they didn't know who the other was. And then they thought they might put three," says Warren.

"What am I going to do when I'm at the board table and I'm talking about our plans for the future with respect to letter-carrier operations? Almost every second item on the purchasing thing has to do with equipment or trucks or something or other. I mean this is just ridiculous."

"He didn't like that at all," agrees Ouellet with a laugh. "He didn't want this. He tried very much to resist this, but the difference between he and I is that I was sitting in Cabinet and he was not.''

The unions didn't even have to ask, much less twist Ouellet's arm. ''There was absolutely no deal. I repeated publicly my desire to see three union representatives on the board. Frankly, I would have liked to see Parrot on the board. I thought originally that there should be three union representatives on the board, to co-opt them and say, 'Look, you have a responsibility, you have to be part and parcel of this organization. You have asked to have it turned into a Crown corporation. You have asked to change the rules. We'll do it, but you're no longer on the outside. You have to be inside and play a role.' But in the early stage, the unions themselves didn't want to be involved.''

Lang says the original intent was to have spokesmen from the broader labour movement only at the beginning. ''It was a deferred issue. It was my understanding that at some point down the road, I would be replaced through a process of direct representation [members of the postal unions]. That was the understanding I was given by the Congress when they first put my name forward.''

Parrot still says no union involved in the post office should have members on its board of directors. He saw the danger of being co-opted, as Ouellet hoped, and prefers to operate as always without any responsibility to help run the corporation.

The letter-carriers were more pragmatic. Putting McGarry on the board gave them that much more of a chance to use the system, to collect information useful to their goals, and to block management moves that made them unhappy. ''McGarry and Findlay have their own way of sort of trying to disrupt the management system, very subtly, in a very sophisticated way, by playing one against the other. They'd achieved it in spades by getting one of them on the board. That became something else to get managed,'' says Warren.

Warren used every means he could to fight Ouellet's proposal. With some help from allies in the Privy Council Office, the postal president did get a hearing at the Cabinet committee on government operations, but his pitch did no good.

"We tried all the different ways of dealing with this thing. And really what came out of it was yes or no on McGarry. So I ended up putting together a ten-page memorandum to him and I sent a copy to the Prime Minister, just saying I think this whole thing is very destructive and you haven't thought it through. If you're going to do that, then there's some quid pro quos you've got to introduce, and I went through the whole argument," says Warren.

"Ouellet didn't like it. He was very mad when I said I was going to go to the PM. I said: 'You and I have a disagreement. How are we supposed to solve it? You win every time?' " The battle raged for eight months.

"Warren went through all sorts of contortions, rationalization, lobbying, pushing ministers over there. Every goddamn place he could push, he fought against Bob McGarry's appointment to the board. It was goddamn disgraceful sometimes to see the kind of antics that he would go through to try to block McGarry's appointment to the board. No way he wanted the man there," says Lang.

"I respected him for it, because he told me," says McGarry. "I told him I'd see him at the meeting. And he said, 'Over my dead body.' And that was probably all it was going to be. The best was sitting watching Ouellet try to console him, telling him I was going to be there."

Warren's efforts were in vain. Ouellet had his own goals and his own reasons for putting McGarry on the board. In the crunch, he proved that the politician was still boss.

McGarry felt that the balance of power on the board limited his role. "Nine to two, you can't do much damage unless you can convince some of the business people of your arguments. The only thing you couldn't say was that they didn't understand labour's position. I've had some tie votes, and the chairman pissed off having to make the deciding vote. But not that often. They usually are on side."

Warren had already run into problems with Ron Lang over the issue of confidentiality. But, then again, the rough-tongued, cigar-smoking epitome of the union man and the smooth, autocratic executive never did see eye to eye. Lang feels that the board should be in a position to tell the president what to do and not the other way around. ''In my opinion, the chief executive officer of Canada Post ought not to be a member of the board. He ought to be responsible to the board, but when he comes to the board, he should not have a vote on what the hell he's bringing to the board. To me, that's a conflict.''

As far as Lang was concerned, Warren simply manipulated the board to get his way. He and his executives would show up for every meeting and took part freely in the discussion. ''The chairman recognizes them before he recognizes members of the board to speak. I think to myself, What the hell is this? Is this a meeting of officers of the corporation, or is this a meeting of the board of directors? Where does the administration start and the board policy decision-making begin? It was so blurred in there. The administration ran the goddamn place as if there was no board. The board, as far as they were concerned, was quite irrelevant.''

Marin, he says, proved no barrier to Warren's dominance. ''Michael Warren would manipulate him, and when he said, Jump, René would say, How high? and When can I come back down?''

Lizotte, however, says any co-operation between Marin and Warren was only on the surface. ''His relations with Warren were not good. I don't know why, but we could tell. . . . There was a war between Marin and Warren.''

McGarry says that whenever they disagreed, Warren always came out on top. ''Whenever it became a battle between the president and the chairman, [Marin] just took the side of least resistance. You could make all the arguments you like and the chairman might even agree with you outside of the meeting, but once it got in the meeting, you just lost it.''

Once again McGarry thinks it was a question of personalities. ''It was a matter of, not size, but who had the biggest ego. I think that one guy kept saying 'I'm the chairman' and the other guy kept saying 'I'm the president.' They both walked around with the title, but Warren ran the corporation.''

Marin, who felt McGarry's appointment was good for the corporation overall, says he and Warren would work out any disagreements before going to the board. ''We never split on a board decision once. . . . My chief executive officer, I have to support. We had no choice but to be friends.''

Lizotte says that whatever Marin's qualifications and the reasons for his appointment, the chairman worked long hours at the office just like everyone else. ''Maybe he practised his putting, but he was there. . . . He really tried to do a job.''

Lang also criticizes Marin for not protecting his board members from management's attacks. ''I know he didn't protect this one, protect me from himself and other members of the board. I was attacked from the day I went in there until the day I left. I was attacked for having a conflict of interest because I was a labour representative. I was attacked because in their view I broke the confidentiality rules. I made it clear when I was there, Ouellet made it clear when I was there, that when I was appointed to that board, I was representing labour's interests on that board. I didn't have to apologize to any goddamn soul in this world for being appointed on that basis. I told them, You represent no one on this board, you only represent yourselves. I have a constituency. I represent more members in Canada Post than all of you put together. And I speak for that interest.''

Lang would sit down with the postal unions before each board meeting. They would run through their current list of problems, and he would talk about the board's agenda. ''I wouldn't give them the documents, but I would talk about them, and say, Look, these questions are coming up at the board. Where the hell do we stand on these kinds of things? And having got the feedback from them, I would then go into the board, and these are the positions that I would take at the board.''

Lang says Warren was never able to understand how Lang could both be a conscientious board member and work for the postal unions. ''Day after day after day I was accused of breaking confidentiality. I said I'm governed by the Canada Business Corporations Act, and the Canada Post Corporation Act, and my duty is to represent and make decisions in the best interests of the corporation as I see them. Now, if I think it's in the interests of the unions and the corporation to have certain information, then I'm going to give them that information. That's my role on this board.''

The most explosive fight between Warren and Lang over confidentiality came during André Lizotte's final days. Lang says he went to bat for Lizotte at the board after hearing of his troubles. "Nothing happens over there that the unions don't know about, sooner than anybody on the damn board knows, and I had a personal relationship with André Lizotte. We were damned good friends. I could fight with him, and I did, but that didn't make any difference. I respected him, he respected me and he respected the unions." Lizotte, he says, "got one royal shafting, one Jesusly royal shafting from Warren."

Lizotte says he had tried to cultivate good relations with the unions, and that led some of his colleagues to accuse him of "playing footsie with the unions. . . . I treated all the unions the same. I was straightforward. They came into my office any time they wanted to. There was nothing under the carpet."

But Lizotte says he never told the unions about his decision. "I had informed Warren I was leaving. And we had a meeting with the unions with Cooke and the rest of the guys. And believe you me, I had never spoken with the unions. But at that meeting, I think it was Ron Lang who said to Warren at the meeting that the unions could not understand why Cooke and Harry were not responsible to me. . . . You can imagine the atmosphere after the meeting."

Warren seemed to think that Lizotte was just sowing confusion in his wake, and that Lang had spilled the beans to Lizotte, passing on the board's discussions about Canada Post's problems with its chief operating officer.

Lang says that at the next board meeting, "every member of the board, the chairman, and Warren went after me and attacked me for two hours and tried to make me admit that I had gone to see Lizotte and told him what went on at the board meeting. I hadn't, and I said that I hadn't. I said that was not my affair, but I said I'll protect him at the board, and I'll tell you that I think you're a rotten bunch of bastards at the board for what you're doing, but that's as far as that one goes. To me that's just a question of clean conscience. But it's a funny thing when all the business people around the board won't protect a chief operating officer because it's up to a labour representative to do it. It's a question of fair play, that's all it is."

Lang was so upset that he actually wrote to Ouellet to complain. "One of the toughest things I've ever done was to sit on a board as a labour representative. You're not accepted."

If Lang felt that he was not accepted, Warren prepared an even chillier reception for McGarry. When the leader of the letter-carriers arrived, "then the board really had to change the way it operated," says Warren. Even basic functions of the board such as talking about the corporate plan were affected.

"You're not going to talk with the unions about exactly how many people are going to be laid off in certain areas until you get to the point where you formally consult about that. So when we presented the corporate plan [to the board] when McGarry was there, I had to kind of stop it at a certain level of detail, so the board gets denied a certain level of detail."

When Warren tried to arrange special rules for the labour representatives, McGarry put up a stink. That forced Warren and Marin to set up a committee of the board, without McGarry or Lang, to deal with all matters of labour relations and personnel.

Warren admits that McGarry's presence helped in some ways. "It acted to some extent in my favour, ironically, because they had to give me disproportionate support in front of McGarry. So every time McGarry raised a question, they'd let me answer. Sometimes others felt that there were issues that they wanted to raise about our stewardship, about how the place was running, but they would sort of hold back. They would come and see me afterwards, or they'd see me at lunch, because they'd say, I don't want to raise this with McGarry around."

And if Warren was worried about leaks through the labour pipeline, he was not above using it himself as a disinformation device, dropping misleading hints about management's goals and bottom line in labour talks.

None the less, Warren is convinced that McGarry's appointment was a fatal blow for the board. Since his decision put politics ahead of the corporation's needs, Ouellet had "undermined the confidence of the rest of the board that the government was really serious about Canada Post."

The decision on McGarry left both managers and board members shaking their heads, says Warren. "How can we win on this broader issue if we have a shareholder who puts something like

direct labour representation ahead of effective functioning of the
board to make a little short-term gain from a press release? It
can be powerfully negative. . . . After a while, we ended up
managing it, but it's the kind of thing that makes the private-
sector people who came in really wonder. It makes them cynical
or it makes them frightened.

"It was a small thing in some respects . . . but it leaves a little
scar. It was such a political thing, it was so crass, that the board
was never quite the same. What wasn't quite the same was their
ownership of the corporation.

"It wasn't as serious as the problems we had for months
trying to get the Conservative government to come to terms
with this. That was very serious stuff. [But this] left one with the
feeling that the shareholder can do anything he wants."

For Warren, greater frustrations lay ahead. In the meantime,
he could not afford to sit and sulk in his office over Canada Post's
internal troubles and the foibles of its minister. Outside his door,
unions, customers, and critics were vying for his attention. And
in his strategy for winning the public battles over the post office,
he had put himself on the front line.

15
Warren
Peace

■

To the old-style bureaucrats of the post office, the idea of baring their collective chest in public was both novel and distasteful. When Warren listened to their plans at Gray Rocks, he found plenty of useful bits and pieces, but he says their overall approach did not seem to recognize the chance for a new start that the corporation gave them.

"It was an approach that was very close to the vest and would continue to be close to the vest," he says. "When I started asking them about sharing some of the plans with the unions, that was one of the most sensitive issues at the meeting. I think I really frightened them."

For Warren, openness — or at least the appearance of openness — was not merely a good idea. It was the only approach that gave him a chance of staying on top of the shaky Canada Post raft without being up-ended by one of the circling sharks he called "stakeholders" in the post office. His strategy for keeping the post office afloat on the uncertain voyage to its promised land was a matter of feeding enough tidbits to the public, the politicians, the customers, his managers, and the unions to keep them all mollified, if not sated. It was a plan driven by public relations — a process he called "managing the stakeholders".

"One of the dilemmas from the beginning was that there are so many stakeholders surrounding Canada Post. And they have some quite different interests and they don't necessarily have

very much patience with the interests of some other stakeholders. And to try to get a rough consensus of all those stakeholders
— I don't mean an absolute one in every detail, but a broad
consensus of those stakeholders as to direction, priorities,
emphasis — is a very difficult chore.

"And I felt that it was better to try to do that. So use the
media, use lots of meetings with your major stakeholder groups,
with the unions, with Cabinet, with all the stakeholders, and try
to get them to see the issues, try to get them publicized, and
somehow out of that try to lead a consensus which says, this
year, here's the balancing act. *You* don't like it and *you* don't like
it but can you live with it? And that was the strategy."

The danger of such an approach is that it involves promises,
very public promises. Canadians are very good at remembering
promises that relate to the post office. "Some people say that I
would have been a lot better off not to have spent so much time
externalizing all of this and simply to have got on with it and had a
style that created less expectations." The most dangerous
promise of all was that of financial results. Promising to break
even within five years set up both expectations in the public and
fears in the unions.

The process began with the big jump in the price of a stamp,
because resistance to higher prices would increase as time passed.
"What I was aiming for in the last couple of years of the five-year
mandate was to have almost no price increases and all of the
work towards break-even coming from improved productivity.
And service through all this was to get increasing attention."

Putting the deficit up front was the only way of telling the
unions that labour costs had to be controlled. Controlling wage
rates and boosting productivity was the only way to give better
service later without raising stamp prices. Public relations would
have to fill the gap between what the public wanted and what he
felt was possible.

"That was the original order of priorities: deficit, labour
relations, and service, the bottom-line orientation being the most
important element for the start-up period. That doesn't mean
you didn't do anything about the other two, you did a lot about
them, but the deficit reduction was the thing, you had to say,
things that you did had to answer that all the time."

Put another way, the process of managing the stakeholders was one of giving them attention they did not expect to make up for the fact that better service would take time. Reporters found that not only could they get access to Warren for quotes, but he would even seek them out for lengthy interviews. Consumer groups and major customers alike were courted for their opinions and suggestions. Letters might lag as before, but flip charts and fast talk gave that crucial feeling of progress.

He did not take long to come up with a seemingly bottomless pit of facts to convince the sceptical. Hugh Mullington, a veteran of years of dealing with the post office at Treasury Board, remembers that when Warren was new to the job, he asked for a chat. "I brought a briefcase full of stuff. I was prepared to be totally open and candid with the guy, tell him exactly what the Treasury Board's concerns were and why.

"I think I said about three words in the conversation. It was a sermon from the mount and I went away shaking my head. I was prepared to tell this guy everything he wanted to know and he didn't ask any questions. The trouble was that it was all conventional wisdom. He had all the solutions. This was his first week on the job and I didn't think he knew the problems yet."

As the Warren whirlwind of publicity spun across the countryside, the president rather than the post office itself became the centre of attention. That was exactly his intention. The strategy for the first couple of years was a matter of "using me as a means of buying time. Part of my job in addition to interacting with the shareholder and making sure we kept our priorities clear was to be out communicating with the key constituencies and buying some time for the corporation."

While Warren may have been director, producer, and star, his good initial reviews were due to a carefully picked handful of people playing supporting roles. These people, concentrated in the president's office, helped him look good and sound good.

Warren began building his own office almost as soon as he accepted the job in the spring. His first move was to find someone with good contacts in the Liberal government. Warren, as a long-time deputy minister in the Ontario government, was well connected with the provincial Conservatives, but he did not know Ottawa or the people in the ruling party. "He wanted a Liberal," says Jonathan Goldbloom, the man Warren picked as his executive assistant.

Goldbloom had all the right political credentials. He was an active Liberal himself, and had worked for former secretary of state John Roberts. His family was Liberal: his father, Victor Goldbloom, had been an influential Cabinet minister in the Quebec provincial government. The younger Goldbloom had a knack for getting to know people, and was well plugged in to the party at both the provincial and federal levels.

Warren picked up Goldbloom's name during the spring of 1981, and looked Goldbloom over during a dinner one night at Toronto's plush La Scala restaurant. He liked what he saw, and hired him. Goldbloom says his job was to make sure that the highest-profile stranger in town met the right people.

The postal president says Goldbloom soon showed that he could do more than that. He may have been well connected in the Liberal Party before, but he quickly developed a network of contacts within and around the post office as well. If Warren was off to do an open-line radio show in Vancouver, Goldbloom managed to find someone in the Vancouver union local to tell him what sort of questions the union was likely to toss onto the airwaves. When Warren left one of his many meetings, Goldbloom often stuck around to talk to people and sort out some of the practical matters that stemmed from the meeting's decisions. "He was somebody who could help me find out what was going on, good, bad, or indifferent, both inside and outside," says Warren. "He was an exceptional eyes and ears as a senior advisor."

His other job was to control the flow of information to the politicians. "Political interference was directed at the president's office so that managers could get on with their jobs," Goldbloom says. "I always tried to prevent the minister's office from talking to anyone but me. It was an advantage being a known Liberal, but I always had a Tory in my office."

Goldbloom's alter ego in the president's office — a known Tory — was Ted Ball. He had worked for Ontario Cabinet minister and later provincial Tory leader Larry Grossman. Goldbloom says he loved working with Ball, whom he describes as "a little off-the-wall but always coming up with ideas".

In the early days, Ball was Warren's shadow as he traipsed through meetings and interviews. If Warren stumbled over a fact or fell short of an example to illustrate his point — which happened rarely — Ball was at his elbow with the missing bits.

Ball's real job was back at the office. He was the man responsible for Warren's speeches, delivered regularly around the country and distributed with vigour to all those Canada Post wanted to reach. "What I needed there was somebody who could organize speeches, take dry, difficult planning scenarios and convert them into punchy pie charts that would work on television or in a roomful of people," says Warren.

The other part of that job was as Warren's communications strategist. He had to figure out what was going on in the corporation and how to present it in public. He introduced a new level of discipline to Canada Post's communications by looking ahead six months and figuring out what Warren should be talking about then.

In that function, he really reported to the third key player on Warren's communications team, André Villeneuve, a smooth but jolly professional who projects the air of a beardless Santa Claus in a business suit. Warren recruited him as his vice-president for communications from Bell Canada, where he had plenty of experience at coaxing employees to think of their gargantuan employer as Ma Bell rather than "ma boss".

Villeneuve, unlike many communications vice-presidents, sat on the senior management committee alongside Lizotte, Harry, and Cooke. While he was tuned in to the potential for marketing and advertising outside the corporation, he would make his mark on the communications efforts within Canada Post.

Dealing with outsiders remained very much the preserve of the president's office. Warren says that in Canada Post's first year, he was getting more mail than the Prime Minister's Office. "We were doing about 5,000 a month for a while. It was just incredible. And we eventually had to get the whole thing computerized, and we had eleven or twelve people that did nothing else but deal with my correspondence, which is part of the outgrowth of that open approach."

The surge of mail going to Michael Warren also reflected Ouellet's attitude to the new corporation. The minister had set it up. Now he wanted to be free of it, or at least divorced from its problems. "We told Warren, You're going to make your plan, you're going to make your recommendations," says Ouellet. "Obviously, you won't take me by surprise, you'll let us know, but if we think it's unacceptable, we'll tell you. But if it is, I'm not going to announce it, you're going to announce your plan . . . and you'll defend it."

As far as Ouellet was concerned, problems with the mail were now problems for Canada Post Corp. and its new president. "If you have a problem with your luggage, you don't write the minister of Transport. You call an agent of Air Canada and tell him, Find my luggage. The same thing with the mail: If your letter is lost or a parcel is lost or delayed, don't write the minister, write the company and complain directly to the company."

The same rules also applied to the unions, which had been accustomed to ready access to the postmaster general, especially under Ouellet. "The creation of the corporation clearly established that from now on, the employees were dealing with the Crown corporation, period. The political intervention was finished," he says. "Although the union came to me on numerous occasions, complaining that they were not happy, I always said, Look, you wanted this Crown corporation, go back and see Mr. Warren. I never accepted to be involved personally in disputes. If the union leaders wanted to meet me, I would receive them and listen to them, but I never put myself again in the ring."

The intent of Ouellet's political strategy was to put himself in a position where he could claim credit if the Crown corporation worked, but avoid the fallout if it blew up. Events did not always work out that way. Warren had similar goals for his own image.

The two came into direct conflict over the announcement of the huge jump in the price of a first-class stamp, from 17 cents to 30 cents, at the beginning of 1982. Both the government and the corporation agreed that the increase was needed if the five-year plan was to be anything more than pulp fiction. Indeed, the rate hike was supposed to have taken place before the Crown corporation was set up.

But while Warren would prove willing to take credit for the sudden drop in the Canada Post deficit that followed, he was not anxious to be tarred as the villain by consumers. Ouellet wanted Warren to hold the press conference to announce the rate increase. Warren wanted Ouellet to do it. In the end, an angry Ouellet had to join Warren at Ottawa's national press theatre and they made the announcement together.

When it came to patronage, Goldbloom and his team did their best to soothe the politicians without giving away much more than explanations. "But that didn't stop the pressure. It sort of nullified it for a while," says Warren. "And Ouellet was not beyond exercising, as some other ministers and members did, the phone call or the 'Gee, Michael, why can't we get this done any more. It looks to me as though it's needed.' I used to see a lot of MPs."

Sometimes the politicians were looking not for handouts but for better service to quiet the complaints of their constituents. Those Warren had to handle carefully. It is not easy to explain to a politician that, yes, a certain block of houses will now get door-to-door service by letter-carrier after months of waiting, but that service would still stop at a certain street. This kind of "very nitty-gritty political stuff" would become an increasing problem as time went on and a new batch of inexperienced MPs came into the House of Commons after the 1984 election.

In the early years, however, Warren's domineering approach to public relations simply overwhelmed politicians who had been used to getting no information from a troublesome institution. He refused to feed them contracts, so he stuffed words and charts and figures down their throats until they choked and admitted that he was right. The abrupt new tactics forced them to pause. Much as they wanted to solve political problems, they did not want to be caught looking like obstacles to success.

Warren sometimes went too far, and antagonized some politicians who simply felt baffled by the barrage of facts and figures. They were rightly suspicious of their reliability and frustrated when they could not penetrate the smokescreen. Part of Warren's communications strategy was to make sure that all queries were intercepted by his office. He alone spoke for the corporation.

With the politicians contained, the media marvelling, and postal customers mollified by a series of measures to show some small but quick improvements in postal service, the toughest challenge lay inside the corporation with its experienced and wary unions.

This is where Villeneuve came into his own. Despite his years in the big-corporation surroundings of Bell Canada, "the creative juices hadn't been squeezed out of him, and he understood how you could go out and work with something like Employees' Week and end up with more good will out of that than getting ten minutes on national television with ads."

Warren assigned Villeneuve to mastermind what he calls "the hearts and minds war". Essentially, the corporation had to convince workers that the people and the attitudes at the top had changed for the better. "We had to win the hearts and minds of a bigger number of employees who essentially had looked around at all the players and said, Who has the best chance of winning? And they quite consistently voted for Parrot and McGarry and the other union leaders who looked like they were in the best position."

Warren and Villeneuve looked for other ways to bypass the union structure and its isolationist leaders. "You start it with a Christmas card to every employee at their home, that was in December of '81. I got hell from a couple of union leaders for sending Christmas cards to the employees," says Warren. "And to get the Christmas cards to our employees' homes was an unbelievable [problem]. We didn't have the home addresses of all the employees. If you took the temporary, part-time people as well as the permanent, you might have 60,000 people. . . . It was absolutely scandalous, the basic level of preparation."

Villeneuve's communications team started advertising the things that were going well, both inside and outside the corporation. He used the creation of the Crown corporation as an excuse for holding celebrations like Employees' Week, and used the corporation to raise money for charities, which CUPW had abandoned with the rise of the militant ethic.

Communications plans by themselves were nothing new. John Paré had been a big fan of the technique, and the post office department tried several approaches in its latter years. "Cascade", for instance, was used to spread the word about a particular issue. A basic package of information would be put together at the top level. Each manager would go through the material with a small group of people under him. Each of them would turn around and pass the message on to some of their underlings. The chain would continue down to include workers on the plant floor.

But, aside from the usual union hostility, these methods were not always objective. In a briefing to Ouellet in 1980, for instance, postal officials noted that the Cascade approach had been used successfully to spread information about the issues during contract bargaining "to correct inaccurate or incomplete information" from the unions. Goldbloom says the effectiveness of those old communications tools had been destroyed because they had been used for such partisan purposes.

In practical terms, there was little regular communication between the corporation and its workers. On the bulletin boards in the plants and postal stations, "you'd see notifications and all that stuff from the vice-presidents of the unions telling them all about Blue Cross and telling them about this, that, and the other thing. And nothing from management. Management didn't even talk to itself," says Cooke.

On the plant floors, the union communications network was, as always, more efficient than management's. If a worker wanted to know something, he asked his steward, because the stewards were the first to know or could find out the fastest. And the union, of course, coloured the information with its views of its importance and consequences for the workers.

"The union always beats us to the punch," the supervisors complained to Warren. The new president figured there were ways to deal with that. As Villeneuve sat in on the senior management meetings, he was always trying to figure out when and how he could tell employees — through the corporate chain of command. "I mean, the supervisors almost died across the country when we had some big combination — we had a rate deferral, we were not going to have a rate increase — they got that all in hand before we let it out. We didn't make it every time, but they started getting the information maybe half the time ahead of anybody else. That was very important."

Parrot told Warren that CUPW felt that the postal president should not even be trying to talk to his union members, that if he wanted to pass a message on to the workers, the union would take care of it. Warren went right ahead with his communications plans.

"When you put things in magazines and send them into the homes of 65,000 people, that was the sort of thing that Parrot didn't want me to do and McGarry didn't want me to do." He says eventually it started to loosen the union choke-hold on the flow of information. Warren and his managers had their ideas about how to save the post office, and the unions had different ideas, but at least ordinary workers were getting a chance to listen to both sides.

Even when the intentions were good, the means sometimes caused confusion and outrage. Warren still recalls vividly his first meeting with Parrot after he moved in as president. Parrot came into his office with one of his union vice-presidents, refused an offer of coffee, and started talking. "He just dealt with me as if I was a person that was completely without value, just a total antithesis of what he thought was useful."

The focus of Parrot's anger that day was a small colouring-book. "And he threw this in front of me, and he said: 'Take a look at that. Take a look at that, Warren.' So I looked at this thing. 'The management of this place make that and give that to all my members to go home and act like fools and to have their children colour the mistakes of their parents.' What this thing was was a colouring-book for the first Employee Week in the province of Quebec, which is where it started. And the colouring-book was pictures of postal employees having different accidents, slipping on the ice and all that sort of stuff. It was designed to get the safety message into the house, so the kid would actually colour this thing, and say, What's happening here, Dad, what is this about? And there were about five of the most common accidents at the post office.

"So Parrot was incensed, and the only point I could see was, 'I think it's a good idea, but maybe they ought to show them doing things safely rather than unsafely. But what's wrong with letting the children . . . ?'

" 'We'll worry about the children,' cut in Parrot. 'Don't you worry about the children. You let us worry about the children, all right? You let us worry about the employees as well. You've done nothing for them.' "

Two or three years later, Warren says he was able to sit down and have a meeting with Parrot and other CUPW leaders and talk about the deficit or problems in the plants without an explosion or the union people walking out. "For about a year, for every hour I met, at least half an hour dwelt on the past, who was wrong, the damage that had been done. I used to kid them after a while and say, Look, we're doing pretty well now, we've been here half an hour and we've got another half an hour to go, can we turn the past off now?

"So those early meetings were meetings that left you with the impression that maybe the rancour and the ill feelings and just the hatred was so deep that there was no hope of ever bringing this together, and what you had to do was become an expert in conflict. I thought early in the game that there was going to be very little chance of setting up something akin to normality in dealing with these unions and therefore in addition to raising the prices early, maybe I had to get this whole labour-relations scene into some kind of an early climax and deal with it that way, because there was no other way to deal with it."

Ouellet, however, was not interested in confrontation, and neither was Warren. He showed that in his dealings with the supervisors, who were also unionized. One Friday night he held a meeting with supervisors in Vancouver to talk about how the corporation could help them. The Vancouver local was known to be tough and to have strong ideological leanings going back to its leading role in the first illegal strike in 1965.

At first, says Warren, the supervisors who stood up were just shaking. "If we're going to be down on the floor we need a baseball bat or something, I mean we're being threatened physically; my car last week, the aerial was broken off and the windshield broken in and I know exactly why." In effect, the intimidated supervisors were asking Warren for physical help. "We don't control that floor, they do. So what we need are billy sticks, or we need some security people down there or some goddamn guns, that's what we need. So let's quit pissing around." That was their message.

After a while, Warren asked: "Are you telling me that you want to be custodians of these people, that we're going to have armed guards down there and you're going to be with them?

That's what you want to do?'' They got into a talk about how supervisors managed in other tough industrial plants. Why couldn't postal supervisors do the same thing?

The response was that union stewards were taking workers off on weekends to teach them about the contract and how to enforce it. The average worker knew more about the agreement than did the supervisors. By the time the meeting ended a couple of hours later, Warren had offered them the same deal that the unions gave their members.

"We put together at that meeting the outline of a supervisory course that eventually 6,000 people were put through. The essence of the course was designed right there. They fought like hell to get themselves trained, to get themselves through the system, and that worked pretty well. And it has also modified the balance of power on the shop floor.''

Training was extended into middle management. Managers were sent off for an intensive two-week course to help them deal with the workers on the floor. "They were astounded that we would take them, and put them into a training mode, in a motel, and pay their accommodations and their meals, and have an instructor that would talk to them and tell them what co-operation was,'' says Cooke.

Eventually, Warren pulled back from many of his direct dealings with the unions. As the honeymoon with the public ground to an end, his public-relations talents were needed elsewhere. The hearts-and-minds war was left to the new team of labour-relations professionals under Stewart Cooke.

One of Cooke's first moves was to try and force the unions to deal with management, rather than go looking for sympathetic ears on Parliament Hill. "Tell ya what, Bob baby, you're going to deal with me and my guys. Nobody else,'' he would say to McGarry. "And they got to know that. I never resented that the union leaders go and try to lobby. That's his goddamn job. But he shouldn't resent it if I trip him as he goes by me.''

It is a typical Cooke sally. He is no stranger either to Crown corporations or to tough unions. A compact, squarely built man with neatly trimmed white hair, he still bristles with energy and moves quickly and abruptly. In an interview, he tends to talk into his hands when he is being careful, but becomes expansive and gestures emphatically when he gets excited. His carefully controlled facial expression disguises an underlying tension. He can't sit still for long. Every now and then he jumps up from the couch and paces back and forth.

It is a manner clearly shaped by years at the bargaining table. There are words and tones for every occasion, but meaning is sometimes buried by manner. Perhaps the mood is shaped by the room. By a fluke of booking, we are talking in Room 291 of the Château Laurier in Ottawa. Two years earlier, the same room was Canada Post's control centre for its contract talks with the postal workers. The rich wallpaper was covered by endless sheets of computer printouts, the furniture scattered and buried under coffee cups. Now there is once again elegance and order, but the memories remain.

Ironically, Stewart Cooke came to Canada Post to get away from high-pressure haggling before it killed him. Cooke had worked for Canadian National Railways for thirty-seven years, starting off as a railway telegrapher, next a station agent, and then a train dispatcher. Then CN noticed that three-quarters of its middle managers were going to retire within five years and started a crash program to train lower-level people. Cooke was picked for the program and went through a series of jobs in various divisions, where he used to swear at the restrictions imposed by the labour-relations people. So CN made him assistant vice-president for labour relations and then vice-president. "I was eight years in that job. There were a lot of accomplishments in that period, but it was a killer. All my predecessors ended up with health problems. I wasn't about to have that happen. . . . I was determined I was going to leave the goddamn job." He vowed to get out as soon as he hit fifty-five, when he could collect his full pension. He says his bosses didn't believe him.

That all changed in September 1981, during a stay at the Château Laurier. He got a phone call in his room from Pat Rourke of the head-hunting firm Rourke Bourbonnais and Associates. Rourke wanted Cooke to suggest some people who might be suitable for a job he had to fill. Cooke asked if he was far away. "He said no, he could be there in five minutes, which told me he was in the lobby." Cooke had a lunch date in fifteen minutes, but told him: "If you can be here in five, I'll give you five." Within three minutes Cooke had figured out what the head-hunter was up to. "You didn't come here to get names. You came here to see what I looked like." Rourke agreed, and then told him the job was with Canada Post.

Cooke said he was interested. He wanted out of CN, and the challenge intrigued him. He had done well in labour relations at the railway because he knew the company inside out. He wondered if he could do the same in a new company. Although he knew the postal unions would be tough to handle, he figured that as executive vice-president, responsible for personnel as well as labour relations, he would be senior enough to stay away from the bargaining table. "I swore that never again would I go to a negotiating table." Political events put those plans to rout.

The government's "6 and 5" program for restraining inflation made that a forlorn hope. By effectively legislating wage rates — as well as the price of a stamp — the program put real contract talks on hold, and some of the issues that might have been handled during the corporation's honeymoon sat and festered. Some unions fell behind others simply by an accident of timing: some settled before the legislation took effect, others got caught.

By mid-1984, every union in the post office was ready to talk at once. Cooke had hired plenty of people in his labour-relations shop, but there were not enough to go around. He had to deal with about a dozen negotiating tables, including the big ones: the postal workers and the letter-carriers. "We recognized that we were going to have to pool our resources. So I got the short straw and I got the CUPW."

Through months of contract talks, he found himself doing daily tours of downtown Ottawa. "There were two negotiations going on at the Delta hotel, there was one going on at the Westin hotel, I had a crew down here in the Four Seasons, I had a crew over here in the Skyline, and I was here," in the Château Laurier. "We negotiated night and day, and I had to keep track of all of these, and I would start out here at eleven or twelve o'clock at night and go to each of these places. It goddamn near killed me."

The talks were a new experience for both sides. "They did seem willing to negotiate. They never did that before," says one union official. To the postal workers, used to facing a stolid group of bureaucrats, Cooke was something completely different. "This guy flies into the hotel suite, plumps himself down, peels an orange, and says, 'Let's make a deal.' What a character."

"CUPW had never negotiated in their life, because they knew they were doomed to failure," says Cooke. "I felt that we had to build bridges of trust."

Jean-Claude Parrot says having people on the other side of the table with the power to make decisions made a real difference. "In 1985, that one, there have been real negotiations, and this is why we were capable of settling. Because if the other side negotiates, we're going to get down to the real issues at some moment or the other. It's when they don't negotiate that you just keep your position, you don't move."

The combination of Canada Post's new status as a corporation and the effects of the recession made the postal workers realistic about money. "They knew it could not be the big issue," says Parrot. With settlements all around them at 3 per cent, a big wage hike was clearly impossible. Instead, they went after other issues.

That suited Canada Post just fine. Its major objective was to control the labour costs that still eat up more than two-thirds of its budget. The corporation had settled on a dental and vision care plan as its major concession, and most of the talk was over work rules. The corporation wanted more freedom to deal with lurches in the flow of mail without incurring big overtime bills. The union was looking for job security.

"They settled on that without a strike because they knew we were strong with the public on that," says Parrot. "The issue of more service that creates jobs, the public is not against that idea. The government talks about creating jobs all the time, and here we are, offering a possibility of reducing the deficit of Canada Post and providing more service and creating jobs. My God, if it's possible to do that, why not?"

Canada Post did not have any problem with granting a job-security clause. "I think at the beginning there were tremendous suspicions about that, that no union should talk about a layoff," says Cooke. "Jesus Christ, you have to be practical. . . . [But] I believe sincerely that you should be able to have a no-layoff policy if you've looked at your attrition rate and it's sufficient to carry it through. And we did.''

Attrition rates were down to about 5 per cent. Even at that rate, much lower than the triple-digit turnover in some plants during the 1970s, the age distribution of the employees meant that the corporation could tell that about 8,000 employees were due to leave over the next four years or so. ''A lot of people got mad at us. The government said we shouldn't have a no-layoff policy. They never looked at it. We managed attrition.'' Canada Post also used ''buyouts'' to get rid of another 3,000 administrative jobs.

If the sheer number of talks stretched managers to the limit, they were working with unaccustomed authority, and they had the tools they needed to compete with the unions' formidable research efforts. Cooke says that, for the first time, postal negotiators could call up on the computer the costs and benefits of any wrinkle the union might suggest, and figure out, for instance, whether adding five minutes to a break would be more costly than a few more cents an hour.

His people had also studied the past pattern of union demands and moves during negotiations. ''We had our game plans and our strategies laid on. We actually plotted the CUPW negotiations, and we missed her by three days. Right through, all the way along, what would happen, and we missed it by three days. Not bad.'' The postal negotiators surprised even themselves.

In the end, mediator Stanley Hartt was able to bring the two sides together for a deal in March 1985, just in time for Prime Minister Brian Mulroney's national economic summit, where Mulroney needed both union good will to create the image he was seeking of a Canada united in pursuit of growth, and the presence of Hartt as chairman of the televised conference.

Canada Post was able to trumpet the progress it had made in restraining postal wages: an average of 2.9 per cent a year, below even the shrunken rate of inflation. The union, however, had both guarantees of no layoffs during the pursuit of break-even and pledges that Canada Post would create jobs in new areas.

Yet even as the labour talks seemed to bear fruit, Warren was running into trouble on the public-relations front. Canadians were proving to be a tougher sell than he had expected. Warren might put in long days of talking and planning, but he simply could not deal with all the stakeholders and what they wanted and expected. "There really was a need to have about four of the Warrens out talking all the way around," says Cooke.

The strategy of buying time could only work if the corporation did start to produce results. Warren's brave promises came back to haunt him. When his currency ran out, his stakeholders proved all too reluctant to lend him the support he needed to buy more time.

"I think the government felt that it had got rid of it, this tar baby, and therefore everything was going to be wonderful," says Stewart Cooke. "And that's bullshit. Because the biggest goddamn miscalculation ever made was the size of the job to be done and how long it would take. . . . The expectations of all parties got up too high, too soon."

16
Licking
the Deficit

■

It was Canada Post's first big gaffe. In the legalistic prose of the *Canada Gazette*, the new Crown corporation let Canadians know what it thought a letter was. And it told them that once the government accepted its definition, it would enforce its monopoly.

The definition left few loopholes. The new regulations, published July 3, 1982, said a letter was "any available matter in any form, the mass of which, if any, does not exceed 500 grams, whether or not enclosed in an envelope, and intended for transmission to any destination or delivery to any addressee." The list of exceptions was short.

At first, post office spokesmen were blunt about the extent of the new definition. A heating-oil company could bring a bill at the same time it delivered oil, but other utilities such as natural gas, hydro, cable television, and phone companies could not use their employees to bring their bills to customers. A secretary could take a memo down the hall within a company, but would break the law if he or she passed on a written message to someone in another company, even if it was in the same building. A department-store delivery man could bring a person's bill with goods being delivered, but the customer would not be able to hand over a cheque on the spot or to go to the store and pay by cheque there. Even walking up and down the street to deliver party invitations to friends would have been illegal. All sorts of increasingly popular habits like paying bills at bank branches or automatic teller machines would have been ruled out.

While admitting that there was "a grey area that the courts would have to define," a Canada Post spokesman at the time confirmed that a person who took his cheque to the store to pay a bill would be "clearly carrying something that Parliament intended to be sent by mail. . . . We fully expect [customers] will adjust their activities to conform."

People who broke the law by violating the tightened monopoly could be sent to jail for as much as five years. Even the post office admitted that trying to enforce the law would be impossible. "You're not going to see any kind of post office police hanging out in the shopping centre to see if you hand-deliver your bill payment," an official said.

Within the sixty days after publication that are set aside for comment on proposed regulations, the government had received more than 300 letters and briefs. By October, Canada Post settled for less. Personal correspondence like Christmas cards and invitations delivered "occasionally" by a friend were excluded. So were cheques and other forms of paying bills. People like plumbers and electricians were allowed to leave a bill at the house at the time they did their work. The post office had tried to reach too far and been slapped down.

Canada Post was not the first to try and stretch its monopoly. In 1973, for instance, the United States Postal Service proposed new regulations to expand the definition of a letter to include all tangible, hard-copy messages except unaddressed circulars. The definition included magnetic discs and tapes holding computer data.

Canada, like other industrialized countries, has largely stuck to threats of court action rather than risk the outcome of a trial. In recent years, other governments have also conceded that the monopoly should not cover services that the post office won't provide. In particular, they have granted exceptions to the monopolies for time-sensitive documents carried for a high price. Although post offices have since entered the high-speed courier business themselves, it has become a booming sector of its own. The lack of reliable postal service has been a major factor.

For Canada Post, the attempt to tighten the monopoly was its second move in a year to boost its revenues. It came on top of the 76-per-cent jump in the price of a first-class stamp in January. The first was more effective in the short term, but the combination ensured some rapid progress on the road toward break-even.

In its first full year of operation, the fiscal period ending March 31, 1983, Canada Post drained only $262 million from federal coffers. Although it actually lost $315 million during the year, it took the rest out of the $2.2 billion in assets it was handed on October 16, 1981. In any case, the loss was well under its target for the year of $400 million. Canada Post looked good.

The big jump in postal rates in 1982, however, could not be repeated. The "6 and 5" restraint program kept the next rate increase to another 2 cents, and the market itself put a lid on further rate increases. Customers had had enough.

In September 1983 the marketing and sales group said Canada Post should not even try to put through another rate increase in 1984. "As indicated by current volume performance, a sluggish economy and aggressive pricing in the past two years have weakened customer demand for postal service generally," it reported in a confidential memo.

The overall flow of mail had risen, but only because of unaddressed admail, the kind of "junk mail" delivered to every house on a postman's route. Because it does not need sorting, it creates no work for the postal plants. It is also much cheaper to send, and therefore brings in less money. In the first eight months of 1983, unaddressed admail was up 18.1 per cent from a year earlier. The parcel business was showing marginal improvement, but all other categories were slipping.

And the number of first-class letters, which make up 60 per cent of the post office's revenue, dropped 1.2 per cent. Canada Post handled fifty-six million fewer letters than its planners had forecast. "Until some improvement in customer demand is seen to be occurring, price increases could fuel further volume reductions and continue the erosion of the corporate volume base. Fear of continued volume loss is supported by current intense competition in major markets" such as admail and parcel post.

Canada Post could have been wrong. It was not the first time that the post office had thought that its postal rates were hitting the limits of what Canadians were willing to endure. In a brief to John Fraser in 1979 and again to André Ouellet in 1980, postal bureaucrats had argued that the post office had already reached the point where higher prices would only drive down the number of letters people sent. "Canada Post has gone almost as far as it can go in using rate increases alone to close the gap between revenue and costs." That was two years before the 76-per-cent jump.

Warren, however, announced a rate freeze that would be maintained as long as possible. Higher costs started nudging the deficit back up. In 1983/84, the post office had an operating loss of $300.1 million and collected $306 million from the government, $44 million more than a year earlier and a hair over its $300-million target.

The government then raised its deficit target for the following year to $350 million, an admission that Canada Post was unable to make ends meet as planned. It still intended to get the deficit down to $200 million in 1985/86 and then break even in 1986/87.

Warren was left with some basic choices. If he wanted to cut the deficit, he could either raise revenues or cut costs. Collecting more money meant either increasing the number of letters and parcels or raising its fees for each. He had already tried higher prices, and that in turn was holding down any increase in volume.

The pattern became clear. When postal rates went up, the deficit went down. When postal rates held steady, the deficit rose. Despite all Warren's brave rhetoric about shifting the burden of deficit-cutting away from customers, the results showed that he was not getting the internal savings he had promised would flow from better productivity.

If the volume of mail did not increase much and productivity did not improve, cutting costs meant going after either wage levels or jobs. Contracts prevented the first, and his own promises in search of labour peace stopped any move to lay off workers. Jobs would be cut only through attrition, the regular process of people leaving the post office on their own. The ill-paid jobs that had once turned over so fast had become sinecures where barely 5 per cent left or retired each year.

There were savings to be had in other areas, of course. Even if salaries and benefits chewed up 73 per cent of its $2.7-billion spending each year, more than $700 million was spent on other items that were easier to cut. That led to some hard-headed renegotiation of contracts with major carriers such as Air Canada. "Mail yields were also severely affected as sharply lower rates were established under an April, 1983, agreement with Canada Post Corporation," Air Canada squawked in its annual report that year.

Warren was only giving as good as he got. Air Canada and CP Air asked for attention on the corporation's first working day. "On that very day, October 17, I received two letters, sent by courier," says Warren. "One was from [Air Canada chief executive] Claude Taylor, and the other was from the then-president of CP, both of them congratulating us, just saying, since you have now become a Crown corporation, we want to advise you that the passes that used to be made available to your senior personnel" would be taken away. Warren didn't know that the passes had existed in the first place, but he was struck by the abrupt, businesslike tone of both messages.

When the airline contracts came up in the second year, Warren wrote back. "I started the letter saying, Now that we are a Crown corporation, we should conduct our business together in a far more businesslike manner, and you would appreciate that." Warren figures he saved $20 million a year on the Air Canada deal alone, and was able to use it to twist the arms of other carriers for another $8 million in savings.

But as some costs were cut, others kept on going up, and the overall savings in the transportation account came to only $6 million in 1983/84, a tiny fraction of the budget. Even the big gains in junk mail caused problems. They masked the decline in other product lines, but brought in little money. And they tended to clog the delivery system. A letter-carrier can carry only so much in his or her bag at once.

Stewart Cooke had spent some of his years at CN as general manager of marketing for its parcel-express service. He had brought in rates that discouraged the "cornflakes" — packages that weigh little and are not worth much, but take up a lot of space. "I knew where the cornflakes were. They were over here in Canada Post."

The attitude he found, among both old-style managers and the unions, was that the volume of business was the key to success. "From a union standpoint, a whole lot of volume meant that you were really making money. There was no understanding that the more volume you got, it could well be the more money you were going to lose if you got the wrong kind of stuff coming in."

Former chief operating officer André Lizotte felt that volume, together with profitable pricing, was vital to success. "If you want to make money in the post office, you've got to get off your ass and get the business. If you just reduce expenses, and you're not that aggressive in getting the business, you're not going to make it. You've got to increase the units that you sell and then increase the margins on each of those units."

Canada Post's customers caused more problems. As each set of labour talks came to a head, large-volume mailers dumped everything they had into the mail system at once, hoping that their messages would make it through the system before a strike. That just clogged the plants in unexpected waves, and the service numbers started to fall. Again, by going public at the beginning, Warren was cornered by his own results. Just as customers got fed up with higher prices for stamps, his own figures started to show that service was getting worse.

The result of all this was to push Warren in the direction that people like Ouellet had intended from the beginning: the move into new services that would increase revenues and maintain the post office as a good provider of jobs. If mail growth was stagnant, make money on something else. "A plain post office service will not be profitable in any country and I don't see how it could be profitable in Canada," says Ouellet. "You have to allow the post office to provide some other services to pay the difference . . . if we want to have a good service for everybody at the same price."

There was no shortage of ideas for expansion, but even the early attempts ran into resistance. One experiment was called

Consumers Post. It allowed a sampling of small rural post offices to act as catalogue stores on behalf of Consumer's Distributing. Customers could walk into the local post office, browse through the catalogue, choose what they wanted, order it, and have it delivered by the post office. It brought big-city merchandise choice to small-town Canada. Many customers were happy, but local businesses were horrified.

In theory, using small, money-losing rural post offices as catalogue stores was one way to make better use of one of Canada Post's greatest assets: a distribution network that penetrates into all but the tiniest communities in the country. In practice, local merchants saw the post office and its private-sector partner as unfair competition. Politicians whose definition of fair is shaped by the people who elect them were quick to agree.

Even Ouellet, who insisted that the way to break even was by moving into new businesses, says Consumers Post was a mistake. "The idea was right, but it was implemented badly. We had difficulty in accepting that the Crown corporation could do things other than deliver the mail. At a different time, it might have been acceptable."

Other experiments also got off to shaky starts. Warren agreed to help keep up the number of jobs for postal workers by trying a new concept at the retail level. Instead of having postal counters run by news-stands or pharmacies, Canada Post would open stores of its own in major shopping centres. These "New Directions" outlets would be more than post offices. Customers could not only mail letters, but buy stationery, wrapping paper, and a variety of Canada Post knick-knacks, including the infamous "World's Greatest Postal System" baseball caps.

The idea was to bring in more customers and get them to leave more of their money behind. The unions argued that these outlets, staffed by knowledgeable postal employees in high-traffic locations, could be more profitable than having agents paid by commission in sub-post offices. Their angle was more job security in more pleasant surroundings and on day shifts.

It did not take long for the wrangling to break out. To prove their point, the unions wanted the best possible locations. To placate their friends, the politicians did not want the most lucrative sub-post offices to be replaced by postal workers and corporate stores. In the end, postal workers would trumpet one major success in boosting revenue by far more than the higher costs of using CUPW members behind the counters; the rest would lose money. The union blames the failures on inferior sites, forced on the post office for political reasons.

Meanwhile, Canada Post's marketing group was never short of new ideas. A 1983 list of proposals included a meter-reading service, selling travellers' cheques, insurance, and lottery tickets, census services, rental of lobby space, and, in the longer term, variations on electronic mail, including printing of bills at postal plants closest to customers, banking services, electronic funds transfers, and delivering goods from stores to customers within cities.

Most of the retail proposals would run into the same problems as Consumers Post. Other merchants providing similar goods and services would scream about unfair competition. If Canada Post was losing money, it was being subsidized. If it was subsidized, it would be unfair to private-sector stores which would have to close if they lost money.

The two big areas for postal expansion were also expensive. One was the parcel business, a traditional preserve of the post office that had been all but wiped out by private-sector carriers. The other was electronic mail, which was seen as both a response to competition and a crucial investment for the future. Both proposals had serious pitfalls.

The parcel business was a simple lesson in competition. Where the post office had once dominated, its own reputation for lousy service had brought its downfall. By 1984, the post office was handling less than half the number of parcels it carried in 1960. The Crown corporation estimated its share of the parcel market at between 6 per cent and 8 per cent. And attempts by post offices in other countries to keep and expand their parcel business had been summarily executed by hard-driving private companies.

The most dramatic example came in the United States. After being turned from a federal department into a state-run corporation in 1970, the United States Postal Service invested a fortune in new mechanized parcel-handling equipment.

It spent nearly US$1 billion to build twenty-one huge bulk-mail plants for handling parcels and bulk second- and third-class mail. The system, finished in 1976, was originally expected to save more than US$300 million a year. By March 1976, however, the General Accounting Office said savings "would exceed $138 million annually," and that only if parcel volume stayed above 400 million pieces a year. In fact, parcel volume that year fell to 338 million pieces, and the Postal Service was expecting a further drop to 137 million pieces by 1985.

The U.S. post office at first predicted a rate of return on its investment in the parcel plants of more than 30 per cent a year. It told the 1977 review commission that its savings that year would be only $40 million, for a 4-per-cent rate of return. If parcel volume fell even further, as predicted, there would be no return at all. The post office had lost business because the long-established United Parcel Service had been able to undercut its rates. The United States Postal Service must, by law, charge what it costs to provide each service. If its costs rise too high, so must its prices.

The Canadian post office has argued that the parcel business proves the need for its monopoly. Its parcel service suffers from "massive cream-skimming", bureaucrats reported to Ouellet in 1980. If Canada Post had to charge its costs on all the routes in its network in order to stay competitive with the private sector in the major corridors in southern Canada, its prices on some routes would have to be multiplied twenty times.

With no monopoly to protect it, a massive investment by Canada Post in new parcel-handling equipment seemed like a risky proposition. Nevertheless, Warren decided to go for it. In 1983, André Lizotte picked Graham McDonald, one of the bright people he had found in the post office when he arrived, to take charge of the parcel project.

Meanwhile, Canada Post was also looking at the electronic-mail business. Unlike parcels, electronic messages in one form or another remained a relatively untried field. But Warren, like Blais before him, could see the disquieting signs of competition that were closing off the future of the post office.

Mail is effectively a mature industry. The post office may keep its monopoly, but letters are only one way to talk. Technology keeps coming up with new ways to communicate. If the post office restricts itself to letters, its share of that communications market can only fall, even if technological advances mean that more people communicate more often overall. In the communications business, the post office has been in decline ever since Alexander Graham Bell made it possible to talk rather than to write or visit.

More recent high-tech wonders are threatening much of what remains in the mail. The greatest danger to mail volumes lies in financial dealings. Electronic funds transfers are becoming more and more common, and could replace billions of letters on which the post office now collects revenue.

Payments from the federal government are only the beginning. Many companies now put pay cheques directly into employee bank accounts. They have also allowed customers to pay their bills at bank branches, and more recently at electronic teller machines. Regular monthly bills such as cable television charges or mortgage payments are often deducted from accounts automatically.

Each of these transactions takes business away from the post office. There are still plenty of bills sent out by mail, of course, even though they may be paid electronically. But the convenience for both business and customer of electronic transfers threatens a large chunk of the post office's business in the long term.

A 1978 Canadian study of the different options for setting up a Crown corporation estimated that, by 1995, electronic data transmission, word-processing, funds transfers, and messages sent by facsimile machines (which scan sheets of paper, send their contents over the phone, and reproduce the paper at the other end) would handle 8 billion messages a year. That would be one and a half times the total volume of mail at the time. "Should the post office be unable to retain its share of the market through the provision of an effective and competitive service, its very existence is in question," the report said.

In 1980, postal bureaucrats reported that the only growth in first-class mail had been coming from financial transactions, which made up 40 per cent of the total volume of mail, or more than 2 billion pieces of mail a year. Between 1985 and 1995, they estimated that electronic funds transfers could grow to account for 2.1 billion transactions a year and become a major competitor for the post office.

"To be successful, major corporations around the world have got to diversify," says Lizotte. "At the post office you're talking about a $3-billion business. If you want to be successful ten years or twenty years from now, a corporation has to diversify."

But the United States Postal Service abandoned its electronic-mail subsidiary in 1985 after losing too much money. The private sector fared no better: Federal Express gave up on its Zapmail service after losing a fortune.

Warren was undaunted by these uncertainties. By 1984, with his deadline for breaking even heaving over the horizon, he was ready to invest $1 billion in the parcel business and electronic mail. There was only one problem. In the summer of 1984, there was an election.

17
New
Terra Tory

■

September 17, 1984, should have been a good day for Perrin Beatty. Two weeks earlier, he and his Conservative colleagues had swept into office with the biggest majority in federal history. With Brian Mulroney as their leader, they had all but wiped out John Turner's Liberals, taking a majority of the seats even in their Quebec fortress. For those like Beatty who had tasted the fruits of Cabinet power for a scant few months in 1979, there was a luscious sense of vindication.

As the golden boy of the Tory Cabinet, Beatty was ready to move. He had been first elected to the House of Commons at the tender age of twenty-two, and was handed his first chance at the Cabinet table under Joe Clark at twenty-nine. He had spent the frustrating years in opposition poking away at the unfairness of Canada's tax-collectors and turned federal harassment of hard-pressed Canadians into a major election issue. He led a Conservative task force that toured the country collecting horror stories and suggestions for change.

Now he was ready to be sworn in as Canada's new minister of National Revenue, the head taxman himself. He would take those hard-hearted gougers and show them the error of their ways. He would be gentle, of course, for Beatty has always been a master of public relations, as smooth and reasonable and tasteful as a nip of Bailey's Irish Cream at the end of a pleasant dinner. But the public would see justice being done. The powerful bureaucrats would be brought to heel and taught to answer the phone with "please" and "thank you". Alas, youth also has its perils.

Beatty used to tell friends that as the new ministers-to-be sat around the table, Prime Minister Brian Mulroney looked up from one of the papers he was signing: this one, he said, would make Beatty the new minister responsible for Canada Post. Beatty's reaction was: "What's this?" To which Mulroney replied: "If I had told you before, would you have taken the job?" It was the gesture of a clever politician who knew the problems that can be caused when subordinates get better press than their boss.

Beatty had to endure as postal minister for less than a year, but it is not a memory in which he takes any delight. In fact, the pleasant man known for quickly returning calls to reporters on the slightest excuse flatly refused to be interviewed for this book. Whatever thoughts passed through his head, his brief stewardship did not lack for excitement. As he took office, Warren's five-year plan had run half its course. As it turned out, Warren himself was near the end of his.

It didn't seem that way at first. Warren was optimistic. After all, he had pretty good Tory credentials himself from his days with the Ontario government. And an earlier chat he'd had with Mulroney had persuaded him that the Conservatives would be more likely to smile on his efforts to act like a business rather than a federal service.

"In a way, I was looking forward to the Conservatives coming in," says Warren. "I had this impression, for better or for worse, that what we were going to see was a shareholder who would probably come in with a fairly major majority and be just the kind of shareholder that we needed to give some backbone to the last third of a mile in turning this place around, and that they would view Canada Post as one of those ones where a lot of the work had been done and they could pick up the win that Trudeau had started to put in place."

The first shocks were not long in coming. Like a school of penned piranha suddenly let loose at a crowded beach, the new MPs, many of them rookies in the Commons swept along by the Tory wave, came looking for the goodies they knew perfectly well the other guys always got. When Warren tried to tell them that times had changed, they merely scoffed. "I think the Conservatives expected that there would be a hell of a lot more patronage going through Canada Post than there was," says Warren. "This group of Quebec MPs, almost none of whom had been in government before, they were used to a philosophy of patronage which was widespread. I was absolutely inundated."

After meetings with MPs, he would always get one or two who would buttonhole him privately. "For Christ's sake, Michael, you're nothing but a goddamn Liberal, and that's the reason we're not getting these. You can't tell me there's no patronage in the post office," ran the typical sally.

"What a lot of the local politicians would say is: 'Well, maybe you've got the deficit down, but nobody cares about the deficit. You should know that. You're a big boy. Hardly anybody in my riding gives a damn about your deficit. But they do care that I can't get them any jobs in Canada Post and the service isn't that much better and so what that you haven't had a strike. You're not supposed to have any goddamn strikes anyway. You've got your priorities mixed up. You should go and think this thing over.' "

MPs hungry for vote-getting goodies were at least a familiar plague. What Warren found truly disconcerting was the attitude of his new minister. "I just went through a series of periods where I was just shaking my head for a number of weeks after they did come into power. First of all, it seemed to me that Perrin Beatty didn't really have much interest in Canada Post, and was frank enough to say so right at the outset."

He knew he could make political hay in the tax department, where he had spent two years preparing, but solutions to the post office problem were less obvious. He did not bring any strong feelings to the job, but knew he would have to move carefully. He wanted to learn the rules of the game before he called any plays.

"We had dozens and dozens of meetings," says Warren. "And I pushed him I think fairly hard to come to terms with some of the issues that were facing us, and I was never successful in getting him to commit. It was a long, long process.'' Warren saw Beatty's silence as a stubborn lack of support that would stymie any move to get Cabinet approval for his plans.

The Canada Post president got his first taste of the new government's careful approach to touchy issues within a couple of months. He decided right after the election that the time had come to end the rate freeze. He asked for another two cents. The answer was no. On October 18, Canada Post issued a press release announcing that it had graciously decided to extend the rate freeze for six months.

A former Canada Post executive says Warren's biggest mistake was taking the new government at its word and expecting it to make businesslike decisions. ''Perrin wants to be prime minister and didn't want to get egg on his face. As a result, when Canada Post asked for an early rate increase, Brian said no and Perrin didn't fight him.''

Before any moves were made, Beatty wanted Warren to give him a complete set of options for the post office. That suited Warren fine. Canada Post eventually put together a package of five options. They covered the full range of possibilities.

On one end, there was the post office as carrier of last resort. It would pull in its horns, leaving the parcel sector entirely, removing its monopoly on letters and inviting private companies to bid for the right to serve its major markets. The bids would begin with Toronto and expand over three years to cover the rest of the areas in which the private sector expressed an interest in running the postal service. Canada Post would serve the rest as cheaply as possible. Warren figured a post office like that would lose about $120 million a year.

At the other end was an ambitious plan to move aggressively into new lines of business such as electronic mail, to expand the corporation's role at the retail end, and to fight back against the competition in traditional areas of strength such as parcel post. It would mean investing a large amount of borrowed money.

The talks between Canada Post and Beatty's office went on through November and December. ''I had biases, of course,'' says Warren. If the government decided to shrink the post office into a carrier of last resort, ''I'd like not to be around a whole long time, because I don't want to be a person laying off 12,000 or 15,000 people over a couple of years. But it doesn't mean that those options were not properly analysed." Beatty had his doubts about that.

Mulroney seemed to have no strong feelings either, but did not want any distractions until the labour talks had been wrapped up. He did not want a rate increase to put more money on the table while the talks went on, and figured that longer-term options could also wait.

When Cabinet did not deal with his options, Warren decided to push for his favourite. He wanted to take his best shot at reaching break-even before his five-year contract ran out, and that meant using the jazzy approach. He suggested breaking even in 1986, a year ahead of schedule. It was an approach that relied on an accountant's tango through the balance sheets rather than sudden improvements at the plant level, but it looked good. Besides, Warren figured Beatty was never strong on balance sheets anyway.

Warren wanted to spend $1 billion on new parcel-handling equipment and machines for electronic bulk mail. (The latter involves sending an advertisement electronically to equipped post offices across the country. There the messages are converted to hard copy, stuffed in envelopes, and mailed out. Because all the mailing is local, the messages arrive in people's homes more quickly.)

The key to breaking even faster while spending all that money was borrowing. Canada Post had no debt, and could borrow either from the government or from the capital markets of the private sector. If borrowed money paid for all Canada Post's spending on new buildings and machinery, the corporation's capital budget would disappear from the deficit.

Warren even lined up a British investment banker prepared to put together an unusual loan deal. The package would have given Canada Post the full amount in cash up front, even though the spending would take place over five years. Furthermore, loan interest would be capitalized so that Canada Post could "break even" for at least one year before the deferred-interest costs blew a hole in the corporation's results. The loan, of course, would be guaranteed by the government.

There were other wrinkles. With the new financial structure in place, he wanted to start selling shares to employees and then, within three years, as much as 10 per cent of the corporation to outsiders. To coax people reluctant to take a chance on a money-losing corporation with a record like Canada Post's, he suggested preferred shares that would have a guaranteed and attractive dividend.

Beatty didn't buy it, and the key bureaucrats in Finance and Treasury Board knew it. They sensed that Beatty had yet to be convinced that Canada Post was doing its basic job properly and was not keen to move into even chancier areas. "It was just a little bit of fantasy drawn up by the three wise guys down there," said one official. "This plan would not have solved anything . . . even if everything went the way they wanted it to. It was just ludicrous."

"Basically I think it was a good plan," says Marin, and the board approved it despite some worries about the corporation's ability to meet the higher interest payments down the road. Beatty, however, stopped it cold. "He asked probing questions because he was a minister who probed a lot, and we couldn't stand that. In retrospect, he was dead on." As Opposition MPs, the Conservatives had seen the results of fancy manipulation of balance sheets at Canadair Ltd. under the Liberals. They did not want to be responsible for another billion-dollar write-off.

Beatty sent in two consulting firms to take a look at the corporation's plans. Their reports confirmed his doubts. They said Canada Post had no ability to forecast accurately and wanted to get into businesses it didn't know. They recommended that Canada Post clean up its existing mess first.

With his grand plan shot down, Warren tried a more conventional approach. By then, the labour talks had been settled and the corporation was again panting for its rate increase. Beatty stalled. "He would go through periods where he would try very hard. And then it would just kind of evaporate. There would be nothing there," says Warren.

Beatty was not Warren's only stumbling-block in the government. In the Tory back-benches, another group had emerged after a few months of relative silence: long-time critics of the post office who had pushed and tormented the institution while in opposition and saw no reason to stop.

The group included party stalwarts such as Don Blenkarn and Bob Horner from Mississauga, Bill Attewell from Don Valley East, and Dan McKenzie from Winnipeg. They were mostly on the right wing of the party. Many came from ridings with large suburban populations, the very group suffering most from Canada Post's moves to cut back its costs by refusing door-to-door delivery to new subdivisions. And they were well acquainted with the publicity value of the post office as a political target.

"The Opposition mentality had not left. These guys were clearly not going to be in Cabinet. They were not Cabinet material. So they just continued as government members in this Opposition mode, which is to find an easy target and then flail away at it. So McKenzie and Blenkarn and some others chose the post office, and they just kept it up as if they were Opposition members."

Because of the resistance to a rate hike, Warren tried reviving the idea of Consumers Post, but that didn't sit with rural Tory MPs any better than it had with their Liberal counterparts.

The most irritating case of political interference was that of Aditya Varma, a postal clerk with a feeling that much was rotten in the state of Canada Post. When he went public with a series of accusations about bad management decisions, untendered contracts, and faked mail-testing, he was fired. Dan McKenzie led a back-bench bid to rescue him.

The Prime Minister's Office forced Canada Post to rehire Varma. "It turned into a huge process of negotiation over this one employee who had been the source to McKenzie the year before," says Warren. "That was such a bizarre occurrence, that whole thing, that I've almost blotted a lot of that from my mind. It's just so difficult for me to believe . . . the meetings back and forth about what Varma wants and what he doesn't want and could we negotiate an agreement with this guy, and I'm saying look, he's before a tribunal and he's got his eight or nine points, his accusations, let's get them out, I want them out now, I want them all fully aired."

The key player in the PMO was Pat MacAdam, Mulroney's special assistant for caucus liaison. MacAdam said his role was "horse-trading on the telephone, arm-twisting, but not threats of any kind. I mean, Canada Post could have said no and I would have been left high and dry. What am I going to say? I didn't have the authority to order them."

But once he had Canada Post's agreement, he leaked the story to the *Toronto Star* to make sure the post office didn't change its mind. MacAdam denied that he or the Prime Minister's Office was interfering in the corporation's affairs. "There was no interference. . . . There was persuasion."

For Warren, the PMO's action was publicly humiliating. The government was saying in the bluntest possible terms that it did not trust post office management. Canada Post had to hire back Varma and then endure an investigation by Toronto consultants Laventhol and Horwath into his various accusations. The six-month investigation found that none of Varma's accusations could be sustained except the one about mail tests' being faked, but it painted a scathing portrait of the post office none the less.

"This other group over here, the Blenkarns and McKenzies, they were just using their government-member status to come back and even some scores, or try to. And in the process it got very bizarre," Warren complains. "It was a new government, and they were very concerned about doing anything wrong in public-relations terms. And the net result was that it was handled in a very awkward sort of way."

Warren, however, had left himself vulnerable. The series of labour talks had brought sudden surges of mail in the days before strike deadlines, and Canada Post's performance numbers were down.

"In those days leading up to a final resolution of those disputes, [the number of letters stacked up in the plants] went from an average of 12 million pieces, which is our normal inventory in the system, to in excess of 24 million, 27 million, and 28 million," he explained to a parliamentary committee in May 1985. "We have had four years without any major labour interruption, and I think both labour and management at Canada Post can be proud of that. Unfortunately, we paid a short-term price on the reliability of our service." To the politicians, such explanations meant little.

What they saw was Canada Post asking for higher prices while its service was getting worse.

On the broader question of corporate direction, Warren was running out of options, and running out of patience. When he couldn't get a deal with his shareholder on how to run what was supposed to be the last phase of the five-year plan by the spring of 1985, he started looking for ways to get around Beatty.

"I found myself having to report this to my board. My board had directly elected labour people on it who were very interested that the government was not supporting the corporation's general direction over the last little while." They saw a chance to reopen the whole public debate over whether the post office should run a deficit. When they tried that during the labour talks, Beatty quashed it quickly.

By spring, the nag factor was already at work. Some ministers were tired of Warren's complaints and presentations and arguments. Warren was reduced to writing letters to Beatty, pointing out that Canada Post was late with its annual report and didn't even have a deficit target for the fiscal year already under way. One letter in early summer pointed out that the delays were so bad that Canada Post was breaking the law, failing to meet the terms of its own legislation and the Financial Administration Act. There was a growing sense on both sides that the combination of Warren and the Conservatives was not going to work.

"I was sort of running the corporation through all this without a corporate plan and with a minister who was trying to somehow find the perfect political way of handling the post office. That was Perrin's approach. And I don't think there is one." The closest thing to perfection, Warren felt, still meant taking some knocks first.

"I just couldn't get a direction or a decision out of him. And I think he probably felt that I didn't come up with a Teflon solution to the next steps in Canada Post. And I kept telling him, that's not the nature of this beast. He would say, 'I never asked for this responsibility,' and I would say, 'Well, I did, and you've got it, and we've got to get on with it.' "

When his manoeuvrings didn't get much of a rise out of Beatty or the government, he decided, "rightly or wrongly, that maybe it would be a good time for me to exit the scene. I had a shareholder who didn't really know what they wanted to do and they weren't overly concerned that I was leaving.''

The government's decision on the rate increase in June, almost eight months after he had wanted it, capped his decision. Along with the rate increase, Beatty ordered a thorough review of the corporation and its fundamental mandate by a private-sector committee headed by Alan Marchment, president of Guaranty Trust Co. of Canada. He tried to get Warren involved with the committee's work, but Warren wasn't interested. ''I just said that the task force was not a good idea, that there were other ways to accomplish this, and he felt that it was.''

Warren says he thinks the task force was the price exacted by Tory back-benchers for going along with higher stamp prices. ''The task force became a quid pro quo for the rate increase. That's what it came down to. . . . I think he honestly believed that that was the price, the only way he could get rate increase through caucus.'' Whether caucus was twisting Beatty's arm or not, the task force was Beatty's way of telling them that he was serious about solving the post office problem. He saw it as the equivalent of his taxation task force, an independent body that would give him the kind of look at the options he had not been able to get from Warren.

Beatty downplayed the level of tension among his fellow MPs. ''The members of caucus have been very responsible. What they've said to me is that they want to see improvements made in the service, and I certainly agree with that, and that they want to look at this whole question of how you finance the corporation.''

Warren's attitude wavered. Some days, he would tell himself that it was still just a matter of a new shareholder coming to grips with a controversial institution and looking for ways to solve its problems that Warren hadn't seen. ''Probably I'd been in the trenches too long and I should remember the guys who were at Gray Rocks, who should have been kind of sent home for a vacation. Maybe that's where I am. So I would go for two or three days with that kind of a frame of mind, saying, Why not have the task force, why not be open-minded about it and partici-pate in it and get a fresh perspective to deal with this new shareholder? And then I would sort of come back the other way and look at the terms of reference of the task force.''

The task force had been told to study all the possible options for the corporation. Warren figured he'd already offered the government the full range of options six months earlier. Warren went and made a presentation to the task force in July and told it that the board of directors had been given only a day's notice of the decision and had not been consulted in advance. "The whole thing scared the shit out of Warren," said one official.

Warren insists that his departure was his own decision. "Nobody suggested to me that I leave. I never had that even remotely. I think I got some indications from a couple of back-benchers that maybe Warren's done enough damage here, both publicly and privately, but from no other source."

Beatty himself remains coy on the subject. At the time, he said only that Warren and the government had both agreed that it was for the best, but that kind of diplomatic language is used to cover up even the most brutal dismissals. He and Warren had talked several times, and "there was a natural demarcation during the summer."

"You don't see someone get a compensation package when he quits," observed one member of the Marchment committee — and Warren made no secret of his six-figure severance pay.

In a hastily written reply from Quebec City, where Beatty was taking French lessons when the news broke, the postal minister said Warren and his employees could be proud of the achievements they had made. "The successful transformation of the post office from a government department to a Crown corporation is almost complete."

News of Warren's resignation leaked to the media just in time to disrupt his marriage to Elizabeth Mylrea. He ran the gauntlet of microphones and cameras on the way into the Nicholas Street courthouse in good humour. Afterwards, when one of his aides asked him if she could do anything for him, he cracked: "Yeah, you could arrange a private wedding."

Inside, on the way to the chambers of his friend Senior District Court Judge Keith Flanagan, the couple bumped into a court beadle, a sheriff's officer. "I know now why you quit, Mr. Warren," he cackled. As Warren looked at him sharply, he added: "She's gorgeous."

As Warren spoke his vows, Jean-Claude Parrot was delivering

his comments on the resignation to reporters in the national press theatre. For the union chief, it was his twenty-fifth wedding anniversary. Warren, smiling, said nothing about his reasons as he slipped away to his farm north of Toronto.

He wrapped up his four-year stint at a final two-day meeting of the board of directors in August. Five months into the fiscal year, Canada Post still didn't know its deficit target. ''In August of 1985, my impression was that most of the big questions about Canada Post were all up for grabs. The business we were in was up for grabs, how it was to be financed was up for grabs, how tough we were going to be in terms of some of the hard issues of labour relations, that was up for grabs. How we wanted to run it, who should run it, up for grabs.''

He was not the last to leave. ''The tragedy of having it in neutral is that some of those people are just slowly exiting and so there is an unseen but critical momentum which has to do with doing things well, making things happen, which comes from hundreds of new people. . . . They will stay for a certain period of time. They're not quite as leading-edge, they're not going to jump out just because of [a year's delay] but if it goes on too long, those people just lose heart.''

In Warren's wake, the Marchment committee was writing his corporate epitaph. It was less than flattering. The task force found that many of the fundamental problems that had plagued the old department seemed untouched by Warren's attempted cures.

The same old abuses were still very much in evidence. For instance, there was the story of the large, multi-storey sorting plant where moving the mail depends on a large elevator. ''On the midnight shift, these guys take fork-lift trucks and ram them into the elevator doors so that you can't get them open. And in this post office, you have to be able to run the mail up three levels. So it means that the whole thing just shuts down for the midnight shift and they all just go and have coffee,'' says committee member Alix Granger, a tough-talking, no-nonsense executive with the Vancouver brokerage firm of Pemberton Houston Willoughby Bell Gouinlock Inc.

The accident statistics told them that postal plants were more dangerous places to work than steel mills or coal mines. That didn't sound right, so the committee checked out some of the accident records. "Some guy had twisted a finger. He took six weeks off. Six weeks for a twisted finger. If I took three minutes off I would be astounded. The union's claim is, well, the Workmen's Compensation Board allowed it."

The committee was also bothered by Warren's attitude. He had not pursued a truly businesslike approach. "He in essence went completely along with this idea of the post office as a giant employment machine." The committee members were not impressed by Warren's presentation to them. "He came with all kinds of charts and made a great presentation. The feeling that everyone had was that it was just a snow-job."

It was Warren's proposals for the billion-dollar move to revive the parcel business and get into electronic bulk mail that really dumbfounded the task force. The investment in the parcel business alone would have cost $191 million. "Now they had absolutely no market studies to indicate that that was possible. And the information that we had seen talking to various people in the States and UPS and people up here was that that was just impossible. It had gone too far to ever get back. It was just throwing money away, that's all it was."

The lack of studies was even more evident on the electronic-mail side of the proposals, which would need $791 million over the first five years and another $2.3 billion in subsequent years. "On the $791 million, in five years' time it would generate $79 million in revenue over the five years." Granger recalls an astonishing conversation with a Canada Post executive.

"Where did you get the $79 million from?"

"Well, it's 10 per cent of $791 million."

"Even I could have figured that one out," said Granger. "But what's behind it? Where's the market analysis to back it up?"

"Oh, we didn't have any."

"You mean to say it's just a figure out of the air?"

"Yeah, well, I guess, sort of."

When Granger asked how much of the expected revenue would be left after the costs of running the electronic-mail service, she was told $25 million. "Where did that come from?"

"Well, we had to come up with a figure, so we just said that."

That proposal, Granger says, was what Warren took to the

board of directors, the board passed, and Perrin Beatty threw out. "We asked them for market studies and things like that to justify this thing and they didn't have any. So there was just nothing to back anything up."

The questioning by committee members had some Canada Post executives squirming, especially Ken Harry, whom they suspected had been the architect of the plan. "We had a — how shall I describe it politely — a very interesting meeting with Ken Harry, the chief financial officer. When I shook his hand when he arrived, it was very damp. And when I left, his whole face was damp. It was not one of Ken Harry's better days, and I'm sure he would agree with that."

Granger pushed him during the interview on the financial reasoning behind the parcel and electronic mail plans. "I've seen a lot of corp finance deals, and if I had heard the numbers that I heard within the first minute there, and I was in a corp finance deal, I would have just picked up my briefcase and walked out. I would have just figured it was some skid trying to promote something crummy on the VSE, that's all I could think of." Granger, however, does not put all the blame on Harry. "I think these are the numbers that he was asked to come up with, and so he did."

The committee got little satisfaction from its attempt to get to the bottom of the proposal by talking to the board of directors. "We had a very unpleasant meeting with the board, to the point where René Marin wrote a very rude letter to Alan Marchment after the meeting. They did not appreciate our whole approach on the subject at all. And they were totally unable to justify any of this rubbish. . . . They just rubber-stamped Warren's pipedreams."

The lacklustre performance of the board, however, was partly a result of the way Canada Post was set up and then run. "They still had a phenomenal amount of political interference. And that never ceased. The corporation itself has been set up in a very bad way because the president is accountable to the minister, not to the board of directors, and the board of directors don't have that much power or responsibility, which is probably part of the reason why they don't act as if they have any responsibility."

In the end, the committee still had lots to say. Its two-volume report included forty-three recommendations for rescuing the post office. Many were simply common sense and had been heard before. It suggested a stronger, more independent board of directors. It said stamp prices should be set by an independent commission. The task force felt Canada Post should forget about electronic mail and stick to its basic business of moving the mail.

The bottom line, however, was blunt: "Shape up or shut down." Its key recommendation was that the Crown corporation get another five years to reach the break-even point. "However, if Canada Post fails by 1990 to achieve its objectives of service and financial self-sufficiency, privatization should again be reconsidered." The monopoly on carrying letters should be maintained until then, but "its extension beyond that date be dependent on its ability to provide reliable, efficient and effective service and achieve financial self-sufficiency."

By the time the committee delivered its report in October, however, Warren was not the only departure. Beatty actually left before Warren. On August 20, three days before Warren's resignation took effect, a Cabinet shuffle rescued him from the job he never seemed to want.

His replacement was Michel Côté, one of the new crop from Quebec who had Mulroney's ear and a good reputation both as an accountant and as someone on his way up in the Cabinet. Once again the post office had to break in a new minister. The result, once again, would be more than a year of confusion.

18
The Crown Corpse

■

Michel Côté was pleased at first with his new Cabinet job. The Department of Consumer and Corporate Affairs was headed for a high-profile role in changing the rules on patents for drug manufacturers, and the addition of the post office job was matched by an appointment to the inner Cabinet, the Priorities and Planning committee. It was a sign from the Prime Minister that he was on his way up.

The Marchment committee, then in the middle of its hearings, was less impressed with the change. Even before it delivered its report, some of its members thought about quitting. When Beatty was relieved of the post office job halfway through the committee's work, they were left hanging, unsure of the whole point of their exercise.

"We just felt it was a complete waste of time. It was set up for a very good reason by Perrin Beatty, to deal with the problems of the post office, and then, before we knew it, he's been pulled off," says committee member Alix Granger. "We wanted to have one minister throughout the whole thing, especially someone we thought would try and run with the report."

The Marchment report was released in the same week that Laventhol and Horwath delivered its inch-thick tome on the accusations made by Aditya Varma. While the consultants found little or no evidence to back up the specific accusations he made, they had few nice things to say about the state of postal management.

The twin releases could have been a springboard for dramatic change. The air was already filling with rumours as to the identity of the new postal president, and there were hints that Côté was only waiting for the Marchment report before making his moves.

The new minister did not want to waste time. When he took over the post office, he saw that it needed a plan of action fast. That in turn coloured his feelings about who should become the new Canada Post president. The early sampling produced several names, including that of Robert Bandeen, the combative former president of Canadian National, and André Lizotte, the former chief operating officer who couldn't live with Warren's style of running the show.

The serious discussions came down to Don Lander and Gil Bennett, the outgoing president of Canadair Ltd. Bennett was the favourite of the Prime Minister's Office. The bureaucrats of the Privy Council Office also approved. Not only would Bennett be good for the job, they said, but hiring him would save hundreds of thousands of dollars. If he got the post office job, the government could save the year and a half's severance pay he was due as he left Canadair.

Bennett, however, wanted too much money and too much independence. Côté wanted someone he could control, and he backed Lander. The minister and his staff wanted an executive who could move fast once picked, who would not sit around for months figuring out how the post office worked. They also wanted to be sure that the new president would not be the kind of person who would chicken out on a tough decision because of the impact it might have on his career.

Lander qualified on both counts. He was in his sixties, and nearing retirement. Despite some worrying health problems, he was still energetic. He had handled a large company in Chrysler's British unit. And he was already working at the post office. Côté felt that he was the sort of person who could quickly gather up the reins and whip the beast into motion. Lander's acting title was quietly confirmed in February 1986, seven months after Warren's resignation.

It was clear from the outset that Lander was not going to be another Warren. Communications between Canada Post and the outside world almost ground to a halt after Warren's departure. Lander didn't give interviews and he didn't make speeches. That seemed reasonable as long as his own future was up in the air.

But, as president, the style remained the same. He gave no interviews and returned no phone calls, even social calls to congratulate him on his appointment. Reporters noticed the difference, and so did postal customers, Members of Parliament, and the unions. The president's door was closed.

"Don Lander refuses to meet the unions," says Lang. "We had lots of differences with Michael Warren, but we knew exactly what the differences were. My job was a go-between, as a member of the board, to say to Michael, Let's have a meeting with the unions on such and such a day, and here's the issues, here's the agenda. Now let's knock heads and see if we can't iron out some of these problems, at least understand why we have these differences. You try to do that now.

"I mean, Ouellet's door was always open. Every postmaster general's door was always open for meetings. Côté refuses to meet with the unions. He will not meet with the unions. It's not necessary. Don Lander's the same way. He'll fluff it off down the line."

There was also no question that, unlike Warren, he would do what he was told by his political masters. He would sometimes take suggestions literally. When Côté told him it would be nice for the post office to have the best advertising program around, meaning a communications plan that would sell Canada Post's message to all its stakeholders, Lander obediently went away and came back with plans for a massive advertising campaign.

That much of his style meshed with Côté's. Unlike Ouellet, who preferred to distance himself from Canada Post unless he wanted something and who let Warren take the flak from postal critics, Côté seemed afraid of what might happen if he let the post office loose. Côté wanted a tight leash on his unruly new pet.

The style fitted Lander's reputation as a hands-on manager who just wanted to run the business. There was no doubt about his ability to get results from his subordinates. As one of his colleagues put it, he may be affable enough on the surface, but "deep within that smile is one hell of a son of a bitch who could tear my throat out if I did the wrong thing."

Lander, said another, "established a climate of fear." As he increased the pressure for results, some executives left, others were fired, and most of the rest silently chewed their fingernails. By early 1987, Canada Post was boasting about a 26-per-cent cut in the number of senior managers.

As head of the post office, Lander could not avoid politics, but he hated it. Political demands made no sense to him. He had no patience for "mickey mousing", as one colleague puts it. For instance, extending letter-carrier service to new neighbourhoods is something that depends on the number of houses, how close together they are, whether enough postal stations exist to serve them, and other factors related to the workings of the post office. Ordinary Canadians just see the postman walking down one street and not the next. Lander had to be pushed into altering service boundaries to ones that made more sense to the common man, and the process frustrated him.

The new president's dislike of politics was compounded by his lack of feeling for public relations. He saw no reason to talk to the politicians or to the public. When he was forced to, he retreated into jargon and refused to be trapped into committing himself. His favourite word is "value", as in: "I think it is important that we who become involved in establishing a mature corporation transfer the value relationship of a true corporation."

When he emerged from his office for his first appearance before a parliamentary committee in May 1986, MPs flailed around for an entire evening trying to pin him down on what Canada Post was planning to do. By then, almost a year had passed since Warren's resignation, and there had still been no public indication of a new corporate plan. Lander gave them no satisfaction.

In answer after answer liberally sprinkled with his favourite term, Lander said he had no idea what Canada Post was planning to do, how it would meet its deficit target, and what options it would choose for reducing costs. "I can only determine that after I hear from the shareholder the direction he wants Canada Post to go."

MPs asked about alternate-day delivery, and group mailboxes, and higher stamp prices. "It is always, as far as we are concerned, a value relationship to see whether we can provide an alternative relationship that is acceptable." Meanwhile, he told MPs, "there is no plan as such. There are elements of a plan. There are options that will go to make up a plan. . . . I do not have a direction in relation to a plan." Canada Post had sent a variety of options up to the minister's office, but the plan itself was being devised by people in other departments. Whatever the result, he said, "this is not a Canada Post plan."

This was a dramatic change from the original intent of the Canada Post act. The post office was supposed to put together its plan and then send it to the government for approval. If approved, the corporate plan became its mandate, says one former bureaucrat. "If it's not, it allows the government to give direction without officially giving a directive. And a directive, of course, is a public document. So the government can refuse to approve the submitted plan, and give indications as to what it would find acceptable and what it would likely approve." That process still allows the government to give under-the-table orders.

But this time the process seemed to have gone one step further. Union leader Bob McGarry was stunned by the contrast between Lander's style and that of Warren. "He [Warren] would go down to the government and tell them where he was going. And he would make them throw out his business plan. This guy waited for the government to write it for him."

Insiders say that, behind the scenes, Lander had a clearer idea of what he was doing than he let on. He was just being typically cautious, unwilling to say anything that might get either him or his minister into trouble.

The basis for the plan had been laid down by Finance minister Michael Wilson in his budget that February 1986. It gave up on the original five-year schedule for breaking even, and added another year. Canada Post was to wipe out its losses by March 31, 1988 — one year later than Warren's original deadline.

That alone told Lander much of what he needed to know. The deficit target meant that efforts to cut the number of employees had to go on, that extending door-to-door delivery to all new suburbs was out of the question, and that the post office had to move ahead with plans to buy newer, more efficient machines for its plants.

Wilson's target date became the unshakable factor in all the planning efforts. Canada Post looked at every possibility within that limit. Its executives and the minister's office looked at ideas from sensible to silly. The options included delivery of the mail every second day, having all delivery converted to group mailboxes instead of to the door, sending letter-carriers on their routes by car instead of on foot, and rolling back wages and salaries at the corporation by 6 per cent across the board.

Aside from the financial target, Lander had to stick to two other principles. The Conservatives were not going to let the post office move into new lines of business such as Consumers Post, and they wanted its move into electronic mail halted while they watched to see what seemed to work best in other countries.

As the planning efforts continued through the spring and into the summer, Côté's chief of staff, Julien Béliveau, was playing an increasingly crucial role. Béliveau is a businessman who only came to Ottawa because he is a friend of Côté's and Côté asked for help. He became intrigued by the post office and then immersed. When Côté was moved to the even more important and complex Industry portfolio in June 1986, the time pressures on him increased and Béliveau's role became more pronounced.

It was Béliveau who huddled with Canada Post executives to hammer out a framework for reaching the target. Côté's move to the industry department delayed the planning process, but Mulroney felt that the delays would have been worse if the postal job had been shifted again. The result was, Béliveau once confessed, that he became "the deputy minister of the post office".

Whether intentionally or not, his choice of phrase reflected both his growing role in running the post office and the sense that Canada Post was once again operating as a department of the government rather than as a Crown corporation.

Lander's behaviour in public, disowning responsibility for the corporate plan, was only one sign of the change. Another came in early summer, when Ron Lang's noisy departure from the board of directors signalled a feeling that the board was being squeezed out of any real role in making decisions.

In late May, after Lang sued Marin and Lander, saying they were denying him information he needed to do his job as a director under the Canada Business Corporations Act, he was quietly dropped from the board, along with two other Liberal appointees, Derek Oland of Moosehead Breweries and Adélard Savoie, a New Brunswick lawyer. (Savoie was later reappointed for another six months because there were too many vacancies on the board.)

Because of the tight government control, Lang said, Canada Post had been "staggering from crisis to crisis" over the previous year and a half. "The whole idea of setting up a Crown corporation was to put it at arm's length with the government. . . . In my view, they could do away with the board of directors completely. The government is now acting as the board of directors."

Oland, as he left, quietly expressed similar feelings. Board members were frustrated by the government's inability to make up its mind what it wanted to do. "Ron's not saying anything that isn't felt by others."

"When the Tories came to power and Warren subsequently resigned, nothing came to the board," says Lang. "Nothing came to the board about what was going on in terms of developing a one-year or a five-year business plan. Nothing came to the board in terms of policy issues. It was just coming there, looking at the monthly performance charts, with maybe forty or fifty contracts which had to have board approval."

If that flap was annoying, there was much more in store for Côté. As the fall unfolded, Canada Post turned into a public-relations disaster.

Even René Marin's long-expected departure as chairman came as a surprise. His contract expired on October 16, five years after the Crown corporation was set up. But the announcement that he would be replaced came as part of a shuffle of deputy ministers in various departments of government in August. Côté got no warning of the change, and knew nothing of Sylvain Cloutier's appointment as the new chairman until it was passed by Cabinet.

He had not paid much attention to the chairman's role, since Marin was not involved in the crucial affairs of the business. The Prime Minister's Office and the Privy Council Office obviously felt the same way. Cloutier was moved to the post office from his previous job as president of Export Development Corp. That was apparently to make room for Robert Richardson, the deputy minister for international trade, who was being shifted out of that job to make room for Gerry Shannon, the former senior assistant deputy minister in the Finance department whom Trade minister Pat Carney wanted as her deputy. Such is life at the senior levels of the bureaucracy.

The only public evidence of the casual nature of the shift came a little later, when someone noticed that Cabinet had told Cloutier to start his new job on October 1, before Marin's contract ran out. Cabinet had to pass a second order-in-council on September 18 amending the date that Cloutier's appointment took effect. Marin was kept on staff, as chairman of the stamp advisory committee, for an extra ninety days before being dropped.

The big embarrassment for Côté was still to come. He was already beginning to suffer from an image problem as a minister who had trouble reaching decisions. That image was not helped by his cautious, nervous manner in public and his occasional verbal slips, the result of his trouble with the English language.

But more than a year after he took office, there was still no five-year plan. Côté may have picked Lander for the post office in the hopes that a quick plan would follow, and yet what was once promised for the spring slipped into June, then July, then September, then October. By October it was finally ready, and he scheduled a press conference for the afternoon of November 5.

As the plan was developed, the options were discussed repeatedly with a committee of the Conservative caucus Côté set up shortly after becoming postal minister. The committee included all the Tory hard-liners, the ones who loved to take shots at the post office. By the time the plan was ready, they had agreed to go along with it, and Côté figured that if they were convinced, they would have passed the word on to their fellow members.

On the morning before the press conference, the Conservative caucus met for its usual weekly session. Caucus meetings, held behind closed doors, are a chance for ordinary MPs to complain about things they don't like and to make proposals to their colleagues. This meeting went quietly until about 12:45.

Suddenly Côté was ambushed by a string of back-bench MPs. Mulroney and deputy prime minister Don Mazankowski had already left for lunch. Tory insiders say the assault was led by Léo Duguay, the MP from St. Boniface and chairman of the Manitoba PC caucus. Others followed, with one scathing attack on the plan after another.

Côté had assumed that if he kept the MPs most interested in the post office on side and well informed, they would tell their colleagues what was planned. They had not. As a result, the rest of the caucus had no idea what was planned, because Côté had never consulted them directly.

There may have been another factor. Côté's plan came before caucus just five days after Prime Minister Mulroney insisted that the billion-dollar maintenance contract for the CF-18 fighter planes be given to Canadair Ltd. in Montreal instead of to low-bidder Bristol Aerospace in Winnipeg, a decision that aroused outrage and disgust in the West. Côté was the first Quebec minister after that to wave a proposal in front of them that looked like an easy and satisfying target for their frustration.

Whatever the reasons, the force of the caucus assault was more than Côté could withstand. He agreed to hold back on the two-cent rate increase that was supposed to be announced right away, and to allow a parliamentary committee to review the whole plan before Canada Post was allowed to charge more.

The press conference was postponed, and Côté's aides and Canada Post officials hurriedly ripped the announcement of the rate increase out of the press kits. Late that afternoon, an embarrassed Côté faced a curious press corps anxious to know how a Cabinet minister could have been forced by caucus to make changes to a proposal so late in the game.

The plan itself was fairly straightforward. It promised new equipment to move the mail faster. It stuck to the deficit target by nibbling at service in several directions. It made community mailboxes, touted with much fanfare as Supermailboxes, the look of the future for houses in new suburbs. It cut back some rural delivery service. Rates would go up each year in line with inflation. It was a plan that seemed to show that the government just wanted to get Canada Post to the break-even point in the way that would cause the least fuss from the fewest people.

It was a plan that said Canada Post could break even without getting into new businesses by using what it had. Stewart Cooke, who finally got his wish to desert the bargaining table, took over administration, real estate, contracts — and much of the chore of selling the plan to the public. He says that, inside the post office, improvements were already taking hold.

Bids were under way for $1 billion worth of new and far faster postal machines. "The next generation is just staggering, the difference between the DC-3 and the Concorde," says Cooke. The optical character-readers now in plants can only sort letters into 18 different slots at once. The newest models can split the mail 250 ways at a time.

Part of the plan involved changing the "topsy-turvy" network of retail outlets, the counters in post offices and news-stands and drugstores that sell stamps. Locations will change, along with colours and layouts. So will ownership. Over ten to fifteen years, Canada Post plans to turn many of its post offices and sub-post offices into franchises, a move guaranteed to irritate the union members who covet the jobs behind the wickets.

"We have a plan now. That wasn't easy. It took a lot of my goddamn life in the last year and a half. It was well thought through," says Cooke. The three basic themes of the Warren era — money, people, and service — are still there, but now the emphasis is on sticking to basics.

"We're not in the retailing business. We're in the business of collecting the goddamn mail and sorting it. And we're not in the transportation business either. We should have people do that that know what they're doing. Our job is to be the processors of the mail, make sure we make money on it, and get stability in the workplace."

The unions, of course, saw things differently. In their eyes, the Conservative approach looked like an attack on the quality of service, and they decided to spend $500,000 on an advertising campaign to get Canadians to complain. The letter-carriers want door-to-door delivery for everyone. The postal workers and post-masters don't want to see the jobs at the wickets end up in the private sector.

There was criticism even from unexpected quarters. Alix Granger of the Marchment committee said its members feel most of their advice was ignored. There has been no move to bring in legislation that would set up a stronger board of directors or independent rate-setting. "We're all disappointed, extremely disappointed. We all had the feeling at the end that we had really wasted our time."

The committee hearings forced on Côté by his caucus were abruptly wrapped up after only four meetings, and before some MPs had even finished questioning Lander, the first and only witness. The committee report put a couple of the measures on hold, but approved the rate increase.

Côté agreed not to cut laneway service to 100,000 rural residents and not to raise rates for small weekly newspapers. He agreed not to close any rural post offices without ninety days' notice and local consultation. The committee agreed to hold more hearings in the spring, but the back-bench revolt seemed to have run out of steam.

In the meantime, Canada Post had done its best to add to the frustration and confusion. When the new plan was published, it unveiled a new name and image for an old idea—the Supermailbox. Warren had begun installing them quietly three years earlier with the less exciting label of community mailboxes.

They are supposed to be a less costly alternative to door-to-door delivery of the mail. Warren told a Commons committee in 1985 that it cost $58 to $60 to have a letter-carrier cover 450 addresses. It would cost only $15 to fill the 10 or 11 old green group mailboxes needed to cover the same number of houses. The new community mailbox, later dubbed the Supermailbox, was an attempt to make the old green boxes look more attractive.

The Supermailbox stands on legs, so that customers do not have to bend over to open their little doors. There is a slot so that the same box can be used to mail letters as well. And there is a big parcel compartment. Customers with delivery to their door have to go to the post office to pick up a parcel unless they are home when the postman rings. With the Supermailbox, the letter-carrier simply leaves the key to the parcel compartment in the letter-box of any customers receiving a package that day.

To save money, Canada Post wanted to use these community boxes in all new subdivisions. As far as customers were concerned, they were certainly better than driving to the post office between 9 a.m. and 5 p.m. to pick up mail, but Canada Post invested in an expensive advertising campaign to tell people they were so wonderful that they could even be better than door-to-door service.

It was an advertising campaign guaranteed to bring out the complaints. Some boxes had been delivered with upside-down doors, or with keys that could open more than one box. Then some customers discovered that they could open the whole front of the box and get at everybody's mail with nothing more than a sharp twist of the wrist.

The postal unions raised the plight of the elderly being forced to negotiate slippery sidewalks, pointed out the height of the mail slot, out of reach of the wheelchair-bound, and said that the ungainly structures would lure hydrant-hungry mutts.

A chastened Canada Post tried to make up for its mistakes, promising that all the boxes would be checked for defects but leaving unanswered the question of why the boxes hadn't been checked before being put on the streets and made the stars of an expensive ad campaign. Supermailbox was a public-relations fiasco.

Through all the public flap, there was more tension building behind the scenes. The contracts for the letter-carriers and the postal workers had run out during the dithering over the corporate plan. Parrot says that until the plan was set, the post office refused to begin talks, because it did not have its mandate clear. Now the unions were getting signals that another price of caucus co-operation was a harder line in negotiations. Union leaders say Cooke's breezy style of give and take had been replaced by a repetitive No to every proposal.

And at the board of directors, Bob McGarry seemed determined to follow Ron Lang's recipe before his expected ejection from the board. His term ran out in October, but he received no notice of either his reappointment or his removal. In December he launched his own lawsuit against the corporation, its board, Cloutier, and Lander.

"The decisions that they brought to the board, as I saw them, were in violation of the act that appointed us. The reduction in service, franchising and all the rest of it, were in violation of the very act that we were appointed to uphold. When I raised the issue, they said that may be, but they were there to run a corporation and it was up to the courts to decide whether they were running it properly or not. I was arguing the act, they were arguing that they were running a business.

"A Crown corporation is run by laws that are set up to run that corporation, and you just can't do things as if you were Joe Doakes out there running the gas station."

The Ottawa suburb of Nepean, however, had already tried to get a court injunction against installation of the boxes, arguing that they violated the Canada Post Corp. Act. But on December 12, Justice William Maloney of the Ontario Supreme Court ruled that "there is nothing in the act that imposes a duty to provide door-to-door delivery."

The corporation's board, which had been meeting monthly, seemed to be lurching into limbo. "Since I filed it [the lawsuit], all board meetings have been cancelled," McGarry said in February. In April, Canada Post made it official: McGarry too was out.

Since the Tories took charge, he says, "the board is just there. Unless you raise real hell, nobody listens. They seem to be going full speed ahead, and as long as they comply with Wilson's mandate on the budget, nobody gives a damn what they do. You can do anything you like, even in violation, as long as you don't get caught in the media or in violation of the budget."

Amid the tension and confusion, Lander's lack of interest in public relations became a real problem. Côté, already beginning to suffer from an image as indecisive, had suffered a crushing humiliation at the hands of his caucus. Having been overrun once, he would find it tougher to resist their demands in the future.

Even worse, what was seen of the incident in public looked like a serious mistake on his part. Either he had failed to keep in touch with his own caucus during the planning process or he did not have the backbone and determination to shrug off criticism and carry on with what he felt was right. It looked as if he wasn't in control. In the war zone of the House of Commons, no one draws more fire than a Cabinet minister who looks tentative and out of control.

With the plan in place, Mulroney felt the time had come to take the burden off his embattled Industry minister and let him concentrate on his major portfolio. In February he gave the postal job to Harvie Andre, a spontaneous, likeable, and above all experienced MP from Calgary.

Andre had already shown as minister of Consumer and Corporate Affairs that he could deflect Opposition attacks in the House during his handling of the new drug patent laws. Mulroney figured that someone who could talk to the public about unpopular issues without making mistakes was just the kind of person he needed.

Caucus members were pleased. "I think it's a good decision to have a minister that's had more experience in the House and more experience in Parliament and government," says Dan McKenzie. "It was a rough one for a new minister and a new Member of Parliament. Harvie's got lots of experience, so I think we can see some great improvements."

Andre admits he did not go looking for the job, but took his appointment in stride. "I suppose, in its simplest terms, it's a political problem that has to be managed. And the problems are service, the public's perception as to whether or not the post office does its job, the role of government and the Crown corporation and how they interact, and of course the fiscal situation. It's a political problem as well as a real problem."

He kept his early responses ambiguous. He talked about the need to improve service rather than to focus on the deficit, but he refused even to hint that the deficit target set by Wilson might be relaxed. "You just can't keep throwing money at it. The post office's current problems are in no small measure due to the sort of blank-cheque approach taken by the previous government."

He points to the multicoloured charts of the Marchment committee, which show postal wage rates taking a sudden jump to well above the national average in 1975. "Bryce Mackasey, there it is. He just went in there with a blank cheque, and all of the problems we have today are a consequence of that."

Andre agrees that the object in having a Crown corporation is to remove it from day-to-day political interference. "And yet they still have a monopoly, a state-run, public-service monopoly, and you don't have normal market discipline to regulate its behaviour. And so again there seems to be a demand to me for some sort of opportunity, vehicle, to express their grievances, concerns, and so on, and right now, that's me. How do you keep hands off and by the same token fulfil your democratic responsibilities in responding to the concerns of the public?"

The most aggravating problem facing Andre as he settled into his new job was not what to do, but what to say. "We're in the middle of labour negotiations and we've got the unions running around using the political route as part of their process. What do you do about it? I have a choice. The letter-carriers are running around saying 3,700 rural post offices will be closed.

"That's a lie. I could take 'em on, and I'm not reluctant to do that, and say look, you're a bunch of goddamn liars and stop it. But that immediately puts me kind of on the side of the corporation. Well, you know, if I'm going to be on the side of the corporation and yet not have any direct control of the corporation, then it's at least high-risk, and maybe inappropriate.

"But when the letter-carriers go out doing those things, they're gettin' people riled up, and Members of Parliament are getting concerned, they're raising concerns, it comes up in the House. What's the choice? What's the bloody choice?"

This is where Lander's failings as a public spokesman become a problem. While Warren was around, he would take on the unions in the public-relations debate if necessary. Ouellet could keep his hands clean. Andre does not have the same option. He is a capable spokesman, and for the moment the post office seems to lack anyone else.

For the Conservatives' third postal minister in less than three years, his personal dilemma reflects that of the corporation for which he is responsible. He cannot speak for everyone. He cannot please everyone.

''If I take on the unions, I'm there then as the spokesman for the corporation. If I'm the spokesman for the corporation, who the hell's the spokesman for the clients, the customers? That's the problem. That's the procedural dilemma. I don't know. I don't have any answers.''

Postscriptions

■

After Gordon Sinclair left the post office in the late 1970s, he had a stock answer for anyone who asked him what was needed to solve the problems of Canada's mail service: "Six months of civil war."

Over the years, there has been no shortage of suggestions for fixing the post office. Royal commissions, consultants, task forces, inquiries, and a cacophony of catcalls from the sidelines have produced a steady drizzle of recommendations.

For the past two decades, the post office has been a makeshift raft on a stormy sea of politics, blown this way and that by the blasts of hot air from the House of Commons, while being tugged in other directions by the underlying currents of public opinion, customer demands, and a changing marketplace. Workers and managers each earnestly try to paddle the raft where they want to go, sending it spinning in circles within circles.

More than any other Crown corporation, the post office needs consistent orders. No other public enterprise is balanced so precariously on the knife edge of its dual identity as service and business. Is it the job of the post office to provide a service that will satisfy all Canadians, no matter what the cost? Or should the post office be trying to do the best it can while living within its means? In political terms, the dilemma reduces to one question: Is a postal deficit necessary?

Unlimited spending certainly offers a vision of peace: no expense spared in doing the job right, lots of money around for delightful wages and working conditions and all for a cost that would look small when compared to the overall federal deficit. But the open-ended approach, sooner or later, must lead to a tax bill that Canadians would find unacceptable. The post office would become a time bomb for the unlucky government in whose lap it blows up.

As soon as one admits that there is a maximum price-tag, the whole management approach changes. If there is a limit on resources, there is pressure to make the best use of them. Whether the target is a $500-million profit or a $500-million deficit, it is still a goal that puts limits on spending, on service, and on wages. To tell the post office to cover expenses, neither making money nor losing money, just symbolizes the balance between Canada Post's goal as a public service and its goal as a business. The targets differ only in how hard they may be to achieve.

The Canadian post office has not always run a deficit. In the first fifty-eight years of this century, the post office ran a deficit only fourteen times. It last recorded a surplus in 1957, when the federal government collected $5.8 million. During the previous twenty-five years the post office had made total profits of $115 million, including only three years of losses. By 1974 the annual loss was up to $177 million. Then it jumped to $321 million in 1975, $546 million in 1976, and $575 million at its peak in 1977.

There were all sorts of reasons for the explosion in the deficit: higher wage rates won by militant unions, heavy spending on new machines, and political foot-dragging when it came to raising postal rates in line with inflation. Above all, though, cities and towns were growing out as much as up. More Canadians in more places wanted postal service.

In 1962, letter-carriers carried mail to the front door of some 3 million addresses in Canada. Seven years later, the number was over 4 million. Five years after that, it passed the 5-million mark, and by the time the post office became a Crown corporation in 1981, the number of points of call getting door-to-door delivery had reached 6.3 million, more than twice the number of less than twenty years earlier.

During the same period, Britain and the United States both ran up huge postal losses as well, even though they did what

Canada did not and created state-owned corporations to run their post offices.

The British corporation was told to meet "the social, industrial and commercial needs" of the United Kingdom, and to provide mail and phone services to "satisfy all reasonable demands for them." In doing so, it was to "have regard" (the same phrase used in Canada) to improving its operating systems, new developments in the field of communications, and efficiency and economy. The minister responsible for the corporation kept the power to give it orders in the "national interest".

British author Michael Corby's analysis of that legislation in *The Postal Business* was incisive and devastating. "Its main weakness lay in the vague exposition of the objectives for the corporation, which was made worse by the failure of the ministry and subsequently the sponsoring department to lay down a comprehensive system of performance indicators. This was a serious defect, since it meant that in practice the corporation was as open to government interference of the meddling variety as it had been before corporation status, and equally was protected from the necessity of meeting a set of sharply defined performance criteria, and responding to customer need."

Even though there was no record of the minister's ever using his power to give orders to the corporation, "the weakness of the clause was that it did not bring into the open that range of ministerial control which varies between a wink-and-a-nod and arm twisting." While thus keeping a theoretically unlimited power over the corporation, the minister also had "ample scope for evading responsibility when things went wrong."

The British post office, which lost £5.8 million in 1968/69 as it was turned into a Crown corporation, rocketed to a £109.2-million deficit by 1974/75. As the deficit reached crisis proportions, the government, which had earlier held down postal prices, then nearly doubled them. Within two years the post office was profitable, and it has stayed that way. "Thus, in the name of the public interest, the postal business first had its prices frozen and was allowed to run up a deficit, and then, as the policy was reversed, it was told to raise prices and operate at a profit," wrote Corby.

Turning a huge loss into a profit needs no fundamental change in the way a corporation is run. British Telecom, while still owned by the government, moved, in only two years, from having the largest business loss in the Guinness Book of Records to huge profits. Again, higher prices did the trick. ''The inescapable fact is that most people in the organization are doing much the same jobs in essentially the same way as they were before, and the major part of the improvement has been brought about by requiring customers to dig a good deal deeper into their pockets.''

The other side to the deficit debate is often ignored. When stamp prices go up, the businesses that account for 80 per cent of the mail bear the main burden. When the deficit goes up, taxes pay the bill. Most taxes are paid by individuals. As Postmaster General Jean-Pierre Côté noted in a 1971 debate over higher postal rates: ''Government has to decide if the taxpayers of this country should subsidize services whose main users are business and industry. . . . The principle of successive operating deficits, to be supported by general taxation, would appear to be quite inequitable.''

The key problem remains the lack of consensus among Canadians. To make a choice is one thing. To stick to it is another. No measures to give the post office a clear job to do and the means to do it will be able to get rid of the quiet phone calls from the minister's office or the political pressures that lead to them. And as long as there are elections, politicians will change. Ministers swap portfolios, governments are defeated. As long as politicians have direct access to postal decision-making, there can be no consistent path for the post office.

Consistency in the long term requires a strong mandate, one with which politicians cannot easily tamper. In practical terms, that means entrenching its basic instructions in legislation. Canada Post's current act follows the British model and contains the same fatal flaws. From Ouellet's interest in hiring practices to Côté's influence on Lander's corporate plan, it has failed to keep politicians at a distance. Each year, each minister, each crisis, the orders change.

The trail of commissions and studies is lined with good suggestions. The two most crucial, both included in the Marchment report, are to put the setting of postal rates into the hands of an independent body and to boost the power and independence of the board of directors.

The board of governors of the United States Postal Service by law cannot be stacked with political cronies, and it has the sole power to hire and fire the postal president. The United States also uses an independent commission to set postal rates. So does Australia. Canada uses a similar procedure to set rates for phone companies, and Canada has profitable phone companies, reasonable prices, and perhaps the best phone service in the world.

Canada Post also needs a new, more precise mandate. The U.S. act specifies that the post office "shall provide prompt, reliable and efficient services to patrons in all areas and shall render postal service to all communities," and goes on to say that "no small post office shall be closed solely for operating at a deficit, it being the specific intent of Congress that effective postal services be insured to residents of both urban and rural communities." It prescribes pay levels comparable to those in the private sector and requires postal rates to cover postal costs.

Canada's legislation is vague. The crucial section says that "while maintaining basic customary postal service, the Corporation, in carrying out its objects, shall have regard to" five points: the idea of moving into new areas in the communications field; the need to be financially self-sustaining "while providing a standard of service that will meet the needs of the people of Canada and that is similar with respect to communities of the same size"; the importance of security; the desire to keep employees happy with the corporation; and the need for the corporation to reflect its identity as an arm of the federal government.

The actions of the three ministers in charge of Canada Post during its first five years show that the act has been no barrier to inconsistency. Canada Post is no better off now than it was while still a federal department. New, more specific legislation could reduce the number and degree of political flip-flops.

No matter how clear its marching orders, however, the Crown corporation as it now exists cannot avoid political influence altogether. It remains, as Harvie Andre noted, a political problem to be managed. Only a more radical change in the structure of the corporation will allow true long-term stability.

Canadian politicians have not lacked for suggestions for radical changes to the way the mail is moved, but there has been a feeling that the post office cannot make a clean break with its past without an agonizing conflict which would ripple through society as a whole. Most of these proposals attack the post office and those who work there with a blunt instrument, and the most tempting target has become the postal unions.

It is easy for the government to get tough. The contract imposed in 1978 through back-to-work legislation showed the government's ability to use its power. A really brutal assault on the terms of contracts built up through decades of struggle would probably provoke a more stubborn and violent union reaction. Chances are that the back-to-work bill would be ignored, and the arrest of union leaders might not work. To win, the government would have to be willing to follow in Ronald Reagan's footsteps and fire the lot if they refused to return to work, as was the case when U.S. air traffic controllers refused to end their strike.

The other major approach to radical change is privatization. In its most basic form, this would mean closing down the post office as a Crown corporation and having the job done by the private sector. This could be done through a single contract for the whole country, a series of regional contracts, or deals that divvied up the various functions of the post office such as sorting, transportation, and delivery. The idea here is to get rid of the postal workers and their unions and replace them with cheaper labour.

This approach is rife with problems. No private-sector company has the expertise to step in and take over. There would inevitably be protests and picketing by the postal workers tossed onto the street. And, as the Lapalme experience showed, once a private company was in place, would-be competitors would have a tough time dislodging it. The effect might well be to replace a public-sector monopoly with a private-sector one on a cost-plus contract.

Renting out the post office's plants and equipment to private contractors leaves another crucial question up in the air. Who would pay for new equipment as it was needed? One thing is certain: no company would invest in expensive equipment without knowing it would be in control of the post office long enough to recover its investment with a profit.

An outright sale of the Crown corporation as is to a private-sector buyer poses similar problems. A private-sector company is no better equipped to handle the postal unions than the government is. Again, drawing on the Lapalme experience, a private company would be in a weaker bargaining position, with no chance of passing legislation to end strikes and probably subject to financial penalties when the mail was not delivered.

There is also the indirect method: Abolish the postal monopoly and allow the private sector to move in wherever it wishes. People in large cities would likely get more choice and cheaper prices. Small towns and rural customers would have to get by on whatever kind of service the government was willing to subsidize through the remnants of the old post office.

All the suggestions for radical change seem to have one thing in common: an attack on one group to the benefit of another. The only alternative, at first glance, is to try and muddle through the middle ground, with the results that we have seen to date. The problem is to find a combination of measures that provides the greatest benefit to the greatest number of stakeholders while causing the least possible damage to the fewest.

It is possible for Canada to have a postal system that provides more competition, allows lower postal rates for all Canadians, and still encourages better postal service. It would lead to a slimmer post office, but it would not require any layoffs or cuts in the existing wages, benefits, or working conditions of postal workers.

The core of the postal system is the network of sorting plants and the trucks and planes that move the mail from one to the other. Since most of the transportation is handled under contract with the private sector, the problem to be solved lies in the sorting process.

Plants are costly to build and costly to run. A private company is unlikely to set up a competing network without being sure both of the rules of the game and of long-term stability in postal policy. If the rules were changed to allow open competition, the private sector would likely move only into those parts of the country with the densest population, where it could provide better service at lower cost than Canada Post.

This ''cream-skimming'' has been the prime argument for keeping the postal monopoly in place. Every industrialized country has thought about getting rid of the monopoly. Every one, so far, has rejected the idea. A post office without a monopoly would lose business in parts of the country and lose money in the rest. Simply removing the monopoly would mean a permanent drain of tax dollars to ensure that all citizens got basic mail service.

One of the ways the United States protects its monopoly is to insist that all letters, whether carried by the postal service or by private couriers, bear the same value of stamps. This ensures that even if couriers attract mail away from the United States Postal Service, its revenue base remains stable. Couriers must also charge minimum fees much higher than the basic postal rate, as they do in Canada and other countries.

Canada should adopt the same rule. All letters, whether carried by Canada Post or by couriers, should have to bear stamps. Then Canada should make that the *only* restriction on competition.

It would be a measure simple in concept but far-reaching in its effects. Instead of being forced by law to charge very high prices, private companies would have much more leeway to deliver letters and packages at different speeds and for different prices.

That would give customers more choice, letting them decide whether to pay for speed or reliability or to settle for the cheapest service. The stamp requirement, however, would ensure that no matter how much business Canada Post lost to the private sector, its income would fall only if there was a drop in the total number of letters being sent. There would be no sudden financial drain on the Crown corporation as a result of competition.

Forcing couriers to buy stamps would also mean that the post office would remain the lowest-cost supplier of mail service. Any courier would have to charge enough to cover its own costs, pay the post office, and still make a profit.

This would tilt competition even more heavily into the densely populated regions and along main inter-city routes. Couriers would skim the cream, take the most profitable traffic, and leave the rest to the post office. But instead of leaving the taxpayers to subsidize the unprofitable routes that no one else wants to serve, the competition would have to bear the cost. Couriers would essentially pay a ''stamp tax'' for the privilege of competing for the profitable routes.

There are complications, of course. The cheaper the alternative service, the greater effect the tax would have. And couriers now offer their basic rate on packages much larger than the post office allows for a normal letter. Since the post office has no monopoly on packages, the government would have to be careful in setting the scope of the tax. The easiest approach would be to charge couriers the price of a basic first-class letter for all mail, regardless of size and weight, with parcels of larger than a certain size excluded.

There are other ways to make the tax more palatable to the courier industry. For instance, since the couriers would pay the price of a stamp on each letter they carry, they should have the freedom to use any parts of the postal service they wish along the way. The most obvious use would be to tuck the courier's shipments onto airplanes between cities under Canada Post's contracts with the airlines. Each courier would have already paid the full cost of having Canada Post carry the letter. A courier could deliver its bags to the airport and pick them up at the other end, leaving the airlines to keep track of the bills to be sent to Canada Post.

This has the advantage of reducing the courier's costs, perhaps by more than the price it would pay for its stamps. It would effectively make Canada Post a bulk buyer of transportation space for the courier industry. That could lead to lower costs per letter both for couriers and for Canada Post.

Another option for couriers would be to handle the sorting and transportation themselves, but turn over their packages to Canada Post letter-carriers for final delivery. Canada Post would absorb the costs out of the revenue it would have already collected from the courier. The main complication at that end would be infighting between Canada Post and couriers over whose packages got priority in carriers' bags.

If couriers succeeded in taking away a large part of the volume going through Canada Post's sorting plants, many postal workers would find themselves with nothing to do. The worse the service provided by Canada Post, the more mail will seek out other carriers. Australia's experiment with smaller, decentralized sorting plants shows that they work better than the giant blobs that currently dot Canada Post's real estate. At least one alternative sorting network, using smaller but more modern plants, would likely emerge.

This threat to the jobs of postal workers is matched by opportunity. If they can sort efficiently, private couriers might take advantage of their services and keep volumes high. Similarly, a good service record by the letter-carriers would likely keep their mailbags full of letters. More importantly, a good performance in the plants and on the streets would help Canada Post keep its customers, and the Crown corporation would always have the edge of being the cheapest service in town.

The system would put pressure on the unions at the bargaining table. The greater the extent of competition, the more mail services will remain open for business during any postal strike. Since the stamp tax would keep rolling in, managers would not have to worry about the costs of a strike. This could fundamentally change the balance of power at postal bargaining tables. If the government felt this was unfair, they could even the odds by suspending the stamp tax during any strike to balance the loss of Canada Post's service to the couriers.

The real advantage of this system is that it does not force a battle with the unions. It allows the government to say that no matter how lazy and overpaid postal workers might be, they will not have to work harder or to take pay cuts. Since there would be no cuts in postal revenue, there would be no need for cuts in costs.

As postal volumes decline, Canada Post would need fewer workers, but it could stick to its no-layoffs policy. It could allow workers to leave or retire at their regular rate, now about 5 per cent a year, and not replace them. Or, as it has already done, it could offer individual workers fat lump-sum payments to leave if it wanted to cut its work force faster.

Efforts to ease the impact on workers need not stop there. They could even be encouraged to set up as individuals or groups in the mail business. Government help could range from training in management skills to loans or even grants to help get their new businesses off the ground.

The real effect of the stamp tax is to separate the business problems of the post office in breaking even from the political problems of cutting down the size of the postal work force. This does not take away the government's ability to be more abrupt with postal workers if it so chooses. It merely removes the need to do so.

Because there is a reasonable, even generous, approach to cutting the work force, the unions would stand on dangerous ground if they tried to fight to the bitter end on principle. The unions' real weak point would be their traditional source of strength. If the terms offered to union members are generous enough — guarantees of job security, no cuts in wages and benefits, and an option of cash payments to quit — the union leadership might have a hard time getting most of its members to stay out on a picket line. And if it did cobble together a solid strike vote, the public's view of the stand might make back-to-work legislation look quite acceptable. Faced with a choice between keeping everything they have or being fired without severance pay, most workers would probably back down.

It does not matter whether Canada Post succeeds in being more efficient and winning more business or whether it withers away to a skeleton. Consumers win either way. This scenario assumes that stamp prices would be set not by politicians, but by an independent commission with orders to set postal rates in line with Canada Post's costs. In this case, lower stamp prices would come from the greater efficiency of the mail system as a whole and would not depend on Canada Post's performance alone.

If Canada Post became more efficient, it could expand. Its costs per letter would fall. If Canada Post shrank, it would mean that its smaller overall costs could be split among more letters carried by couriers. Either way, the price of a stamp could be cut and still allow Canada Post to break even without any loss of service to any community in Canada.

The other parts of the postal business lend themselves to some imaginative solutions as well. Because of the high costs of door-to-door delivery, Canada Post has been reluctant to assign postmen to walk the streets of new suburban developments. The struggle for letter-carrier service has become a basic issue of equity. There seems to be something fundamentally unfair when one street gets a mailman and the next street has only a box.

There is another approach to the job of getting mail from the postal stations to homes and businesses. Hand it over to municipalities. Local politicians now complain freely about any perceived lack of service. If their own taxpayers have to cover the cost, they are likely to be more careful in their demands. While this would mean that some cities and towns would have less service than others, the level of postal service would always be within the control of those affected. Nowhere does the voter have closer contact with his political representative than at the municipal level.

There are two possible ways to finance the change. Canada Post could hand over the job without offering any compensation. Municipalities would have to raise taxes, but Canada Post could take the savings and chop postal rates. Instead, Canada Post could hand out a per-capita grant to municipalities to pay for letter-carrier service. Each municipality would then decide how to use the money, whether to provide door-to-door service or some alternative, whether to hire LCUC members or to use municipal employees or private contractors.

Larger cities could even adopt a more flexible approach, allowing individual neighbourhoods to set their own standards and adding or subtracting the appropriate amounts from their property-tax bills. Rosedale matrons could accept their letters from a uniformed chauffeur and a Cadillac, while Pointe St. Charles could hire teen-age dropouts to run around on their bicycles.

This would mean drastic changes for Canada Post's letter-carriers. Giving the job to municipalities would get around union protests about the way private contractors hire cheap labour. Politicians would still be in charge of deciding between public-sector and private-sector letter-carriers, but the federal government and Canada Post would be off the hook.

The least explosive approach would be to follow the Teamsters' model in the wake of the Lapalme affair. Each municipality might or might not hire Canada Post's letter-carriers. Whether or not the LCUC members had jobs waiting for them either with the town or with a private delivery company, they would collect generous severance pay. Canada Post should do everything possible to place its letter-carriers in new jobs. No matter how generous the severance pay, workers with no place to go could disrupt the entire effort. As with the inside workers, the government should offer help to letter-carriers who want to set up businesses of their own.

There would be new opportunities for letter-carriers as well. They would, with the co-operation of the municipality, get the chance to take on extra chores for more money. Whether hired as individuals or as companies, letter-carriers could do other jobs for other customers as well. They could, for instance, act as meter-readers for utilities or as security guards providing a daily check for families on vacation.

In the retail network, the post offices where Canadians buy stamps and pay for parcels, fundamental changes are already under way. Canada Post has embarked on a ten- to fifteen-year program to turn many branches into franchise operations. Postal workers who have slogged through years on the night shift to win comfortable day jobs at the wickets are worried that those jobs will be farmed out to high-schoolers, but the post office sees a big advantage to customers. Privately run outlets will stay open longer and there will be more of them. Canada Post plans to boost the number of retail outlets by 50 per cent.

The postal unions have attacked the plan. They say that post offices will be closed, that the private-sector replacements will not be as good. One way or another, however, there must be a melding of stamp sales and other retail activities. Franchising goes one way, allowing store owners to sell stamps and postal services in addition to their other offerings. The other direction would mean finding more uses for small post offices which do not make money on their own. When Canada Post tried the Consumers Post experiment, local businesses cried foul. Local communities will have to decide whether it is better to let the post office sell other goods or to have private stores run the local post office. It should be their individual choice.

In all three arms of the post office — sorting, delivery, and retail — the government has a chance to change the way the postal business is run. In each case, there are hurdles to be overcome. There will be a fierce public-relations battle at the very least. But the big advantage, particularly of the stamp tax, is that if federal politicians have the courage to move once, the new shape of the postal system would impose its own discipline.

The government would lay down the new rules and then take its hands off. Canada Post managers and workers would then have to decide collectively whether they wished the corporation to grow or to wither away. But at least the rules would be clear. The inconsistency that has plagued the post office for so long and left postal service, postal costs, and postal labour relations in a shambles would be over. These are not changes that could be easily reversed.

Whether through frustration or through pride, the post office is still an institution that binds us together as Canadians. Its sad showing over the past two decades reflects our own identity crisis, our failing sense of where we are going and where we want to go. Whatever its shape, it remains a symbol not only of Canada's government, but of our ability to govern ourselves. Its past encompasses our despair; its future is tied to our fears, our hopes, and our will to succeed.

Notes

This book is not so much about events as about people and their feelings. As a result, much of the material is derived from dozens of interviews, most of them tape-recorded, conducted with people who have worked in and around the post office over the past two decades. I owe a debt of gratitude to all the ministers, bureaucrats, postal executives, and union members who were, in some cases, astonishingly frank.

Most quotations are attributed by name. In some cases, however, I have respected a desire for anonymity. All quotes attributed to the late Joe Davidson, the former president of the Canadian Union of Postal Workers, are drawn from his 1978 autobiography, *Joe Davidson*, co-written with his former executive assistant, John Deverell, who is now a journalist.

An event that seemed significant to one person may not stick in another's mind. Memories also tend to fade with time, especially when recalling conversations that may be two decades old. As a result, the dialogue used in the book may not reflect the exact words used at the time. Rather, it is what people remember being said. Where the words reflect one person's memory, I have so indicated.

I have also drawn on a considerable body of documentary material, including internal post office documents, various Canadian studies, and reports and publications concerning foreign postal operations. Most of this material is publicly available, but some is not. I have avoided footnotes in the text, and references in the text are not always specific. They should, however, be clear enough for the interested reader to find any relevant document in the following list. I have also drawn information and quotes from the debates of the House of Commons and from various issues of newspapers including *The Globe and Mail* and *The New York Times*.

Selected References:

Canada Post Corp. and Canada Post Office:

Annual Reports, 1979-1986.

Canada Post Office: An Organizational History (1841– 1974). Organization, Planning and Development Branch, October 1975.

Considerations Which Affect the Choice of Organizational Structure for the Canada Post Office (Report of a study group to Postmaster General Gilles Lamontagne). August 1978.

Fultz, J. G. *Coding and Mechanization 52 Months Later.* August 1974.

Hay Associates. *Canada Post: Climate Analysis Report.* October 1975.

The History of Canada Post. Public Relations Branch, May 1986.

Labour Relations in the Post Office: A Chronology. Labour Relations Branch, October 1981.

Mackasey, Bryce. *What's Behind the Lemming Urge?* Public Affairs Branch, June 1976.

Major Organizational and Compensation Issues in Canada Post (Report of the Joint Post Office-Treasury Board Secretariat Study Group). December 1975.

Minister's Information Book. Rev. March 1980.

Ouellet, André. *From the Pen of the Postmaster General.* Public Affairs Branch, September 1974.

Recommendations: Timing of 1984 Price Increase. September 1983.

Uberig, J. E. *Information Paper Re Special Status for the Canada Post Office*, 1975.

Wilcox, George. *History of Rural Mail in Canada*. Public Affairs Branch, 1975.

Other documents:

Auditor General of Canada. Report to the House of Commons, Fiscal Year Ended 31 March, 1981.

Australian Postal Commission. Annual Report, 1983.

Canadian Union of Postal Workers. Negotiations, 1977. Ottawa: CUPW, 1978.

Canadian Union of Postal Workers. National Constitution, 1983.

Corby, Michael. *The Postal Business 1969–79*. London: Kogan Page, 1979.

Davidson, Joe, and Deverell, John. *Joe Davidson*. Toronto: James Lorimer, 1978.

Deutsche Bundespost. Annual Report, 1983.

Emery, Claude. *A Comparative Analysis of Post Office Operations in Canada and Australia*. Ottawa: Library of Parliament, 1985.

———. *Post Office Operation in the U.S. and Britain: An Analysis and Comparison with Canada*. Ottawa: Library of Parliament, 1985.

Gonnsen, August. *Labor Conflict in the Canadian Post Office: An Investigation of Factors Contributing to Its Persistence and Intensity*. Buffalo: State University of New York at Buffalo, 1981.

Johnson, Walter. *Trade Unions and the State*. Montreal: Black Rose Books, 1979.

Kates, Peat, Marwick and Co. *A Blueprint for Change: Canada Post Office*. Toronto, 1969.

Kierans, Eric. Letter of resignation. Ottawa, March 17, 1970.

Laventhol and Horwath, Management Consultants. *An Investigation of the Allegations Made by Postal Clerk A. N. Varma*. Toronto, 1985.

Pearson, Lester B. *Mike: The Memoirs of the Right Honourable Lester B. Pearson*. Toronto: University of Toronto Press, 1972-75.

Report of the Commission of Inquiry into Mail Transport in Montreal. H. Carl Goldenberg, Commissioner. Ottawa: The Commission, 1970.

Report of the Commission of Inquiry Relating to the Security and Investigation Services Branch within the Post Office Department. René Marin, Commissioner. Ottawa: The Commission, 1981.

Report of the Commission on Postal Service. Washington, D.C.: The Commission, 1977.

Report of the Review Committee on the Mandate and Productivity of Canada Post Corporation. Alan Marchment, Chairman. Ottawa: Government of Canada, 1985.

Report of the Royal Commission of Inquiry into Working Conditions in the Post Office Department. André Montpetit, Commissioner. Ottawa: The Commission, 1966.

Reynolds, Steven Huntley. *The Struggle Continues: An Analysis of Conflict in the Canadian Post Office* (M.A. Thesis). Hamilton: McMaster University, 1981.

Vadeboncoeur, Pierre. *366 Days and As Long As It Takes: Long Live the Lapalme Guys.* Montreal: les Ateliers de la Librairie Beauchemin Ltée, 1971.

Index